BULLETS IN MY
BOTTOM DRAWER

PALMETTO
PUBLISHING
Charleston, SC
www.PalmettoPublishing.com

Paperback ISBN: 979-8-8229-5085-6

BULLETS IN MY BOTTOM DRAWER

the lighter side of combat

JOHN MONTALBANO

Contents Road Map

Author's Note

Like many of you, I've read a lot about and watched documentaries relating to the Vietnam War from personal, military, historical, or political perspectives. Even went there on vacation a few years ago. I'm not surprised by the amount of information available, though it's still considered an unpopular topic of conversation. Opens too many wounds. I think it has to do with embarrassment, maybe even guilt. Mention the word Vietnam in a crowd of guys and you immediately hear silence, the end of a conversation, or excuses, "I wanted to go but . . ." fill in the blank—college, a bad knee, allergies, you've heard them all. James Fallows, a Harvard educated, successful journalist and author, who, when not protesting the war or going to class, studied regulations for the draft and found ways to purposely fail his physical. For his effort, he received a draft exemption. Years after the war ended, he published a confession for himself and others who chose ways to avoid the call to a citizen's most basic duty. In it, he confronted the truth of his earlier actions, concluding with: "On the part of those who were spared, there is a residual guilt, often so deeply buried that it surfaces only in unnaturally vehement denials that there is anything to feel guilty about... there was little character in the choices we made."[1] Others gained our respect being conscientious objectors who put on the uniform and served or spent two years working at a VA hospital.

Without the public validating our personal involvement, not to mention the reception we returned to, it's been a tough pill to swallow for all these years. We find solace and pride when people like Joe Galloway, journalist and co-author of We Were Soldiers Once... and Young, stated at one of our reunion dinners, "I was proud to be there with you because you were the best Americans of my generation... When our country called you answered, when our country said GO you went..."[2]

Yet, with all that's been written, it's almost impossible to find anything that might help shake some memories or relieve the stigma placed on so many returning vets. I've never read or seen anything over these past decades about the positive things that shaped many of us—the good times and experiences, the laughs, the camaraderie. It wasn't until I visited the "Wall" in Washington, DC, where I felt anything remotely close to healing. Years later I was revisiting the Vietnam Veterans Memorial one frigid February morning in 1992, just walking along the low-slung monument with the same measured cadence as the other visitors; some searching

---

1   James Fallows. "What did you do in the class war, Daddy?" *Washington Monthly*, October 1975

2   I've included the speech by Joe Galloway published in *Air Mobile*, the 5th Battalion 7th Cavalry Association's newsletter, Volume 7, Issue 3, September 1998.

for names, others for answers; some confused, others lost in thought, staring at the polished stone wall. Maybe they were looking for an etching or inner peace, and closure. When I reached the name of my best friend, I was surprised the tears didn't instantly fill my eyes like they always had in the past. Instead, the hate, frustration, and depression caused by his loss was replaced with a smile, a remembrance of the good times we had had growing up together in Pompton Lakes, a small town in northern New Jersey.

There were so many good memories. It seemed like we'd been together forever—through grade and high school, sports and double dates, working on our cars, and going to the beach with friends. At nineteen years old, it was only fitting that we'd be drafted on the same day, our birthdays being only eight days apart. Fortunately, our friendship and laughs continued through our basic and advanced military training. We arrived in Vietnam together and ultimately were both assigned to the 1st Cavalry Division. Just standing in front of his name made me misty, but I also felt my smile growing broader, as if he had just mentioned an episode I hadn't remembered. I shook my head, wondering why he and all the others had to leave this life so young. A last look before shrugging my shoulders without an answer, and as always, I said aloud, "See you soon, Donny. See you soon."

I continued my walk but with a slightly different mindset while seeing the names of others I had known. I don't know why it happened, but while staring at a name etched into the cold black granite, my focus changed unexpectedly. I wasn't looking at a name but at my own reflection, smiling back with the memory of another fallen comrade. I suddenly started to remember the laughs, the bonds of friendship, and the unconditional trust we had in each other, even though our time together was so short. For the first time since I had left the 1st Cavalry Division back in 1968, the positive events and life lessons started surfacing. I was a Vietnam veteran, and suddenly a proud one at that. As I looked into my own eyes on the Wall, the negative thoughts started to melt away. I had this strange feeling, as if thousands of voices were yelling, "Don't grieve us. Just remember the good times!"[3] It was at that moment I felt compelled to record events reflecting our day-to-day life so many years ago. The good times and laughs, even those on not-so-good days. A few years ago, I read *Pickett's Charge in History and Memory*, a Civil War history book by Carol Reardon. Through her research she found a quote by a 71st Pennsylvania veteran of Gettysburg who noted, "Generals and Admirals win high renown for military achievements of their men, but personal deeds of heroism by simple privates or subalterns are rarely recorded." The following pages are my attempt to record what "privates and subalterns" often faced without recognition.

This book is a personal narrative, but I needed the whole cast of real-life characters to help me tell the stories. Many of the photos of the main characters are used throughout the pages, and most of those were taken during a stand-down[4], our three-or-four-day "break time." I hope you don't get the impression the casual poses were the way we spent our days in the field. The book is trying to convey life conditions, the resilience of the human spirit, and the ability to find laughter in

---

3   Years later I would hear Joe Galloway say something very similar leading me to believe others have heard the voices as well...

4   Stand-down—A few days of rest in a relatively secure area.

the darkest hours. Humor was often our only lifeline during the most challenging times. To be clear, this book is not about politics or body counts unless necessary to make a point. Many of the characters' names have been changed to protect the innocent from embarrassment. I have no intention of ridiculing anyone who took part in a particular episode other than myself. It is not meant to be a historically accurate account of the war. There are plenty of books for those specific subjects. If you would like to read more about a major operation or mission that I refer to in a story, there are references throughout the pages.

Many stories take place in or around the Imperial City of Hue during the Tet Offensive, and other locations within Vietnam's northernmost I Corps region during the first eight months of 1968. I hope the book doesn't give the impression that we had fun every day and war isn't that bad. Just for the sake of perspective, the first few weeks of February alone, our battalion lost twenty-seven good men, and another 203 were wounded. We will never forget them, but there are also the good things I long to remember and share.

The achievements of the 5th Battalion, 7th Cavalry, 1st Cavalry Division have been well documented. Because this was never intended to be a history book, I didn't go to the National Archives in Maryland to get our Daily Journals and Summaries. The short stories that follow are based on my vivid memories, along with specific battle details provided by Charles Baker, the battalion S-3 at the time. As the operations officer, Charlie did much of the planning and initiated many of the Daily Journals. So, he saved me a trip to Maryland. Read his excellent book, Gray Horse Troop: Forever Soldiers, for detailed accounts about the 5/7's[5] involvement during the 1968 Tet Offensive in Hue, Operation Pegasus for lifting the siege around the Khe Sahn Combat Base, and the combat air assault into the A Shau Valley. Many other stories simply relate to the mountains or Rocket Ridge, areas where the enemy had hospitals, spent R &R, stored their weapons, munitions, and supplies.

Take this book at face value. I'm not suggesting war is fun or romantic. The stories relate to general things like food, clothing, and shelter. As such, the stories don't necessarily fall into chronological order. You might find that to be a little confusing at times, as it was for the grunts who had little idea of what day it was or where we were. Only why. Readers will find redundant descriptions throughout the book. It was done intentionally in hopes of giving you a taste of the monotony in a grunt's daily life. The events as seen through my eyes describe what took place when, where, and how written. I have a good memory but used a bit of editorial license here and there for the dialogue. But the happenings are all true and not contrived in any way, shape, or form.

I didn't keep a diary. When you're running on high-octane adrenaline during those moments of high anxiety, you tend to remember things very clearly for the rest of your life. What immediately comes to mind is the book No Surrender: My Thirty-Year War about a Japanese soldier who was found on a Philippine island in 1974, thirty years after the end of WWII. He was able to recall in detail specific events throughout those years

---

5   5/7—Pronounced "fifth of the seventh," referring to the 5th Battalion of the 7th Cavalry.

due to his senses being so acutely attuned while evading the constant threat of capture.

Some events on the following pages happened during actual combat. I chose not to dwell on the casualties, but sometimes they can't be ignored. I'd rather focus on the humor we saw and felt at our own or others' expense. And in no way am I trying to romanticize or glorify war to those readers who haven't experienced the chaos. It would be nice if our governments would go back and use the Middle Ages as a reference. Let's just have a bunch of the warring politicians climb into a ring and beat the hell out of each other. It would save us a lot of money, there would be fewer casualties, and wars would be over in less than a week. Some of the stories will allude to the terror and conditions that sometimes left us living like undomesticated animals. It was simply the way we *had* to live at times, a glimpse of a grunt's daily life and the conditions under which they served. Think of it as personal deeds by simple privates or subalterns *being* recorded.

I read somewhere that it's difficult, almost unimaginable, to think of the words *war* and *laughter* being used in the same sentence. One evokes pain, suffering, and personal trauma, the other joy and mirth. But that's how I remember it—the good, the bad, and the ugly sometimes happening at the same time. The 1968 novel M.A.S.H., by Richard Hooker, hit the nail on the head. Anyone who watched the TV series or saw Robert Altman's war movie by the same name, laughed. It wasn't about political history or the wherefores and whys of war. It was about people doing and living in the harsh conditions in a war zone. And yet when we watched it, we laughed, we cried, and we got close to the characters. Very close. And after all these years, you can probably still recall some of those episodes very clearly, as I do mine.

I want to share with my fellow veterans, our families, the uninitiated, and the just plain curious readers the ordinary moments leading to unexpected humor that often surfaced in the most dangerous situations. Hopefully, this book will reawaken positive thoughts and memories and provoke some smiles. It might bring comfort to some and entertain others. The best result from reading the book would be bringing some war buddies back together. Maybe just look up an old friend and catch up on life, or even just say hi. I'd bet that by just thinking of the name of an old friend, a smile will appear. No media can truly capture the harsh realities and chaos that shaped our lives. But maybe I can help with the ongoing healing process by focusing on the positive. Maybe writing this book is the reason He brought me home.

—John Montalbano

Preface

I grew up during the fifties enjoying a semirural boy's dream life—playing with friends, fishing and swimming in the river behind our house, camping, hunting, ice skating, playing baseball and football. Unfortunately, as is my nature, I especially enjoyed playing in school too. But I wouldn't trade one minute or change one thing from those years. I graduated from Pompton Lakes High School in 1965. Pompton Lakes, New Jersey, was one of those great little self-sufficient towns back before malls came along. It seemed everyone had a sibling that went through the school system before them, and a younger one who would follow. We were the vanguard of the Baby Boomers, and as a result, everyone knew everyone, as well as every store owner's name. We occasionally got into some minor trouble, but the police were nice (mean) enough to just tell our parents. I was truly blessed to have grown up there and enjoyed a good school system that covered everything a young adult should know to make their way in the world.

Throughout those years we even learned about race relations in an offhand sort of way. When there was a lull in class or we were waiting for the bell to ring, it wasn't unusual for someone to ask a teacher who'd grown up in town about an old monument, or the dilapidated boxing ring behind the Elks Lodge, or just some recollections of the past. It didn't mean much to us when we were young, but we grew to appreciate it more through the years as other teachers in later grades also shared their experiences. That old boxing ring was for Joe Lewis, the Heavyweight Boxing Champion of the World from 1937 to the late '40's, a national hero who had his training camp near the lake. Throughout our school years, numerous teachers told us stories of how Mr. Lewis would take ten, fifteen, twenty excited little kids, apparently a lot of them future teachers, to an afternoon matinee at the Colonial Theatre in town. A few parents would try to calm the little devils down and get them in a line so the person standing in the glass enclosed ticket booth could count them as they passed. After the kids were lined up again inside, he'd buy them all popcorn and soda. In subsequent years we'd also heard about some very big-ticket items Mr. Lewis had purchased for the town in the form of emergency equipment. Sounded like a good guy. For those who don't know, Joe Lewis was an African American. We would all learn through life's lessons that people are people, no matter what shade they come in. Some good, some bad. Every combat soldier validated that lesson in Vietnam. Unfortunately, not necessarily back in the base camps where different cultures clashed.

I didn't know much about politics back then; in fact, I probably couldn't even spell the word. Having fun and laughing was always foremost on my mind. Never read a newspaper, other than the comics and sports sections, and didn't know a thing about the war in Vietnam. After graduation a lot of friends and classmates went off to college, but our family had gone through some financial hard times. They couldn't afford to send me, and a loan to a seventeen-year-old wouldn't even be considered. I had a dream and was willing to travel a couple hours each day as my parents had done. Two weeks after graduation, I drove twenty-seven miles to the big city of Newark, New Jersey. And with the help of my Uncle Tom, I was fortunate to be hired as a mechanical/architectural draftsman for Western Electric. The driving was a drag, but with the company paying a good portion of my college tuition, it was worth the mileage. If I really wanted to be an architect, I knew it would take longer, but I'd try to get my engineering degree by going to school nights. But, like so many other guys who graduated high school in the sixties, we had a good run for a couple of years until Uncle Sam sent us a letter. I was nineteen when drafted into the US Army in August 1967.

There were four months of military training. Initially, Basic Training in Fort Dix, New Jersey, which was very convenient for my family and girlfriend, followed by my first airplane trip for Advanced Infantry Training at Fort Jackson, located outside of Columbia, South Carolina. On our first day of AIT, we were informed, almost apologetically by our company commander, a Special Forces captain recently returned from Vietnam on a temporary assignment, that we would all be serving in an infantry unit in Vietnam after we completed training. He was not making it up. He was not trying to scare us. He wasn't going to make us exercise. He wanted everyone to be awake for all of the classes. If we weren't in shape already, we would be after a month in Nam. Everyone. No exceptions, unless you had someone in the immediate family who was killed there, and you were the sole surviving male. At nineteen you always think, "Nah, won't happen me. He's just trying to scare us." By the end of the eight weeks, I had turned twenty, gotten married, and on January 3rd was on my way to Southeast Asia via California as predicted. Some nightmares do come true. After processing in-country, I was assigned to A Company, 5th Battalion, 7th Cavalry, 1st Cavalry Division. I was no scholar, but something in the name sounded familiar. *'Wait, wasn't Custer in the 7th Cavalry?'*

The timing of my arrival and my unit's location could not have been worse. I joined the company in late January after some more intensive training, and by the first week of February, we were outside the Imperial City of Hue fighting for our lives during the communist Tet Offensive. Maybe I'm wired differently, but I was still able to laugh and have fun even though experiencing some not-so-good things on some not-so-good days that changed my life forever. I'm honored to have been able to share some of those good times with you.

Acknowledgments

The original manuscript sat in one drawer or another, when it wasn't boxed for moving four times, for almost twenty years. Except for those moments of inspiration when I pulled it up on the computer and did some editing. Between floppy discs, CDs, and thumb drives, I continued work through I don't know how many computers and software upgrades. You get the idea. There's a lot of dust on it. Back at the turn of the century, I had a literary agent who sent the manuscript to over thirty publishers. One liked it, but the business went under while the book was in editing. The others responded with basically the same reply: "We like it, but no one wants to read about Vietnam." So, there it sat. Fast-forward to 2023.

It would still be a work in progress if not for a lot of people asking if it was published yet. I had mentioned the manuscript to Ken Morgan and Steve Wood, a couple of new friends who had recently moved into our development. Both wanted to read it after some of my anecdotes had piqued their interest. I reluctantly gave them a rough manuscript I hadn't seen in years, and their responses to reading it reminded me of why I wrote it in the first place. "If you don't publish it," they both agreed, very seriously I might add, "it would be a disservice to all the guys who served." That caught me completely by surprise. Surprised because someone actually read it, liked it, and validated the concept. I assumed they were just being nice to a friend, so I put it back in the drawer. Over the following six months or so, they asked how the book was coming, and I kept hedging about research, or finding photos, or anything that might change the subject. I thank them both for their unending encouragement.

When I first came up with the idea of writing about the "lighter side of combat," I bounced a partial draft off Jim Mello, who shared all of my military training and ultimate assignment to the 1st Cavalry Division. For his help and years of friendship, I again say thank you to Jim and his late wife Cindy for editing the early drafts and providing me with constructive criticism, direction, and sage advice, as well as hospitality to my family and me over the years. I can't think about the manuscript without thinking of them.

As a member of the 5th Battalion, 7th Cavalry Association, I've been fortunate to reunite with those I served with. Our continued reunions and ongoing correspondence have helped to relieve some things locked up inside for far too long. My sincere gratitude to the late Lt. Gen. James B. Vaught, a.k.a. JB, Colonel Vaught, Boss. I truly believe that his leadership, intelligence, and compassion are the reason a lot of us are still here to read this. To my former CO, John Taylor, thank you for the continued friendship and overseeing our monthly calls. After so many years, you're still watching over our well-being and helping to show us the way.

To Tim Pasquarelli, my platoon's leader, it was a hoot serving under you. I wouldn't say they were fun times, but I certainly enjoyed sharing them with you. There's a reason you're featured in more than a few stories. To Vince Laurich, the 1st Platoon's leader, your willingness and ability to travel the country to meet, be with, and attend ceremonies for so many veterans, arrange gatherings, and plan fishing trips are astounding. Let's do it again. To Boyd Osler, the 3rd Platoon leader, your shared insight and experiences are truly praiseworthy. You've seen the best and worst of man's deeds, helping us all to remember we're never alone. As the grunt of the bunch, I'm proud and honored to be a part of our brotherhood.

To Charlie Baker, the 5/7 battalion S-3. Your personal input, the Daily Journals in your book Gray Horse Troop, and some detailed behind-the-scenes information were invaluable. As the operations officer during the period when these stories originated, you were able to give me details straight from the horse's mouth, so to speak. Thank you for saving me a trip to the archives and also for including the "little Italian guy" in your historical accounts.

To Larry Hilton, with whom I served, here's another book for you to add captions and page markers noting the 5/7's exploits. It's always good to see you at the reunions after sharing our days together in '68. Even on the not-so-fun days.

To the men of the 5/7 I say, Garry Owen!

To Ed Helmuth, a good friend from high school who is named in one of the stories. By your taking the time away from your studies to write me a letter back in February '68, it helped the guys in my squad, and me in particular, a lot more than you can ever imagine. Thank you, Ed. Still makes me smile every time I'm caught out in the rain.

To Linda Ebel Thomasma, thank you for reaching out for information about your big brother Bill. His photos that you shared with me reside in the 5th Battalion, 7th Cavalry Association's archives as well as in this book. I've printed a couple of pictures of Bill and include him in a number of stories that will keep his memory alive for generations. Your family should be proud of him. I know the guys in our squad were.

To the late Maggie Driscoll, who in her past military career was the highest-ranking female NCO in the United States Air Force. I thank you for your friendship and sharing your experiences. When we talked about me writing your story, you laughed and said you already knew what you would call it. I've changed my original title, and in your honor, I've used yours: Bullets in My Bottom Drawer. We all miss you down here, Maggie.

Thanks to Palmetto Publishing's Troy Otten for overseeing the origination process and to Alexandra Lapointe, my project manager, for her professional assistance in completing the finished product.

To my wife Helen, daughters Michelle and Gina, and grandsons Bowen, Alec, and Aaron, thank you for believing in me and sharing your time at the Wall and our military reunions. The guys you've met over the years always sing your praises and ask about you. It certainly makes for a very proud husband, father, and grandfather.

My motivation to see this book completed is a result of so many people who all have one thing in common:

They want to let veterans know they are not forgotten but still very much appreciated. To my family, friends, troopers of the 7th Cavalry past and present, and even a few doctors who prodded me without using a needle, I thank you all for your welcome encouragement and support.

—John Montalbano

Selected Bibliography

Arnold, James, and Gordon Rottman, The Tet Offensive and the Siege of Khe Sahn. Osprey Publishing Ltd., 2006.

Baker, Charles, Gray Horse Troop: Forever Soldiers. Powder River Publications, 2013.

Bernstein, Jonathan, and Gordon Rottman, Vietnam Choppers and Their Crews. Osprey Publishing Ltd., 2007.

Bishop, Chris, Gordon Rottman, Richard Lanthrop, and John McDonald. US Armaments of the Vietnam War. Osprey Publishing Ltd., 2007.

Bowden, Mark. Hue 1968: A Turning Point of the American War in Vietnam. Atlantic Monthly Press, 2017.

Herr, Michael. Dispatches. Alfred A. Knopf, 1977

Mason, Robert. Chickenhawk. The Viking Press, 1983.

Melson, Charles, and Gordon Rottman. Vietnam Warriors. Osprey Publishing Ltd., 2006.

Moore, Lt. Gen. Harold G., and Joseph L. Galloway. We Were Soldiers Once…and Young: Ia Drang—the

Battle That Changed the War in Vietnam. Random House, 1992.

New York Times. Associated Press. Army Chief Abrams dies at 59, directed U.S. forces in Vietnam." September 4, 1974. p. 1.

Oberdorfer, Don. Tet! The Story of a Battle and Its Historic Aftermath. Doubleday, 1971.

Reardon, Carol, Pickett's Charge in History and Memory. University of North Carolina Press, 1997.

Scannell, Vernon. Not Without Joy. Routledge, 1976

Spector, Ronald H., After Tet: The Bloodiest Year in Vietnam. Vintage, 1994.

Time. Nation: Peer Pattern's. April 14, 1967

Official Records

S-3, 5th Battalion, 7th Cavalry. Battalion Daily Journals: January through June 1968. National Archives, College Park, Maryland.

S-3, 3rd Brigade, 1st Cavalry Division. Selected Daily Summary Reports: January through June 1968. National Archives, College Park, Maryland.

G-3, 1st Cavalry Division. Selected Daily Journals: January through June 1968. National Archives, College Park, Maryland.

Chapter I
This Can't Be Real

At times we find ourselves perplexed, shaking our heads mulling over something we're seeing or doing or hearing, wondering if it's real. Your brain starts running through the archives to see if there's a match. If there is, you have the answer and your mind clears. Until then, your thoughts are rapidly asking simple questions prompting the brain where to look. "Are my eyes and ears deceiving me?" "How the heck did I get into this?" "I can't believe this is happening." "I must be dreaming." "This can't be real." "I must be on Candid Camera." "What the . . . ?!" Happens all the time. You're waiting at a traffic light on the way to work and happen to glance over at the car that just pulled up next to you. Looking back at you is a sheep, his head and a big pair of curled horns hanging out of the window of a Cadillac. Quick, what do you think? What comes to mind? Right, you rub your eyes thinking you're still asleep. But believe it or not, it's a true story. My aunt was taking her pet to the vet. "This can't be real!"

Questioning oneself happens often when you're doing something unexpected or never experienced, may-

be out of character. Sometimes you have the answer
but don't know if it's right or wrong. Same thing happens—short answers. "No way!" "I can't." "Not possible." "Fuhgeddaboudit!" It's those moments in life
when you're painted into a corner. This is especially so
when high anxiety or danger is involved. Like standing
in an open doorway at ten thousand feet and you're
supposed to deplane while the craft is still moving. Or
you told your buddies you ski, and one day you find
yourself at the top of a black diamond trail and the ski
lift is no longer working. "How the hell did I get into
this nightmare?!"

These things happen and you somehow convince
yourself to act, or you chicken out or come up with a
simple answer. If you're in the military and are given
orders, all of the above are still in play, but you only
have one answer: "Yes, sir." I found myself in that position a number of times.

Under a Crescent Moon

About twenty minutes into the mission, I stopped for a quick breather and to shake the cobwebs out of my head. The total silence seemed familiar. Past missions flashed through my mind, and for some reason February 21 rang a bell. Maybe that was it, near Hue during the Tet Offensive. This new operation felt similar but not quite the same. Back then the weather was dreary, with some form of rain every day, and cold at night. Now it was hot every day, with stifling humidity. But there were some similarities, I guessed—not much sleep, crawl out of our hooches in near-total darkness, dress, same rushed light breakfast, then "saddle up." No rucksacks, same weapons, and plenty of ammo. So maybe the two operations weren't the same, but there was something else.

The month near Hue was a much larger operation. We in A Company, 5th Battalion of the 7th Cavalry, along with the three other companies of the 5/7, had moved out in near-total darkness on that dreary morning. Considering the number of guys walking on the well-trodden muddy trail, the surroundings remained deathly quiet. No birds, no frogs, not even a hint of air movement to disturb the leaves on the stunted shrubs. The moment we left the protection of the wood line, a dense fog masked our hunched-over low approach until every man to the front slowly disappeared, one by one. It wasn't a very comfortable final approach, crawling through clusters of tall wet grass, but it helped dampen any unwanted sounds and would conceal any sudden movements until we reached our destination.

Eventually the entire company took up positions behind a low berm skirting a muddy rice paddy about three football fields wide. Beyond that wide open field lay a dense line of bamboo and hardwoods surrounding the village of Thon La Chu.[6] Three companies, coming from different directions with different missions, were preparing for a frontal assault against a well-entrenched NVA[7] force—the same guys we'd been trying to oust for two weeks.

The operation might have ended sooner but for some problems like constant rain and low cloud cover grounding our gunships,[8] no artillery because the rounds were still in transit from the 1st Cavalry's original base camp in An Khe two hundred miles away, and a serious lack of some heavy weapons or armor. So it wasn't until after our battalion alone had lost a lot of troopers, from 475 down to 360 troopers in under two weeks, before the brigade finally found out what we were up against. Through intelligence reports and pris-

---

6   Baker, Gray Horse Troop.

7   NVA—North Vietnamese Army.

8   Gunships—Reference to all helicopter types modified to carry a number of different weapon configurations; helicopters used for attack or in ground support for troops.

oner interrogations, they couldn't blame us grunts in the 7th and 12th Cavalry's for not trying. The enemy force, well dug-in with overlapping trenches and one-man spider holes that we couldn't dislodge, numbered well over a thousand. And based on POWs' assigned regiments, some of which were thought to be in Khe Sahn, that number could be as large as three thousand. As it turned out, Thon La Chu was *the* central hub for all NVA operations, troop replacements, supplies, anything and everything to do with their Hue offensive during the Lunar New Year of Tet. And their guys guarded that stinkin' position really well.

Nah, on second thought, the two operations really weren't similar at all. Can't compare the two. Back then we knew what to expect. This time, too many unknowns. Back then we just made our way to the offensive position on flat ground. This time the terrain was rugged, severe. We had to climb down roughly seven hundred feet of saturated jungle floor on a steep mountain slope in the dark. And not make any noise, we didn't want to wake up Charlie.[9] And this was the easy part of the operation. *Humph.*

I didn't think any of the guys in our squad had taken long to figure out that the descent was very precarious and taking a greater toll on our bodies and minds than the brass had anticipated. I had wedged a foot against a sapling to remain stationary and felt pain radiating from a deep scrape on my right forearm. The burning feeling quickly brought me back from the memory of Hue. *Okay, focus on today. Let's go, break time's over.* Nothing to do now except wipe some dirt out of the

---

9   Charlie, or Victor Charlie—Nickname given to our North Vietnamese and Vietcong enemy, derived from the US military phonetic spelling alphabet for VC (Vietcong).

oozing wound with one hand, hold onto my M-16[10] with the other, and go.

Moving down was easy. I lifted my foot from the sapling and let gravity do its thing, dragging my butt downhill a few feet at a time on the damp leaves while digging my bootheels into the dirt to control the speed. It reminded me of sleigh riding as a kid. In the morning we'd climb a mountain, then go down having no set path and a lot of trees, dragging our feet to slow down and live another day. Unlike those days long gone, I now had a few other options to control my speed, like slowly swinging my free arm back and forth trying to reach something to hold onto, while doing the same with my legs to locate something to put my foot against to stop my descent. I just prayed a sapling didn't sneak in between my feet. Otherwise, I'd just keep sliding until I found something.

Although barely able to see my hand at the end of my arm, each time I stopped, I slowly scanned below for any sign of movement. Pretty hard to do in the dark, so hearing was the only sense available to make sure I wasn't too close nor had strayed too far left or right of the guys below me. I was also praying the guys above and behind me, who would soon be coming down, were finding handholds.

In a matter of time, I could eventually make out ghostly apparitions hunched over within the edge of a tree line, and quickly slowed my butt ride until standing awkwardly like the others on what felt like slippery bedrock on a less severe slope. Each guy was clutching a weapon in one hand and either rubbing burning muscles or rubbing the wet mud off their rear end. I shook

---

10   M-16—Standard-issue semi- or fully automatic assault rifle weighing 7.5 pounds carried by riflemen.

my head a little and smiled, thinking the aches we felt were very different than what many of us had experienced only a few years earlier while in high school.

Knowing most of the guys in my squad and having gone through hell with some of them for the past few months, I was certain they could feel the same pounding in their chest, caused as much from the descent as the anxiety of what could happen in the next pulsating heartbeat. Stifled gasps surrounded me as each guy labored to fill his starving lungs with jungle air so thick with humidity it was nearly impossible to get relief. As much as we wanted to shift our bodies, everyone was acutely aware of our precarious position and fought the natural urges to stretch out cramping muscles. Built into every grunt around me were thousands of years of human evolution that gave us a natural instinct to stay alive, thus preventing any unrestricted movement or loud breathing that might alert a nearby source of food, or an armed enemy.

Nothing in the darkness is as it seems, but the reality was all so clear in each grunt's mind. We were half a world away from our hometowns, and it felt like decades since we had casually passed through early life completely without a care. I again shook my head in disbelief to regain my focus and turned to look to my right at the silhouettes of two guys a foot or so away who were trying to see where we were. No one could be certain how near we were to the first objective, nor did we know if we had awakened Charlie. *Let the high anxiety begin!*

We were on a tight schedule, knowing the rest of the company would be right behind us and depending on us to complete our mission first. Offering words of caution and encouragement to each other, we watched the point man move forward just as two other guys from our squad slid down behind us. Each guy waited to allow for ample spacing from the guy ahead before he followed. One after another, each disappeared into the black void in less than a matter of seconds. It was the rugged terrain's massive umbrella like canopy of leaves and vines that seemingly gave it the ability to suck every last ray of visible light from the night air. Enough to not only conceal our human forms but even the mountain itself. We would have to continue down before we could escape through the jungle's dark green curtain. Until then, we would have to be content with only dim shapes of exotic trees and plants close by, discernible only because of their size.

Without knowing the reason, we found that our ability to identify that which stood just a few feet away slowly improved, while the tropical forest still provided the illusion of protection. We could move a little faster now that convenient handholds could be seen. Just when I was wondering when this mountain was going to end, I was surprised when, as if with only a single step, I found myself no longer under the complete veil of darkness. That made life a little easier. We also no longer needed to hold onto anything to walk on terrain that had suddenly morphed into a gentle slope. But if we could see better in the dim light, it meant we were exposed and vulnerable. That meant movement and sound discipline was even more critical than before. Patience was needed now, both to regain strength and recover our eyesight thanks to the hint of moonlight filtering through millions of fluttering leaves overhead. We could almost see again, and a gentle air movement started cooling our overheated bodies. With the light's intensity having changed so suddenly, I could do nothing more than wait at the edge of the jungle backdrop, frozen in a crouched position until my vision improved, just as the three before me had done.

I was familiar with terrain changes such as this. Having grown up with a river behind my house that flooded occasionally, I saw what water could do over time. Every outside bend in the river was scoured flat for thirty feet or so. The riverbank was always flat and either covered with silt, sand, or stones, depending on its location. There was nothing growing within ten feet of the bank and then only some grasses on the barren, muddy ground. A little farther away from the water, saplings surrounded by sparse vegetation could be seen trying to survive. Beyond them the terrain began to rise, the hardwoods grew taller and larger brush covered the ground.

Just as I suspected, the jagged rock outcroppings and decaying vegetation of the mountainside had finally given way to a section of flat terrain sparsely populated with smaller hardwoods. Where the tree line ended, groupings of saplings could be seen silhouetted by an even lighter backdrop. That meant there had to be an open area in the canopy, and that meant we were nearing our target. As long as no one made any sudden movements, the shadows of the small trees should be able to provide us with enough cover. I thought it fascinating that minutes earlier, when blinded by the dark, we were able to hear faint rustling noises, somehow sense the presence of someone or something nearby, feel and taste the stifling humidity pressing against us, and smell the underbelly of the decaying jungle floor. But when our vision slowly adjusted to what little light the crescent moon offered, somehow our other senses waned.

Beyond the saplings there appeared to be a low-lying, grass-covered, muddy flat about fifteen feet from and less than two feet above a river that looked like it was filled with black ink. I thought if it were not for the moon and the trickling, gurgling sounds we had started to hear minutes before, the point man might have unknowingly slipped into water. I frowned in disgust when I recognized what was lining the water's edge and nudged Big Joe Kochman standing beside me. When he turned, I pointed at a nightmare of spiky, three-foot-tall blades of grass. We had learned from careless contact in the past that the grass had razor-sharp edges that easily sliced any unprotected skin. *Gee, since we left the perimeter, it's just been one good thing after another*, I thought. Still struggling for breath in even denser air and now bleeding in a few more new places, I, like probably most around me, cursed the brass for putting us there. And, like every grunt through the ages, I was pissed because it always seemed to be our platoon or squad or legion or tribe that got the dirtiest or most dangerous jobs.

To conceal ourselves again before leaving the "safe" cover of four-inch-diameter trees, we slowly slunk down into the dew-covered tufts of small grass rising from the mud for our last-minute predawn preparations. I couldn't hear it but knew each of us was clawing at the cool mud and smearing the gritty black coating on our faces for camouflage. Any leftover globs were rubbed on mosquito-ravaged and overheated exposed skin. I welcomed the temporary relief the mud provided in easing the pain of bites, bruises, and scrapes. It was the same remedy I'd used as a kid, gathering mud at the river's edge behind our house. It was much better than going in the house and having my mother make a big deal out of a minor injury while she painted the wound with mercurochrome. *Ouch!*

Preparations continued unabated by each man using his own personal checklist—ammo magazines still packed tight to prevent movement and sound, grenades secured, weapon safeties on, and any last-minute prayers silently offered over still-deafening heartbeats. I shifted my head from side to side, peeking through small separations in the thick grass, straining to see our next destination. Finally, a whispered order was passed from man to man, and we slowly crawled forward to our first objective: the river's edge. Through squinted eyes, I could barely make out our second and most dangerous objective: a flat, completely exposed beachhead across the moving water.

From our new vantage point, we could see flickering shafts of moonlight shimmering across the river's rippling surface. The eerie movements and patterns of light and shadow made the water appear almost alive, as if it were the wrinkled skin of an ancient trembling hand, long spindly fingers pointing toward a shallow gravel beach. Our attention was being directed toward a cutout on the inside bend of the river. The barren area was at least 150 feet wide, and deep, completely devoid of any living vegetation, and appeared nothing like the narrow spit of grass-covered mud we were lying on. The opposite bank's open rocky expanse was strewn with the remains of shattered trees and huge tangled roots devoid of any soil. It was hard to know for sure in the low light whether they were roots or the exposed carcasses of dinosaurs left to bleach in the sun, left there just as a reminder that this was a dangerous land. And at the farthest limits of the beach, away from the water, was an identical copy of the menacing dark wall of dense jungle that stood just steps behind us.

The growling noise in the pit of my stomach made me reflect on the chain of events that had brought me to this point in time, reminding me that we had awoken before four that morning and prepared to move out without much time for a breakfast. Order of march for the day was our 2nd Platoon, followed by the 3rd, then the headquarters or HQ people, made up of the company commander (CO); the artillery forward observer, or FO; "Top," our tough, cigar-chomping First Sergeant, who was already a veteran of two wars; and their RTOs.[11] Coming down last and covering our backs would be the 1st Platoon. Staying on the mountaintop to later help sling the large cargo net with our rucksacks to a helicopter would be a grunt from each platoon and, on this day, the FO's radio operator.

As soon as we had started moving down the mountain earlier, we in the lead squad knew there were going to be problems with the operation. Not only was it extremely difficult to see, but compounding our blindness was the severe angle of the mountain slope that forced us to hang onto any tree, rock, weed, or vine we could locate by touch so as to prevent us from sliding downhill. Lastly, the ground was in a constant state of dampness, common to a jungle floor, thus making our footing even more precarious. After only one hundred feet of progress, I felt our squad could get down without too much danger or noise but didn't think the later squads could. To control our descent, we had to drag our butts and dig in our boot heels to minimize any downward momentum, thus creating a smooth, open trail for those behind to follow. But in doing so, we

---

11   RTO—Radio Telephone Operator.

were not only making it even slicker for the remaining squads, but we were pulling out any vine, fern, root, branch, and rock within arm's reach.

Sam Byrd, our squad leader, had radioed the CO with that intelligence, but because he didn't want to screw up the operation's timetable, he told us to push on. The company was supposed to get down the mountain and cross the river before daylight. Not only did we, the point squad, have to worry about climbing down a mountain in near total darkness, crossing the current of a river, and possibly making contact, but we also had to worry about being crushed by a human avalanche trying to punch a clock for the ole man. The tension in our squad mounted because so many things could go wrong during a questionable exercise like this.

The operation was to be our first "beach assault" without the use of our helicopters. Rather than encountering an ocean or lagoon beach normally associated with beach landings, we were in the middle of Vietnam's mountainous I Corps region, in a place thought to be heavily occupied by North Vietnamese Army regulars—a possible NVA staging area for the Tet Offensive and subsequent incursions. As I scanned our surroundings, I found everything just as our squad leader had described during our briefing the night before. The added intelligence as to what to expect always helped ease the anxiety during the early stages of a mission, when things could change from peaceful stillness to incredible noise and chaos. The other fact that helped us was being proud members of the "First Team," the 1st Cavalry Division. We drew some comfort knowing we had pretty good intelligence reports because of our superb Long Range Reconnaissance teams and also the support of the largest concentration of helicopters assigned to any division in Vietnam. Being airmobile meant they could bring supplies, reinforcements, and firepower and, if need be, could get us to safety or a hospital in minutes, not hours. Despite these reassurances, the mission was something we had never attempted before, and we were all uptight about what we were doing.

Most of the guys near me had survived the near-constant month-long combat on our way to the Imperial City of Hue during the February 1968 Tet Offensive. We had come through many more firefights since, and a lot of Purple Hearts and medals of valor were awarded to validate the experiences. Despite being a seasoned veteran, an uneasy feeling in the gut and unanswered questions before every mission never changed, "Is today the day? I don't feel good about this. Oh, man I'm too short for this shit!"

Adding to the tense atmosphere of that particular early morning was the fact that we had a few new guys who were completely untested in the field. Most were still shaking from their first jump out of a hovering helicopter during the air assault onto the mountaintop less than twelve hours earlier. The very presence of these "cherries" made me feel uncomfortable because it was yet another unknown factor in the operation. At this point on the riverbank, the intangibles didn't matter—there was nothing more that could be done to relieve our anxieties. Everyone had been prepped the previous night and reminded before we had set out that morning what to expect and what to do if contact was made.

While the remainder of our company tried to silently make its way single file down the mountain, our squad was the lead element of the attack and was about to execute the first daring maneuver. Three guys were to swim across the river, two pushing inflated air mattresses carrying their weapons, munitions, and gear, while the third dragged a heavy rope. The plan was to secure the rope to an immovable object on each shore to help the guys in the following squads to negotiate the river current in safety with little or no noise. The CO's ambitious plan was to get the entire company across the river before dawn while still concealing our presence and thus maintaining an element of surprise—a classic US Army Ranger maneuver, I've been told.

There were five of us lying at the river's edge; Big Joe Kochman, from Philadelphia; Jack Teakle, from Waco, Texas; me, from New Jersey; Butch O'Brien, from Boston; and Sam Byrd, our squad leader, also from Philly. While we prepared to execute the plan, I had time to reflect on the long chain of events leading up to this incredible moment. My life's memories played quickly through my mind. *How could it possibly be,* I thought to myself, *after watching war movies my whole life, emulating my father by dressing like a soldier for Halloween, playing war in the woods behind our house in preparation for the possibility of a real day like this, undergoing eighteen weeks of formal military training, and enduring months of intense combat with the best the North Vietnamese Army could throw at us—how could this be happening to me?* Disbelieving the situation, I continued trying to make sense out of the predicament I found myself unable to escape. *Why am I lying here in wet, insect-infested, cutting grass, with streaks of mud, wearing only my helmet, carrying two bags full of munitions, holding an M-16 rifle, and seeing Jackie's butt cheek that looks like a crescent moon?* No, that wasn't it. I shook my head in disbelief. *Why am I lying on a muddy riverbank, in a heavily defended free-fire combat zone, with other men who are also naked?* No, no, no, that wasn't it either. Oh, that was it! *Why am I lying naked on a muddy riverbank in the dark with other naked guys?! How the hell did I get here?! What the. . .?*

Jack Teakle, the author, Big Joe Kochman

The previous day had started out okay. Our four-day stand-down on LZ[12] Jack, a small artillery firebase seven miles or so outside of Camp Evans, the new home of the 1st Cavalry Division, northwest of Hue in the Vietnam's I Corps region, had ended. Soon, we'd board slicks[13] for another two-week operation in the rugged, mountainous area west of Hue. We knew the area as "Rocket Ridge," where the NVA were fond of launching rockets at Camp Evans and the surrounding settlements. We had received three replacements in

---

12   LZ—Landing Zone; airfield, base for insertion or extraction of troops or materials; a remote firebase for artillery to support ground operations.

13   Slicks—Term given to the Bell UH-1 "Huey" helicopters used for transporting cargo, supplies, and troops.

the squad that week, FNGs or Fucking New Guys, as they were called, so my actions as a fire team leader would have to be a little more focused to make sure they didn't get into trouble. The first few weeks for replacement troops were always the most dangerous for them and us. Other than combat action, when someone was trying to kill you, there were many things they had to learn before they were able to survive and eventually be accepted by the old-timers. We needed to be certain they could handle basic day-to-day chores. Not necessarily in order of importance, but could they stay awake on guard duty every night, walk around with a loaded weapon and hand grenades without hurting someone on our side, and of course, did they know how to make hot coffee in the morning before we hit the trail? Much of the stand-down had been spent getting to know them and help them settle in for the long haul. There was Billy Ebel, from Michigan. He reminded me of a guy named Wally Cox, an actor who played a TV character named Mr. Peepers during my childhood, but I guess today you'd say he looked like Pee-wee Herman instead. Anyway, a nice kid with the intelligence to listen and learn, two of the most important traits necessary for survival. He looked like the studious type with his thick, gray-rimmed glasses, lanky build, and quiet demeanor. Like all new guys, Bill wanted to fit in, so when asked if he would like to carry the M-79[14] grenade launcher for a while, he agreed. He appeared to know his own physical limitations, so we trusted his decision. If he wasn't in shape from his four months of Basic and Advanced Infantry Training, he soon would be.

---

14   M-79—Single-shot, shoulder-fired, break-action, 40mm grenade launcher with an effective range of 75-300 meters. When fired, shell activates at or past thirty meters.

The second new guy was Butch O'Brien, from the Boston area. Unlike the reserved and conservative Ebel, Butch immediately came across like a lunatic mercenary who craved combat. Many new guys tried to act that way at first, thinking they were impressing people by showing how tough they were, bragging about how they would act under fire. Unfortunately, they all got their chance and found that words were cheap. But unlike the others who eventually learned the meaning of humility, there was something about that guy that bothered us. He was built solid, like a football running back, and he appeared to be at least semi-intelligent, but he was definitely a loose cannon. He wanted medals and was willing to take chances to get them, and that might mean trouble for the rest of us at some time in the future.

The third guy was from Arkansas, and he looked and sounded like...I don't know, I guess like a pre–Civil War plantation owner would have sounded like. Or maybe more like Foghorn Leghorn, the big cartoon rooster. "Mah name is Shelby Jefferies, sah. Pleashah tah make yah acquaintance." Shelby was a likable guy and quick with a funny joke or story. He came to the army in a slightly different manner than most. He had to make a choice between jail or military service. When asked why he didn't join the air force or navy, he said he was afraid of heights and couldn't swim. We couldn't wait to see him on his first CA,[15] climbing out of a moving helicopter, standing on the skids, and jumping into water. All I knew was I didn't want to be below that 248-pound, five-foot-ten rooster when he jumped, so I made a mental note to myself that on all air assaults, I should jump out *after* him.

---

15   CA—Combat Air assault; troop insertion via helicopter.

Our company walked downhill away from the fire base headed towards an open pick-up area just outside the wire. We were spread out in a long line, segmented by platoon and individual squad in the order we would board the inbound helicopters. It was time for us to go back to work. Until then, we were following standard operating procedures of hurry up and wait, just sitting on our rucksacks, baking under the hot sun, and waiting for the slicks to arrive. As had happened many times before, they would lift us out and drop us off somewhere on a jungle mountaintop. Most of the old-timers—that is, anyone who had already survived a month in-country—were trying to store some last-minute sleep that would be appreciated in the days to come. Others were writing letters that would be given to a helicopter door gunner or crew chief for mailing. I walked over to each new guy to give them last-minute instructions on where to sit in the chopper and what to expect and do at the landing zone. I made sure Shelby understood he would follow me, sit on the canvas seat next to me, and slide his butt as far in as possible. Bruce would climb in before Jack from the opposite side and sit next to me. They both nodded, so at least I knew they were listening. Whether they could remember was yet to be seen. And I made sure they understood the potential danger. "The LZ might be small, and only one chopper at a time can go in. Always remember, when a chopper lands it's a big target. Get in and get out fast!"

While I was trading barbs with Shelby, we heard "Saddle up!" Everyone started climbing into their gear before we even heard the familiar sound of Hueys[16] in the distance. Shelby and Butch would be my responsibility, so I checked their gear insuring everything was firmly attached and not likely to cause an injury. We would be riding in the last helicopter of the first wave and were lined up at the end of our squad's staged formation. It was finally adrenaline pumping time when the increasing volume of Huey rotor blades slapping the air let us know a flight was coming in for a landing.

---

16   Huey—Bell UH-1 utility helicopter; most common helicopter used to transport troops, supplies, and medevac wounded, or modified for use as a gunship.

As their nose raised and their speed decreased to near zero, we could feel the increasing vibrations from the powerful engines, and a down draft of air turbulence pushing us back on our heels. By then, any verbal communications would require yelling to a person standing next to you. And all this *before* they even landed.

The two squads from our platoon quickly headed toward our designated rides as soon as their skids touched down. Every guy moving with a purpose, bent at the waist and trying to shield their eyes from the swirling grit. The heavy backpacks bounced and shifted left and right with each step, making running impossibly awkward, and the full complement of munitions each guy carried naturally slowed their progress. Try as we might, there was no escaping the loose, powdery red clay that filled the air. It stuck to our relatively clean fatigues, coated every square inch of exposed, sweat-covered skin, and threatened to blind anyone fool enough not to squint and shade his eyes.

In less than a minute, the four slicks were loaded and airborne with twenty-eight troopers. I had taken the middle seat in order to keep an eye on both FNGs sitting on either side. Whereas most of the guys in the Huey looked like they were deeply tanned or sunburned from being coated with red clay, Shelby, by comparison, looked a little pale.

When we traveled "heavy"—that is, with our backpacks, or rucksacks, "rucks" as we called them—the worst place to sit in a helicopter was on a seat. Because of its size, the backpack took up the seating area, while your butt was suspended in space, desperately trying to find an edge to rest a cheek on. Shelby sat to my left and Butch to my right, while four others from our squad sat on the floor, two in each door opening, their legs and feet dangling outside above the helicopter's landing skids. We were once again off to the happy hunting grounds, leaving the remaining members of our company waiting for the choppers to return and pick up the second wave. Sam Byrd, our squad leader from Philly, rode with us for a number of reasons. First, he wanted to make sure the new guys obeyed orders, and second, Sam was getting "short"—only a couple of months left on his tour of duty—and liked taking the trailing birds in case of a "hot" landing zone. Very wise. Time spent in-country did that to you.

A fifteen-minute ride through a beautiful blue sky, surrounded by other Hueys loaded with grunts, and helicopter gunships armed with rockets and miniguns[17] flanking the formation, had the same effect on us old-timers as it did on the new guys. It was exciting to be a part of, but we were anxious and tried to keep our minds focused on the job ahead—getting off the damn helicopter with no incoming enemy fire. Like the others, I watched the landscape two thousand kilometers below slowly changing from a flat, lush, yellow-green carpet with occasional burn marks from exploded artillery ordnance to the dark green vegetation of the rugged mountain peaks and valleys we would soon be patrolling. A look around the chopper showed a scene that was all too familiar—sweat-stained, dusty grunts with graffiti on their camouflaged helmet covers and flak jackets.

We typically traveled "light" for air assaults, carrying up to seventy pounds of equipment, centered pri-

---

17   Minigun—electrically operated six-barreled rotary Gatling gun capable of firing between two thousand and four thousand rounds per minute of 7.62 millimeter belt-fed ammunition.

marily on the weapon, munitions, canteen(s), helmet, and a flak vest. If a grunt wasn't carrying the PRC-25 radio, he held a weapon of some sort in his hand— an M-16 assault rifle, the M-79 grenade launcher and a .45-caliber pistol on his hip, or the M-60[18] machine gun. I know, put all of those on a scale together and it doesn't come close to seventy pounds. So let me give you an example of one of our rifleman, me for instance, who typically carried a six-and-a-half-pound M-16. We all carried twenty loaded magazines and some combination of a dozen or so fragmentation, white phosphorus, concussion, and smoke hand grenades. That "basic load" totaled about forty-five pounds. From day to day we alternated carrying olive-green steel ammunition cans about the size and shape of a heavy-duty lunch box. The main difference being the top was flat and they didn't have a picture of Davy Crockett or Mickey Mouse stenciled on the sides. Each ammo can, weighing about twenty-six pounds, contained two paper-thin cardboard boxes with each containing two one-hundred-round belts of linked M-60 machine-gun ammo. Collectively, with three guys sharing the load daily, the machine gunner in each squad would typically have twelve hundred to fifteen hundred rounds for immediate disposal.

If a riflemen wasn't carrying a can of ammo that particular day, he shared the load for other things that the squad needed and for himself, other can't-do-without items in case the rucks weren't delivered. Critical

---

18   M-60—Belt-fed automatic machine gun weighing thirty-two pounds and capable of firing five-hundred to six-hundred fifty rounds per minute of 7.62 millimeter ammunition.

items like trip flares,[19] Claymore mines,[20] an entrenching tool,[21] machete, plastique explosives, blasting caps
and detonation cord, extra batteries for the radio, and
maybe a can or two of C rations[22] for that all-important
luncheon date. Those things might add another fifteen
to twenty pounds to one's load. Oh, almost forgot—a
LAW[23] rocket launcher or two. *But wait, there's more!* I
don't know, how much does a sweat-soaked cotton towel weigh, plus a first aid kit, bottle of mosquito repellant,
gum, the army-issued web or a souvenir belt and bags
needed to carry everything, jungle boots, a camera, eating utensils, watch, knife, bayonet, cigarettes, lighter, et
al., with most of the smaller items carried in billowing
shirt and pants pockets? You get the idea—it all added
up pretty quick. Once everything was divided up, every man, regardless of weapon or radio, carried closer
to the seventy-pound mark. We learned many lessons
during the Tet Offensive, such as you can't have too
much ammo. So that was traveling light, and our rucks
would typically be flown out to us in a sling at the end
of each day. Unless it was raining.

---

19   Trip flare—Metal device roughly seven inches long by two inches
in diameter and used to guard against night infiltration; has a spike on one end
and detonator on the top, triggered by trip wire. When ignited, it will burn
for slightly over one minute at fifty thousand candlepower at 4,200 degrees,
illuminating up to a three-hundred-meter radius.

20   Claymore mine—Antipersonnel weapon roughly five inches tall
by ten inches wide and weighing 3.5 pounds, made of slightly curved, dark
gray-green fiberglass. A Claymore contains a layer of C-4 explosive behind a
matrix of approximately seven hundred steel balls and can be triggered manu-
ally or by trip wire.

21   Entrenching tool—Small portable collapsible shovel.

22   C-rations—individually boxed meal for one, canned foodstuff.

23   LAW—Light Anti-armor Weapon; a disposable sixty-six-millimeter
shoulder-fired rocket launcher weighing 5.2 pounds, accurate to 160 yards
with a maximum range of 220 yards.

Unfortunately, on this particular air assault, we were traveling "heavy." So, besides the above mentioned "light" stuff, we were also carrying our bulging, thirty-plus-pound rucksacks. The olive-green heavy-duty nylon backpack, mounted on a steel frame and worn using two shoulder straps, held all of our worldly possessions not immediately needed for fighting. Stuffed, lashed, packed, and stashed in the bag, side pockets, or on the frame were shaving items, nail clippers, scissors, toothbrush and paste, soap, writing paper, pen, address book, cans or packages of food, Tabasco sauce, Kool-Aid, iodine and salt pills, spices, extra cigarettes, lighter fluid, cookies, candy, toilet paper, small saucepan, canteen cup, letters and pictures from home, *Playboy* magazines, book, out-of-date newspapers, extra socks, maybe a sweater, bathing suit, soft "boonies" hat, towel, poncho and poncho liner, tent pegs, string, rope, air mattress, entrenching tool, gas mask, flashlight, gun-cleaning kit, trip flares, machete, Claymore mine, plastique explosives, loose ammo or frags…these just to name a few of the essential items. Little Joe, our radiotelephone operator or RTO, also carried a twenty-six-pound PRC-25[24] radio lashed to his rucksack frame. On operations when we traveled "light," the bag containing his personal items would be removed from the frame and flown out with the rest of the rucksacks.

So that's what we carried, but what did we look like? Well, we also wore a belt of some sort to carry other things. Either a souvenir NVA or US military web belt encircled each waist. Many supported at least one D ring, a four-inch-long, one-quarter inch-thick oval-

---

24   PRC-25—Battery-operated short-range radiotelephone carried by troops, land vehicles, and riverine craft and aircraft; considered "the most important field item in the Vietnam War."

shaped steel clip that opened on one side. The exceptionally strong little devices are used by mountain climbers for attaching themselves to ropes. In our case they would be used to repel down a rope from a hovering helicopter. Fortunately, we never had to use them. Attached to each belt were combinations of items mentioned above—one or two water canteens of either the one- or two-quart capacity, a bayonet or machete, first aid kits, maybe a pistol. Besides faded, ill-fitting, dusty green jungle fatigues, some guys also wore a faded army-issued green towel perpetually soaked and stained wrapped around their neck. It made it very convenient to wipe the constant sweat from their faces and eyes. Many of us wore our trousers rolled up to the knee for better air circulation and our socks pulled up over our calves for protection against the sharp-edged, slicing grasses, the socks' stretched-out elastic tops held up instead with rubber bands. The large cargo pockets on each pant leg were usually stuffed with extra ammo magazines, a rifle-cleaning kit, a handkerchief, pocketknife, watch, maybe a map and flashlight. Our boot tops were often rolled down, the top three or four holes left unlaced, giving them the appearance of "high black" sneakers.

Shirt sleeves were rolled up above the elbows during the warm months, and flak vests were left open to allow some additional air circulation, unless it suddenly got noisy. If we got to an area with ground leeches, everything would be rolled down, rolled up, buttoned, laced, and tied to prevent the little suckers' easy access to a meal. The four expandable shirt pockets usually held a plastic fork and spoon, wallet, cigarettes, lighter, camera, mosquito repellent, toilet paper, gum, Kool-Aid, iodine and salt tablets, aspirin, compass, and sundry other items, everything wrapped individually or in combinations, using translucent rubber bags to prevent water damage or noise from their movement. Some guys also wore necklaces adorned with water buffalo teeth, rabbit's foot, spent AK-47 rounds, grenade pins, Buddha's, crosses and other religious icons, pictures of loved ones, or anything else they felt might bring them luck. Most everyone wore a P-38 can opener and a dog tag bearing the owner's name, serial number, blood type, and religious affiliation, with a second tag being tied into a boot lacing.

Bill Ebel carrying a M-79 grenade launcher

The helicopter pilot and copilot of a typical Huey "slick" always looked the same—bored. We only saw their faces when boarding, or if we happened to be looking up through the nose bubble when they were taking off. Even then there wasn't much to see—aviator-style sunglasses, a mustache, olive-green flight helmet and jungle fatigues, and flak jacket. The door gunners and crew chiefs—well, they were something different. They, like us, had graffiti on their helmets and flak jackets. They also had graffiti on their arms and hands in the form of tattoos gotten at Momma San's Tattoo Parlor and Dance Hall. They too had mustaches like the pilots, but theirs were truly mustaches—giant handlebar types, Fu Manchus, bushy mothers that threatened to block any air passage to their nostrils. While in flight, some door gunners would hang on their machine guns, leaning out of the helicopter to find something to shoot at searching for potential trouble, while others just tried to take advantage of the cool high-altitude air to sleep off the aftereffects of a previous night's prayer meeting back at Camp Evans, where their sleeping quarters were located.

Like grunts, each gunner was unique in his own way. The one sitting just off my left, next to Shelby and strapped into his gunner's seat, seemed like a regular guy, a surfer type. His helmet cover had a big peace sign on the front, done with a blue ink pen, and was adorned with a few fresh-cut purple flowers held in place with a large elastic band. With his big blond 'stache and the flowers, it was just a matter of time before he'd be back in the World, wearing a ponytail and marching against the war. Why not? He would have certainly earned the right.

As if reading my mind, he turned to face me, nodded, and smiled. He then held up one finger to signal our destination was near. The message was passed on verbally and visually, and we all made our last-second gear adjustments before the guys sitting in the open doorways prepared to slide out and down to the skids. The period of highest exhilaration and anxiety began when the gunships escorting us started to prepare the area for the air assault, firing rockets and machine guns around the LZ to discourage any unwelcome viewers.

Looking down from a couple of hundred feet up, our landing zone looked like a very narrow strip of craggy bedrock at the very end of a mountain ridgeline. Constant exposure to the elements had left it completely devoid of vegetation, but much too small for even a single Huey to land. I scanned the terrain and was amazed at its severity. Mountain peaks in all directions were all well over fifteen-hundred feet and dropped down at angles so severe they'd be difficult climb up or down. The flanks of the LZ where we'd be inserted dropped off sharply around three sides covered with a dense, dark-green canopy of leaves hiding any signs of what awaited us. Far below, a river coiled around the same three sides of the mountain's base, like a huge snake threatening to completely encircle it. It too quickly vanished under the canopy but reappeared at each bend in the river to continue slithering through the deep valleys it had created.

The slicks carrying us started to bank hard to the right, each pilot maneuvering to position his ship for the insertion. I watched in awe each time a slick ahead of us flew down toward the drop area at speed. At precisely the right moment, the pilot would abruptly pull up the Huey's nose to slow its descent, then smoothly come to a hover only a few feet above the ground for the grunts to jump off. We awaited our turn, circling high above, and I started giving orders to Butch and Shelby over the roar of the door gunners firing and the chopper's blades slapping the air. Through the haze of expended gunpowder and aviation fumes, I yelled, "Get ready! Watch the guys in the doorway slide out and jump off from the skids. Follow the guy in front of you fast, and don't wait for the bird to land! When you hit the ground, run! Follow Sam to our defensive perimeter position. Got it?" They both nodded and turned to look outside the ship.

As each chopper in front of us dove into the dust storm created by the departure of those before them, I yelled at each new guy seated next to me, "Get ready to move fast!" Each powerful Huey approached the LZ at speed, pulled up sharply, quickly came to a hover, and began wobbling left to right as the heavily loaded guys jumped off both sides. Moments after it pulled away, the third slick repeated the approach, and we watched the other half of our squad jump off and run into the trees. They would join the others in securing the LZ for the remainder of the landing—us. I remember noticing that as each guy ran for cover, he was almost sliding down the edges of the mountain, because other than the LZ, there wasn't any flat piece of ground to be seen other than fifty feet below the summit where there appeared to be a wide, slopping ledge. I also noticed that the LZ was not taking any incoming fire, which was always a great relief.

Like those before us, the guys sitting on the floor on each side of the helicopter slid their legs out and feet down to a skid while it flew in, nose flared up, and the Huey shuddered from the maneuver. Timing at this point was critical, as no one wanted to stay on the big target any longer than necessary. As the guys were jumping off the skids, I slid hard to the left into Shelby's side, very conscious of his inexperience, fear of heights and not being in the best physical condition. As the chopper quickly started to hover, I kept looking between him, who I was gently shoving off the seat toward the door opening with my left shoulder telling him to go, and Butch off to my right, who was screaming and heading for the right door as if he were kid on his favorite amusement park ride.

Looking back to the left, I watched anxiously as Shelby very methodically slid slowly toward the door opening with his head tilted down as if looking off a skyscraper. Still on the seat, I nudged him a little more with my boot and quickly glanced again to my right and watched Butch dropping down to the skid, and jump. When I turned towards the door opening to leave, I was stunned to see Shelby slowly easing himself down to a skid. Again to my right to make sure everyone and all equipment was off, then back to my left to ensure Shelby finally made it out. He had taken far too much time to get off. I quickly dropped down to the skid. Just as I was about to jump, I felt the chopper pitch to the right, not sure if it was beginning to take off or had suddenly shot up, having just lost Shelby's tonnage.

Usually, the door gunner or crew chief would notify the pilot that he still had people on board, at which point they would lower the chopper to a safer jump level, but not on this occasion. I felt and heard the surge of the Huey's engine and watched the ground getting farther away, hesitating to jump from that height wearing a ruck, thinking the upward motion would be reversed. At about that same time, I also felt the door gunner's hand on the back of my helmet giving me a little incentive to get off his chopper. I vividly remember the scenery spinning as I did either a one-eighty twist, flop maneuver or a perfectly executed three-quarter dive from about ten feet, landing "safely" on my back. Fortunately, I was wearing a strapped-on steel helmet and landed on my soft rucksack stuffed with a poncho and

poncho liner. Didn't break one bone! Then again, it
might be the reason for all of the screws and rods in my
neck and back fifty-some years later.

Dazed, ears ringing, the breath knocked out of me,
and lying spread eagle at the edge of the LZ, I desperately tried to catch my breath in the growing dust storm
from the departing chopper. The concentrated downdraft, whirling turbulence and my heavy rucksack held
me down like an enormous unseen hand, fingers tug-
ging at my loose fatigues in every direction causing them
to flap uncontrollably in the maelstrom. As the Huey
climbed higher above me, it looked like a UFO through
my blurred vision and scrambled brain. Compounding
my confusion, I could faintly hear over the loud ringing
in my ears and the roar from the craft's ascent, sounds
that were alien to me and never before heard on a combat air assault. The strange noise sounded vaguely like
muffled cheering and laughter from a far-off distance.
As James Bond once said, "Out of great danger often
comes great humor."[25]

My stationary, supine, spread-eagle position only allowed me to stare at the ship's door opening with the
sun's glaring rays pouring through, seemingly focused
directly into my watery eyes. The intense back lighting made the apparition appear to have a glowing co-
rona with long waves of blurred hot air escaping from
its top. I continued to gasp for air and watched as the
craft slowly floated away above me. Framed in the door
opening of the ship, as it gained forward momentum,
there appeared an odd looking being with a big head
and purple halo, grinning broadly while offering a peace
sign with his left hand. *Okay, kids, fun's over. Let's go!*

---

25   Timothy Dalton as James Bond, *The Living Daylights*.

The laughing seemed to die down a bit possibly because I hadn't moved yet. From somewhere out of the vegetation Big Joe yelled, "Bano, you alive?" I had to think about it before I could answer. I felt like a turtle trying to right itself as I started to roll over my ruck in a feeble attempt to get up, when Joe grabbed one of the straps and picked me up. No time to check for injuries, because I could still walk. We climbed down to the wide ledge I had noticed earlier, or rather Joe climbed down while holding me up. I was soon able to breathe again and joined up with the defensive perimeter before the second wave of slicks would arrive. Although it was only two thirty in the afternoon, it was too late for us to get off the mountain and climb up another one before dark, as was our normal operating procedure. It's always safer to sleep on top of a mountain than in a valley because a higher position on a mountain is easier to defend.

A few hours after the whole company was inserted, we had already formed a defensive perimeter, set up our hooches or night shelters, dug foxholes, set out the trip flares and Claymores. Once our defense was established, we began settling in for the night, preparing our individual gourmet meals out of carefully selected C-ration units. Our commanding officer, or CO, called the platoon leaders over to his command post (CP) located at the center of our perimeter to brief them on the following day's operational plans and objectives.

While stirring a can of franks and beans, delicately seasoned with cheeses and Tabasco sauce, I was reflecting that so far, the operation was almost like being on an extended stand-down—no hassles, no walking, no pressure. Maybe a little pain in my back and neck, but overall…Soon the squad leaders met with the platoon

leaders for their briefing. By the time I was about to
make some coffee, the squad leaders coming into my
peripheral vision interrupted my concentration and
brought me back to reality. They all looked stunned,
and by the way they were mumbling to each other, it
was obvious we weren't going to like the next day's operation. They separated and each went in a different direction to brief their squads with the CO's orders. Sam
approached our area looking like a madman with his
arms flailing and talking to himself. In a not-too-pleas-
ant voice, he ordered the 2nd Squad to gather around.
Within fifteen minutes, everyone in the entire company was mumbling and flailing their arms.

Like most warriors since the beginning of time, we'd
been ordered to do a lot day after day, night after night.
We'd been deprived of sleep, been offered poor food
supplies, endured forced marches carrying unbearable
weight on our tired backs and shoulders, and braved
the terrifying unknown and harsh environmental elements, not to mention dangerous air assaults and
people we didn't know trying to kill us. But this—this
operation was asking entirely too, too much of us, hitting at the very core of our male psyches, our very being. We all suspected the CO had probably taken too
many rifle butts to the side of his head during Officer
Candidate School, but what did we grunts know.

It would turn out to be a very long night for many,
especially when awake during guard duty, left with time
to think about what might happen the next day. The
strategy and tactics were actually straightforward. Before sunrise, we would get up and prepare to move out
"light"—just our munitions, weapons, and water. Drop
off our rucks in a designated area and queue up to move
out. It was our squad's turn to take point. The lead

force. The tip of the spear, if you will. Or, in defensive terms, the first targets for the bad guys.

The remainder of the company would follow by squad. Simply put, the company, under the cover of darkness, would silently climb down a trail our squad would create. Our first chore as point squad once we reached a river down below was to blow up our air mattresses; remove our clothes and boots; put them, flak vest, helmet, weapons, and munitions on the mattresses; and slowly swim across the moving water to the opposite shore. Once there we would get dressed, re-form into a defensive line inside the cover of the jungle, and prepare to defend the others who would follow. Once the entire company had re-formed, we would start a search-and-destroy mission into a suspected large North Vietnamese Army encampment area. Other companies of the 5th Battalion, 7th Cavalry would be approaching the area from different directions. Same thing we'd been doing since we left Hue in February.

When Sam finished briefing us, everyone sat in stunned silence, spoons full of heated C rations suspended in air inches away from gaping mouths. After we took about two seconds to digest the orders, the words "then take off all of your clothes" finally registered. It hit every guy almost simultaneously, and in zero seconds a cacophony of angry voices began questioning the sanity of the US Army's officers in earnest—a grunt's favorite pastime through the ages.

"If they wanted us on that side of the stinkin' river, why didn't they just land us over there?!"

"Aw, man, I'm too short for this bullshit."

"Ah ain't a-takin' mah clothes off an' let skeeters bite mah Willy."

"Ah believe Ah should tell yah, sah, that Ah cain't swim."

"Hey, is anybody bringing soap?"

Based on the sound coming from the other squads, everyone was already foaming at the mouth, ready to attack the CO. Sam finally calmed us down with perfectly sound answers to all of our questions. Apparently, the squad leaders had had the exact same concerns when they met with CO during the briefing. They didn't think he knew most grunts went "commando" all the time.

No one really cared too much for most of the answers, but the order about dropping our drawers really made no sense. The CO didn't want anyone to drown because they were weighted down with wet clothes and boots. Forget about the possibility of cramping up after getting overheated from climbing down a thousand feet and plunging into cold mountain water, or maybe being swept away in the current of the river, possibly being shot at. No, he didn't want our lightweight, nylon jungle fatigues to weigh us down! *How do they come up with this stuff?*

Keep in mind that dying in battle is not the romantic ending that Hollywood would have us believe. In reality, meeting any violent, traumatic death is horrible, and in war it's especially so. You're not with your loved ones, haven't made your peace with anyone, don't even know what killed you. Dying in combat while naked would also be absolutely humiliating. What do you say to Saint Peter when you're trying to enter the Pearly Gates? Everyone's standing around wearing beautiful white, flowing robes and feathers and they're doubled over laughing because you're buck naked? What if we made contact when we were swimming across the river?

We call in for a "dust-off," and when the medevac heli-copter lands at a MASH unit, all of the casualties being offloaded are nude. Wouldn't you think the troopers' activities prior to being wounded might be little sus-pect?!

Despite Sam's attempts to calm us down, the ques-tions from all parts of the country continued.

"Did dat fuckin' lunatic tink dis ting out all by his-self?"

"Yeah, wait a minute. What about running into the jungle for cover? Did he expect the enemy to see us na-ked and laugh so hard they wouldn't be able to shoot straight?!"

"Hell, that's nothin'. What if we reach the beach-head and start receiving fire? Did he think about what would be breaking our falls if we have to hit the dirt?"

We went on and on, getting carried away feeding off each other's comments, but none of our griping mat-tered. We were going to do as ordered, as good troopers do. At least the atmosphere around the perimeter was a little lighter after the venting. The squad dispersed, and we went our separate ways to ponder the morning ahead.

Nights in the field were always the same. We pulled guard duty in or very near a foxhole for as long as necessary, depending on the number of people in the squad, to cover an entire night. If the squad had a full complement of eleven or twelve, and we were watch-ing from only one guard position, we would stay awake for about forty-five minutes each. But if the squad had been reduced to say seven or eight because of casualties and/or R and R,[26] or even if it was a full squad but each fire team was guarding its own position, then the

---

26   R and R—Rest and recuperation (or relaxation or rehabilitation).

amount of lost sleep for each guy could be closer to an hour and a half. So for whatever reason, after walking through mountains and jungles all day, or "humping a ruck in the boonies," as we grunts called it, and with our senses, emotions, and muscles working full blast at all times, we tended to get a little tired by nightfall. So waking up at two thirty in the morning to pull guard duty until four could be brutal. On the other hand, at least we got some quality time to ourselves to think about life, home, and loved ones. On that particular night, though, each of us also got to think about the family jewels and what might become of them before dawn.

Hand signals just above ground level, a slow, deliberate head nod, and the sound of water flowing over rocks snapped me back to my senses. *Oh, that. What the hell are we doing here?* No reason to wonder why I was naked, or the others; we had a job to do. Our three-point men were signaling that they were ready to enter the water. The small riverbank hadn't given us much room to strip without bumping into each other's butts or getting kneed as we bent over. I mean, think about it: Six of us trying to stay out of sight, make no noise or sudden movements, while undressing in an area only two feet wide by six feet long. If that weren't enough, we were also trying to avoid sharp, cutting grass three feet high that provided shelter for mosquitoes the size of hummingbirds. And to compound matters, some guys were blowing up air mattresses in the same space— no small feat considering we were out of breath from the climb down. We tried as best we could not to alert an enemy of our presence, but muffled sounds coming from behind and above us, deep inside the jungle on our side of the river, would make anyone within range suspicious. Besides the occasional slap at a mosquito snacking on a tender rear end, there were the sounds of a steel helmet rolling into a tree at a high rate of speed, grunts and groans, branches snapping, and the unmistakable sound of a giant rooster bouncing down-hill and questioning his sanity.

We were running a little behind schedule but were ready to execute the plan just the same. At the river-bank, crouched in the razor-sharp grass, were six na-ked, hardened troopers of the 1st Cavalry Division. Each man concentrating intently on the wood line across the river for any signs of movement and being very careful not to lower his eyes below the waist of the guy squatting next to him. Behind us, draped down the mountain in carefully spaced intervals, hung the rest of the company waiting for their turns to complete the descent onto some flat ground where they too would disrobe.

We had already decided earlier that our squad's three strongest, Big Joe, Jackie, and Butch, would be first across. Joe and Jackie, my best friends and survi-vors of many firefights, slowly and without a sound slid into the river like otters, while we got ready to hand them the rope and inflated air mattresses loaded with their helmets and weapons. While treading water, they turned and grabbed the two heavily laden air mattress-es and slowly pulled them into the river. Big Joe had to come back to the shore a little closer to reach for the ammo bags. It was immediately obvious when he stood up that the water was very cold—either that or we might have to start calling him Little Joe. Our third man, the new kid built like an NFL running back, had volunteered to pull the rope across. He claimed to be a former lifeguard, and at that point we had to trust his judgment. He had watched Joe and Jackie's silent belly crawl and copied them perfectly. I mentally went through a checklist of our objectives, making sure we hadn't missed anything. We had come down an incredibly steep mountain in total darkness, made our way through dense jungle to the river, and found the ideal crossing spot. Check. We made our preliminary preparations, stripped, and had all three-point men in the water without our position being compromised. So far, everything was going as planned.

All three nodded that they were ready and turned toward the far bank, with only that portion of their heads from the nose up visible. We watched as they slowly dog-paddled toward the other shore, Joe and Jackie on either side of an air mattress, Butch slightly behind them, releasing coils of rope as he swam, one end having already been secured to a tree on our side of the river. The rest of us could now do no more than move our focus from the dark silhouettes of the little convoy to concentrate on the far tree line, training our weapons in case covering fire would be needed to protect them. A dangerous thing for us to do in the dark, giving away our position, but a necessity.

When finally reaching the shallower water, they began to stumble their way up the rocky beach, crouching to keep their silhouettes low. The contrasting bodies and awkward gaits caused by the rounded river rocks under their bare feet made them look like shaved gorillas heading for the jungle. Joe and Jackie had deeply tanned bodies with bright white butts. Butch, having recently arrived in-country, looked like a ghost by comparison. All three had very defined muscular bodies with no signs of fat, though Joe and Jackie had especially pronounced backs and shoulders after many months of carrying weapons, munition, and rucksacks, plus digging a deep hole every night.

If we weren't so anxious about receiving incoming fire, I'm sure we would have been gasping for air from laughing so much. Here were these three Adonis's—Joe, with long, dark hair, very broad shoulders, tattoos on arms and chest, and heavy muscles from years of weightlifting; Jackie, the tall, lanky Texan with sandy hair, sort of a Kevin Bacon look-alike; and Butch, the all-American football running back. But instead of being impressive, they looked like Neanderthals bent over at the waist, stumbling on the rocks, their arms swaying from left to right to maintain balance. The scene was hysterical and deserved laughter except for the fact that we had to cross next and join the clan.

They piled up the gear on the beach and split up, Joe and Jackie swimming back to get the other air mattresses loaded with clothes and boots while Butch headed toward the jungle to tie the rope to a stationary object. At about the time Joe and Jackie were almost back to our shoreline, and Butch was returning from one of the huge root carcasses to get dressed and pick up his weapon, we heard the unmistakable *thoomp* sound of a mortar round being fired. The instant I recognized the sound, I turned and stared at the shocked horror frozen on the three unshaven, muddied faces huddling beside me. My immediate thought was *God, please don't let us die like this. It's not supposed to happen this way. Oh, God, how humiliating. John Wayne never went through anything like this.* We were all completely naked, just like the day we came into the world, and we were about to leave the same way! *Okay! We get it! Our CO didn't want any clothes or boots dragging anyone to the bottom of a muddy river, so the order of dress for the morning was...nothing!*

We, as the lead element, hadn't called in any fire missions. That meant the incoming rounds were enemy fire, triggering that all-too-familiar knot in the gut. At almost the same instant we heard the round go out, we could hear the muted chatter from our radio cradled on the air mattress about to go across. Word was being passed down through the company's RTOs that a ceasefire had already been called. Apparently, a mistake by our mortar platoon. But it was too late—the second round was already on the way.

We at the river's edge were somewhat relieved to hear it was friendly fire, hoping it was directed anywhere except where we were. I was trying with my best mime impersonation to tell Joe and Jackie that it was friendly fire. Our position hadn't been compromised, but they were already frantically trying to get back to our shore, having also recognized the sounds of mortars. Unfortunately, there was no time or way to tell the new kid on the other side because the first round had detonated inside the jungle from where he stood. Friendly fire or not, there was still another round about to land somewhere.

From the first explosion came the crackling sounds of trees splintering, low-frequency whirring sounds of unseen shrapnel flying through branches and leaves, and the resulting plume of smoke and debris being blown into the air. A very motivated, still-nude Butch frantically stumbled toward the water, only to be cut off by a round landing in the river well off to his left. He spun around toward the right as the geyser of water showered down on the beachhead. Finally reaching the landing area, he grabbed a helmet off the pile of gear on an air mattress and headed toward the jungle for cover, running/staggering as if he were on hot coals. All of us were cheering him on in hushed tones, cringing at what we were seeing. It was like watching a horror movie, fearing what the next instant could bring. Sam whispered to get ready because we might have to get him quick if something were to happen.

It was immediately obvious it wasn't Butch's helmet because it moved around on top of his head like a beanie, spinning and bouncing as he stumbled forward. It was also very obvious he did not want to lose that only piece of protection as he desperately tried to pull it down over his ears. I'm sure he realized by then that he was really in deep doo-doo. With nowhere to go, he started staggering around in circles, bent at the waist and mooning us, desperately looking for a safe place on the open beach, continually switching the helmet from his head to his private parts and back again, over and over. When it looked as if he had found some cover among a huge tangle of washed-up tree roots, he dropped to the ground, assumed a fetal position, and held the helmet down over his ears. The explosions had stopped as abruptly as they had started, but of course he didn't know it was friendly fire that had ceased. Perhaps fearing another round and feeling he was still too exposed, he got up and continued his strange dance in the moonlight.

As the dirt, leaves, branches, and torrents of water settled back to earth, our emotions, as happens so many times during combat, were completely frazzled. Naturally, we were all relieved no one was hit, but we also knew we needed to get out of there fast. As much as we wanted to start laughing and screaming, we knew we couldn't, because strange as it may seem, we still hadn't given our position away to the enemy. The exploding rounds would just appear to Charlie as some wasteful American harassment fire, harmlessly landing in a remote part, of a remote jungle, in a remote valley.

Still, we were having trouble controlling ourselves because of the scene we had just witnessed and the relief we felt. Hurriedly, we all began to slither into the water, pulling and pushing our loaded air mattresses. We swam in pairs, taking turns putting our heads underwater, and I could swear as air bubbles popped on the surface, you could hear the unmistakable screams of garbled laughter. Most of our squad would have probably drowned that morning if we hadn't taken turns helping each other up to the surface, just long enough to get a quick gulp of air before re-submerging.

Butch didn't quite look like the macho warrior he was trying to project when we reached his shoreline. Instead, he sheepishly took his clothes from the air mattress and modestly turned his back as he dressed to the sounds of swallowed laughter and snickers. We put our clothes on, grinning from ear to ear while making faces at the new kid. He had probably just made military history but didn't know it. When we were dressed and loaded up, we headed for the cover of the dense jungle as the other squads following us made their way down and across the river. The others, of course, didn't know what had just happened below them because they couldn't see through the jungle canopy blocking their view. All they knew was that the first squad to cross the river had taken incoming mortar fire and their turn was coming soon. The unknown was always the worst.

From our vantage point, we could see the rest of the guys begin their swims as the sun began rising, dimly illuminating the whole crossing area. The timetable had been blown wide open, so to speak, because of the mortar snafu, the severity of the terrain, and the mudslide that was being created from every sliding butt. As a result, by the time each trooper reached the water's edge, he looked muddier than the guy before him. Because of that, some guys took a little longer than others to cross, washing their hair on the way over.

The operation was in shambles by the time the CO and his entourage reached the river. He wasn't aware that most grunts were always "commando"—just a shirt and pants. Guys were backstroking across, standing in calf-deep water, and lathering themselves with soap, lying on air mattresses to catch their breath and get some rays on the beach, squatting along the gravel beach, washing muddy clothes. Even our battalion commander got to take a bath. Total chaos prevailed. It looked like a nudist beach full of college guys on spring break. You know, I wonder if a CO would use that same plan today if women were allowed in combat. I shudder to think of it.

By ten thirty we had all finally saddled up and were heading into the jungle for the start of another operation into the unknown. Grins, smiles, and laughter ended as soon as we entered the dark, stifling humidity that always brought us back to the reality of why we were there. As we slowly made our way deeper into the cover, Little Joe, our squad's RTO, tapped me on the shoulder and in a very low voice said that one of our other companies on the operation had lost a guy. They were crossing a river while traveling heavy, and one FNG had drowned. Once again laughter and joy were instantly replaced by grief, frustration, and disgust. War plays incredible games with the mind.

An Uphill Battle

We cautiously made our way through yet another deep river gorge, slowly searching for any signs of the NVA regulars we'd been chasing for months. Eight long days into the mission had passed in hushed, uneventful silence, the type of day a grunt always welcomed. And, if not for always being so "wired" and alert, it was turning out to be a great hiking and camping trip, with only an occasional hint of rain in the air. The company was spread out in a long column, with every other man walking on the opposite side of the stream; every pair of eyes scanning the terrain rising above them; everyone either hugging the embankment or, if necessary, walking in the ankle-deep water where the streambed narrowed. It would have been nice to be able to relax, but the sunken riverbed at the foot of rising mountain sides was perfect for an ambush. And Charlie knew it… safe from sight under the triple canopy, fresh water readily available, and encampments easily defended.

Our daily travels kept us beneath an umbrella of enormous sagging tree limbs dressed in translucent leaves in every imaginable shade of green, each one seemingly backlit by the unseen sun. The shape and density of the high, spreading branches reaching over the stream from both sides created a comfortable, shaded boulevard. Occasionally we could catch glimpses of a beautiful deep blue sky peeking through gaps overhead. And in those few areas where shrubs tried to reach up for more sunlight, they invariably weakened after a time and their skinny four- or five-feet tall branches simply sagged over into the water. It would've been very easy to lose one's focus while admiring the beauty of nature, but with the stream bed constantly changing from being fifty-feet wide and having three-foot high dirt banks, then narrowing to twenty feet where the current ran against exposed bedrock, we naturally had to be aware of the unseen danger at each choke point. Each day as we walked along the water's edge, and glancing down now and then to ensure silence with each careful step, we were often alerted to colorful fish in hues of red and orange, their small streamlined bodies flashing with each abrupt turn to escape our intrusive boots.

At the end of each day, we climbed up a mountainside to a "safe" area and set up the defensive perimeter for the night. If there was anything we enjoyed as much as quiet days, it was an abundance of nearby saplings to setup our hooches and nice soft earth to dig our foxholes. Mail, our rucksacks, and a hot meals were flown out when we were in a position to receive them. After all was said and done, as the evening cooled and night fell, we laid our tired bodies down on our air mattresses and were rewarded with a gazillion twinkling stars dotting a black velvet sky until our eyes closed. Sheer nirvana. It didn't take much to make us happy back then. It was one less day before going back to the World.

Each morning we undid everything we had done the previous night, but in reverse. We ate something, took the morning chill off with some hot coffee, disarmed the trip flares and Claymores, refilled the foxholes, repacked everything and dropped our rucks in the cargo net still laid out from the previous day. Then we'd commute to work; saddle up, and head back down the mountain. It was like the movie "Ground Hog Day" with Bill Murray, each day almost identical. Officers knew the when, where, why, and potentially what to expect or look for. Grunts were just flying blind every single day with few exceptions. Literally. *Just get on the chopper and follow me... Yes sir...*

We continued at a snail's pace along the streambed each day, careful not to make a sound or disturb the vegetation. We could only assume the headquarters intelligence staff must have been alerted by our Long-Range Reconnaissance Patrol (LRRP) reports that there was sufficient activity to warrant the operation. The fact that we were in that specific area was not by accident. As calming and peaceful as the surroundings were to us thus far, we also knew the quiet serenity could be shattered in the next heartbeat. *Just a nice quiet walk in the woods. Until a bear walks out from behind a tree...*

No contact with any large enemy concentrations had been reported by any of the other companies working in the other nearby valleys. Naturally, we hoped Charlie had either cleared out of the area or chose not to engage us after hearing the sounds of helicopters landing on mountaintops in every direction. That was one of the nice things about being in the 1st Cavalry. Not only was walking minimized because of our helicopters, but anyone in an area who heard the roar of a large combat air assault taking place might try to avoid making contact. Unless, that is, Charlie was in a stronger position, with more people which was often the case in the tight jungle surroundings.

The morning of the ninth day again brought beautiful weather. We had saddled up and moved off our most recent mountaintop retreat. After eventually reaching the bottom, we continued our walk through the meandering river valley. The serene effect of the sun's rays passing through the gently swaying canopy created contrasting shadows in the otherwise darkened surroundings. When illuminated, the incredible variety of fragrant plant life was at times almost hypnotic. Inanimate objects appeared to come alive, moving with every change in the light's intensity, seemingly trying to break free from their static earthly bonds. Long, choking vines, gnarled and covered with searching tentacles, hung from the treetops for hundreds of feet down to the river's edge. Their twisted shapes transformed into potentially dangerous life-forms, threatening to reach out and strangle anything or anyone who wasn't alert. Shafts of light that reached the river's mirrored surface reflected up and illuminated the bottoms of millions of leaves of different sizes, shapes, and colors, creating shadows where they weren't expected. The only sounds breaking the stillness came from the constant trickle of water bubbling over and between rocks and boot tops, or the occasional bird disturbed in the branches high above.

Despite the enchanting yet threatening atmosphere, the cool, sparkling water and shadows were refreshing. Many operations would have us directly exposed to the sun's intense heat, evaporating every bit of moisture from our bodies and burning any exposed skin. Some days we might be in open areas having absolutely no shade, be it low-lying terrain or in the mountains. Areas with any type of densely spaced vegetation ten feet high was brutal. We didn't think we'd make it through the day. There was nothing worse than the sun beating down and the suffocating closeness of incredible humidity making the air so heavy it was almost impossible to fill our lungs. At the top of the list was going through razor-sharp elephant grass that flayed our arms, hands, and neck. Every little cut would burn like hell as sweat filled the voids. Other operations found us slithering through mud on one cold, rainy day after another. It was on days like those that we would be pissed, our anger and frustration building until we blamed the brass or the army or even the president for screwing with us. We were sure that we'd been sent into those conditions, on that specific day, at that exact minute, because they wanted to mess with our minds. We rapidly learned to be very thankful for the tranquility that comfortable days brought us. In the long run, it taught us to never take anything for granted. All in all, the current operation had been good to us thus far, and this too was shaping up to be another nice day. At least it started that way.

Little Joe, who was about twenty feet or so in front of me, slowly held up his arm, as if signaling a left turn, but in this case, it meant *Halt!* I assumed our point man had spotted something, had maybe come to a fork in the river, or encountered some other obstacle requiring an officer to make a decision. Ordinarily, stops in our nature walks were not unusual, and in fact were welcomed, because if nothing was going on at the front of the column, it meant we could sit and rest, light a cigarette, take a drink of water, maybe even "break for beans" if it was late in the morning. Because it was only midmorning, I didn't think we were stopping for lunch, and I hadn't heard any shots, so I knew we were not under attack, but the surrounding area had suddenly become just *too* quiet. There were no birds making their usual racket, no tree frogs, and no noise at all except for the familiar sound of a heartbeat getting louder. It was at times like those when the hair on our necks started to rise, mouths got dry, and knees started to shake. Experience had taught us old-timers to trust our senses when we felt that something just wasn't right. Be ready. Something might happen any second.

Everyone had stopped and was scanning the slopes on each side of the river for any sign of movement. Little Joe, our RTO holding the radio handset to his ear, waggled a finger on his raised left hand for me to come up to him. Our point man had found a smoldering campfire along a small trail. Orders were for the squads to fan out and head up the riverbank to the right of the stream, and into the tree line for a closer look. I told him to tell Big Joe and Sam, and he immediately started towards them. Using hand signals, we split our squad into the two separate fire teams and began the search. If Charlie was waiting for us, we were in a terrible situation. The mountain growing out of the stream was extremely steep, and anyone uphill would have a great advantage.

The entire company began to climb and sweep the area, but because of the thickness of the foliage, we could only see the guys to our immediate left and right, and only occasionally, someone on the far side of them. About thirty feet to my left was Little Joe, carrying the radio and holding a CAR-15[27] assault rifle with only a

---

27   CAR-15—smaller version of the M-16 assault rifle, having a shorter barrel and collapsible stock.

few magazines. His primary job was to relay communications between us and our superiors, not to engage
in fighting unless necessary. Thirty feet or so off to my
right was Bill Ebel, the new guy from Michigan with
the grenade launcher—a useless weapon in this type
of terrain, but he did carry a .45 caliber semiautomatic
pistol that could come in handy in such tight quarters.
Between the three of us, I was the only one adequately
armed, with an M-16, a full complement of ammunition, and grenades. I couldn't help but think that we
three made a very weak link in our line, and RTOs
were prime targets.

We continued our climb, staying as low as possible
in the thigh-high shrubs constantly glancing left and
right to make sure we were all still next to each other.
When Ebel turned and looked at me for a little guidance and moral support, I noticed his eyes were about
the size of cue balls, and about to roll out of their sockets. They might have if not for the fact that they were
being held in place behind his thick glasses. Under the
circumstances, all I could do was give him a comforting
look, a nod, a thumbs-up, and pointed up for him to
continue. The small gesture at least seemed to calm him
enough to let his eyelids come back into view.

A seventy-five-foot climb from the river's edge
brought me to a vertical bedrock outcropping blocking my climb. About twenty-five feet above the sheer
face was a ledge that jutted out. I stopped to assess my
position, turned, and looked down through the small
openings in the brush I had just climbed through and
could barely see the water below me. While I decided
on the best way to traverse the obstacle ahead, my
mind drifted back to my earlier childhood in the early
fifties when my friends and I used to play "guns" or war

in a small, forested area near my house. We had always set up our machine-gun nest in this type of position to ambush the Japanese trying to find us on that far-off, make-believe tropical island in the Pacific.

I glanced over toward Little Joe, who signaled me over to him by holding out the radio handset in my direction. We very slowly crouched and quietly started to make our way toward each other while Ebel also tried to traverse the mountainside to join us. In a few minutes, we were kneeling close together, with Joe passing me the handset, saying, "Bano, I think you oughta listen to this. The other squads are finding all kinds of NVA signs! All over the place!" I grabbed the handset and pushed it up and under my helmet to listen while LT was telling the radio operators to notify their squads to use extreme caution. I caught a slight movement off to the left out of the corner of my eye and noticed Sam trying to get my attention. He gave me a three-ring sign with his fingers, followed with a thumbs-up, signaling he had gotten the message, and everything was okay. He then jabbed a finger a couple of times in front of him, indicating he was taking his team farther uphill. I saw him signaling the unseen guys to his left, making a sweeping motion of his left arm and then waving his downturned palm toward the ground. He was letting them know they should continue climbing, stay low, and be very cautious. I also noticed that Sam looked nervous, being that he was "short," so close to going home.

Returning my attention to Ebel and Little Joe, I told them my plan of action, which Bill would then have to relay to the rest of our team to his right. I suddenly detected something odd about the ledge above me that I hadn't noticed earlier. Maybe it was because the angle of sight was different in my new position, or the heightened anxiety had cleared my mind, or maybe it was my Hollywood training bringing me back to a Japanese-infested island with John Wayne. But for whatever reason, what I suddenly saw was not just a ledge but a real, honest-to-goodness machine-gun nest, complete with a camouflaged bamboo-and-thatch-covered roof. I was staring up at it when I heard the new kid whisper, "Hey, Bano. Is everything okay?" I blinked a couple of times to rewet my irises and adjusted my pants, which had suddenly ridden up a few inches.

Not wanting to influence anyone's imagination, I looked at each of them and asked if they saw anything unusual about the ledge just above and to the right of us. Ebel's glasses were so thick, I didn't think he could even see the ledge, but when Little Joe's eyes started to bulge, I knew what I saw had just been confirmed. He shifted his attention back to me, mouth hanging open, and before he could even say a word, all I could do was nod and frown. While Ebel kept studying the mountainside, trying to find a ledge, Little Joe described the "nest" the same way I saw it. He also thought he could see a gun barrel or something poking out of it.

My mind began to race almost as fast as my heart, so I sat back, lit a cigarette, and tried to think of the best way to approach the formidable obstacle without giving my position away. *Hello? You just lit a cigarette!* If the three of us just stayed put, we'd be safe because we were so close to the ledge. If anyone tried to fire at us, they'd have to unnecessarily expose themselves by leaning out from their protective covering, and I knew that would never happen—Charlie was extremely patient when it came to an ambush. We couldn't flank it because Sam and Big Joe had already started moving the guys up to the left, and I didn't know how far up the rest of my team had gone off to the right. Given our current situation, my options seemed limited, because Sam and the others would be sitting ducks if we didn't act fast. I decided the best and only thing to do immediately was a surprise, one-man frontal assault on the machine gun.

The new kid was whispering, "How are we going to get out of here? What'll we do now, Bano?" Having formulated my plan in an instant, I told Little Joe and Ebel to listen up. Little Joe would stay where he was to provide covering fire for me if I needed it and to radio LT immediately if I "hit the shit," as we called a firefight. Ebel was to give me his .45, take my M-16 and ammo, and leave the useless grenade launcher with Little Joe, then go back to the right to notify the other guys of the machine-gun position and what was about to happen. Having given the plan to Little Joe and Ebel, they acknowledged the order, and we began the weapons exchange. Before Bill and I started making our way to the right, I looked down to check my footing and noticed a pile of cigarette filters. So much for formulating instant plans. *Maybe they were they from the machine gunner...*

After a few more nervous seconds, we were all in position, Ebel signaling me with a thumbs up that the rest of the guys were ready. A million things started racing through my mind foreseeing the possibilities of something going one way or another, and what were the options. I took out a concussion grenade from my bag in the event the position was built over a spider hole, a one-man defensive position that was a common NVA practice. *Well, here goes nothin'.* I thought. *Is this the way I'm going to "get it"? What'll Judy say about her dumb husband thinking more about himself and strangers than his own family? I'll never know if my unborn, fatherless child is a boy or a girl. Mom might die of grief. Dad? He'll be sad but proud—his only son had answered the call and followed in his footsteps. Just like his six brothers, from WWII through the Taipei Crisis. I guess someone gets the Purple Heart. Won't do me any good...* My mind was on overload and started screaming at me. *Enough already, let's go!* Then the smart side of my mind kicked back in: *No, wait! One more cigarette. Damn, I don't have any!*

With the grenade in my left hand and the pistol in my right, I crawled up the slope and stayed close to the outcropping to remain out of sight. When I reached the lower left corner of the gun emplacement, I stopped and listened for any sound but heard nothing. My plan was simple: do the same thing Bill Phieffer did in Hue. Crawl up and over the ledge, gaining the element of surprise, use the .45, and, if necessary, pull the pin and drop the grenade in the hole. I hadn't heard any shots yet, so I didn't want to alert Charlie if he was in the neighborhood. Why shoot first? Take the prisoner or I might feel like an idiot if no one was in there. At least I thought it was a good idea at the time. I took a deep breath, turned my head to look down to see if everyone was in position. It was going to have to do because the new kid still seemed to be having trouble locating ledge and me. I popped up and over the ledge with a blood-curdling yell, or maybe more like, "Boo!" I didn't want to talk to the guy, just scare him.

I thought my heart would explode with all the adrenaline pumping through it, but instead, what I found almost made it stop beating altogether. While I leaned over the nest with the pistol pointing at no one and the grenade held at the ready, I could only stare dumbfounded, frozen in a John Wayne pose. It was not a machine-gun nest in the classic military form. It was more like a...well, it was shaped like...I still have trouble with this. Okay, it was an outhouse of the finest North Vietnamese construction! It had a tightly woven organic floor and roof reinforced with bamboo poles. In the center of the floor was a one-foot-square hole for doing what I thought I had just done in my pants. The "gun barrel" we had seen was a piece of split bamboo, anchored about a two-inches above the floor, pitched forward and down from the hole and ending a few inches past the front end. That probably explained why my footing kept getting worse the closer I got to the nest. The split bamboo "trough" was used to channel pee off the end. *Great,* I thought, *how can I tell the guys I single-handedly took an unoccupied one-hole shitter?* I thought about it for a minute and realized I was the only one who knew what it was. *Hey, why tell anyone anything? I* reasoned. *That's probably how legends are made.*

I waved off Little Joe and the new kid so they could continue going straight up instead of trying to reach me, figuring we could straighten out the weapons exchange at a better place. Ebel signaled the rest of the guys on the right to start moving up the mountain, knowing that I had "cleared" the obstacle in their path. I started climbing up again, only this time my legs were a little stiffer. When everyone had reached the top and joined up with the rest of our squad, I was relieved to find that I could only see the covered roof of the "nest" below us. Totally awed, Little Joe explained to Sam why it had taken us so long. "Bano cleared a machine-gun nest that was blocking our way. You shoulda seen it. If I was in there when he came over the side, I would have shit in my pants! Man, you shoulda seen it!" About that time everyone was looking at my back while I relieved myself in the bushes. Young Bill Ebel probably mistook my cool, speechless demeanor as selfless bravery. The old-timers knew better. And in due time, Bill would too. Hey, don't tell me we didn't have fun over there.

With the chatter coming from Little Joe's radio keeping him informed of the great stuff everyone was finding, we headed out to join in a treasure hunt. As it was, we had found a North Vietnamese R and R complex, complete with all the comforts of home. Charlie had apparently had to cut his in-country R and R short, taking only the weapons and munitions he was carrying, but what he left behind was a gold mine of war souvenirs, from an accordion to uniforms. There were certainly more comforts in that jungle encampment then we had: a generator and lights, movie projector and tins of reel-to-reel films, musical instruments and sheet music, flags and hammocks, fresh, clean clothes and sneakers. If I remember correctly (or it was just a myth?), a crate of brand-new automatic pistols and munitions was found, then placed in a pile with the rest of the valuable equipment to be destroyed later by engineers who would be flown in. There was almost anything a grunt could want to take advantage of a few days off before getting back to the war. It was immediately apparent to us dumb, non-logistically minded grunts that Charlie was living and being supplied a hell of a lot better than our newspapers back home were telling the public. His newspapers and letters were only a few days old!

Little Joe, our RTO

We Were FNGs Once . . . and Dumb

It's probably not fair to the guys mentioned in the previous chapters, singling them out because of their inexperience at the time. We all went through it. Before we learned the importance of teamwork, getting things done as safely and efficiently as possible, and the comradeship to have someone there to cover your ass at all times, we were all "cherries." That is, we were new kids, affectionately known as a "fucking new guy," or FNG for short. It didn't take most of us very long to realize we weren't fighting for Mom, apple pie, and the good ole US of A. Nope, we were fighting for our own survival, and for that of our squad and our company. Most grunts, I'm sure, remember how simple life was then. None of the complexities we had/have in the real world. No other issues mattered to us—race, religion, politics, nationality, sexual preference...Well, back then sexual preference did sort of bother a lot of guys. That is, it bothered them until the "questionable one" proved himself worthy of the brotherhood. Anyway, our goal in life as a combat soldier in Vietnam, consisted of base human survival for twelve months, until such time as one could return to the world, and pick up life where it had been left on hold. Sure, like tens of thousands of other grunts, I too was a new kid once. I remember my first lonely days with my new family, as I'm sure every one of my brothers can recall his first awkward steps.

My life as a grunt started for me on January 25, 1968. I had traveled for hours, flying north on an olive-green C123, a two-engine propeller-driven transport/cargo plane, leaving from the 1st Cavalry Division's base camp at An Khe, and landing at the Phu Bai airport south of Hue. From there I was directed to hitch a ride on any one of the heavily laden olive-green trucks lining the street in front of the terminal. I was told they were just one of many convoys relocating the whole 1st Cavalry Division to its new area of operations up north. Because their new base did not yet have its own runway, everything was leaving Phu Bai by truck convoy to get there.

It was no small feat moving twenty thousand men, 450 helicopters, artillery, munitions, and supplies from one base to another. I looked up and down the line and climbed onto one that was not too close to the front, and not trailing too far to the end. To me, it looked just right. It took a while for the trucks to load up, so I waited, sitting atop a steel shipping container under the broiling sun, watching other guys up ahead and behind me doing the same thing. Good time to get a tan, I thought. I wouldn't look like I just got in-country. What I didn't count on, was the blowing soot, dirt, and sand coating every exposed piece of my sweat-covered skin until I looked like a piece of sandpaper. We all sat for hours until the long line of trucks fired up their powerful diesel engines, and finally roared out of Phu Bai on Highway 1. The convoy was escorted by helicopter gunships, and MPs in jeeps having a M-60 mounted behind the front seats.

We passed small clusters of thatched houses and barren rice paddies before reaching the Imperial City of Hue, with its large Catholic church, hotels, and university campus. *A beautiful place as far as cities go*, I thought. There were numerous examples of the French architectural influences, like those buildings found in New Orleans, standing in stark contrast to the traditional buildings decorated with Oriental motifs, having bright splashes of reds, yellows, and gold. The colorful streets were alive with mopeds, rickshaws, and quaint old Renault and Peugeot cars that looked like early 1930s Fords. Vietnamese guys that appeared to be my age, wearing white shirts and black ties, rode bicycles to and from campuses. I assumed they were students, because I didn't see any of them carrying a Bible. That revelation certainly pissed me off. My own college education had to be put on hold so I could instead do "field" studies at the University of Vietnam. What's wrong with this picture?

The convoy continued through flat countryside; a route dotted with small hamlets consisting of more thatched houses, framed by more barren rice paddies. Occasionally there were colorful pagodas and cemeteries breaking up the boring scenery, a reminder of the years of hardship the country had endured. Lined along the roadside, in front of each hamlet we passed, were the smiling, happy faces of young Vietnamese kids yelling, their arms held up for the chance to catch the ever-present GI candy bars being thrown from most of the trucks. I felt a little bad because I had nothing to give them. I felt worse because they and their country were again being violated by war, evidenced by the occasional burned-out remains of a helicopter or the wreck of some other type of olive-green military vehicle.

We eventually reached Camp Evans, located in the military's northernmost I Corps (pronounced *eye core*) region. The new base camp, fifteen miles northwest of Hue, would be home for the 1st Cavalry Division (Airmobile). Cargo planes and truck convoys would continue transferring tons of supplies from the "old" base at An Khe, located in II Corps, Vietnam's rugged Central Highlands region. It was where the infamous Ia Drang Valley[28] battle took place in 1965, the first major head-to-head confrontation of the Vietnam War, fought between US forces of the 1st Battalion, 7th Cavalry, 1st Cavalry Division (Airmobile) and thousands of VC and NVA regulars.

Scanning the surroundings from my high perch, I was surprised that the old and new base camps were so different. An Khe had a swimming pool, drive-in theater, USO and Red Cross club, baseball diamond, NCO and officers' clubs, boardwalks, and most importantly, a tarmac full of helicopters protected between sandbagged revetments. Overlooking the base was an enormous gold-and-black 1st Cavalry patch carved into the side of "Hon Cong" mountain. Whereas the new 1st Cav's base being erected was little more than a sparsely populated, dust- and sand-blown olive-green tent city being vacated by an outgoing convoy of empty trucks. I jumped off my searing, hot-metal perch that looked

---

28   Ia Drang Valley—A battle lasting three days where 450 men of the 1st Battalion, 7th Cavalry were surrounded by two thousand North Vietnamese soldiers. The events are detailed in the book by Lt. Gen. Harold G. Moore (Ret.) and Joseph L. Galloway and the motion picture of the same name, *We Were Soldiers Once . . . and Young.*

like a Sears garden shed, one of the two olive-green, ten-feet-square steel shipping containers, stenciled with a large white star on each of its corrugated sides. I felt more like I'd been dragged behind a truck, rather than ridden atop one. Adding to my initial coating, that had started in Phu Bai and continued along Highway 1, were plumes of creosote-laced road dirt kicked-up by the departing trucks.

My face, neck and arms were streaked by trickles of sweat flowing from my temples, armpits, and forearms. Each rivulet created a lightning-like design as it cut its way through each gritty layer. Good Lord it was hot. My mouth and eyes were both dry and full of grit. I felt and surely looked like the skinny guy on the beach getting sand kicked in his face, like the Jack Atlas ads adorning the back cover of almost every comic book. After climbing down from the truck, I started to brush the road dirt from my nice new olive-green jungle boots and fatigues, but the fresh coating of creosote made it difficult. *Well, I'm really here*, I thought. *The training is over.* Continuing my preening, I slapped at my flopping clothes and wiped the sweat and road dirt from my face with my filthy shirttails and sweat-soaked rolled-up sleeves. I'd been taught to always try to make a good initial impression because it might make life a little easier. So I naturally tried to get as much dirt off me as possible. I mean, I didn't want my new friends to think I was a slob—you know, someone who might screw up their barracks during inspections. When I looked up at the surroundings, trying to get my bearings, I noticed the truck driver had a puzzled expression on his face. I'm sure I did too, and asked him where my unit was located, or at least in what general direction. His eyebrows shot up and expression changed to a wide-eyed stare, as if he were about to ask, "What?!" He then frowned, and shook his head, shrugged, and shared some off-color names relating to my newness. Turning towards the truck's door, he, like so many guys before him, emphasized the number of days he had left in country before he went home. I still had over three-hundred and fifty, so I remained quiet.

Obviously, I hadn't made a good first impression. So, I too did an about-face and headed out on my own. In no time at all I was lost, lonely, hungry, and exhausted from carrying a heavy duffel bag stuffed with newly issued olive-green clothes and gear. Not a good start. I shuffled around in the intense sun, collecting another coat of grit and creosote for what seemed like hours. I asked every guy I passed if he knew where my barracks were located. At their request, handing them a copy of my damp, wrinkled, dirt-and-creosote-laced orders. Each one answered with a shrug and a confused look and pointed me in a different direction. The longer I wandered, the more concerned I felt about being AWOL. Definitely, not a good first impression. So, I tried to move faster in spite of the heat, dehydration, and exhaustion handicap slowing me down. I finally located my assigned company late in the day by chance. I hadn't seen any water fountains and had reached the point where I desperately had to stop, get out of the blinding hot sun, and address my thirst. Scribbled with black paint, on a broken piece of pallet wood, hanging from the closed flaps of a large, creosote-laced, dirt-covered, faded olive-green tent, were numbers and letters that matched the sweat-stained, creosote-laced, dirt-covered travel orders I held balled up in my hand: "5th Bat/7th Cav, 1st Air Cav Div.—Supply."

I cautiously pulled a flap back and was instantly blinded the moment I stepped into the dark, hot, cavernous tent piled with stacks of equipment. I heard a voice but couldn't locate the body until my eyes adjusted to the dim light. I eventually "reported as ordered" to a young sergeant sitting on an old wooden artillery box, reading an article in a *Playboy* magazine. He told me to drop the formalities, pull up a box, grab a cold Coke, and cool off. He seemed like a nice guy, with a friendly smile that certainly made me feel a little less anxious. During our small talk, I asked how he'd gotten such a nice, cushy job. In an instant his nice smile turned into a scowl, and he informed me that he had been in the field for over eleven months. He was in the rear to work in supply while he was "short" and would soon to be "boarding that big silver bird heading back to the world." I couldn't help but notice that although he was only a year or so older than me, he looked much older. Maybe he just looked harder, like the guys in the black-and-white WWII photographs. They always looked like they were closer to forty years old instead of twenty, didn't they?

With the conversation ending abruptly, he moved around the tent gathering things I'd need in the field: a rucksack, air mattress, poncho, poncho liner, and two-quart canteen; magazines and ammo for my "16"; high-explosive, concussion, and smoke hand grenades; flak vest; gas mask; and some toiletry items. He casually mentioned, "Just stuff everything in your ruck for now; sort it out later." I set the empty coke bottle on a crate and started packing, wondering how all that stuff could fit into the pockets of the small bag hanging off the frame. While I kept trying to rearrange things, he picked up my duffel bag and dumped everything onto the wood-pallet floor. He looked over at me and said, "Don't worry, you'll figure it out. Everyone has their own way of doing things." I was just wondering how all that stuff, plus anything he pulled out of my duffle bag could fit in the pack, and how much it was going to weigh. In the meantime, he was making piles out of the duffle bag's contents while talking. "You're not in training anymore. You're on your own. After a while you probably won't need or want to hump some of that stuff anyway. Your squad leader and some of the guys in your squad will help you out." As he talked, he took the majority of items I had carried around in the duffel bag, including the bag itself, and threw them on a pile of similar items in a back corner of the tent. "I don't know why they keep giving you guys all this crap. They were probably never in the field. God, look at this stuff." He continued while the pile in the back grew higher.

In keeping with my naivety and/or stupidity, I asked him where my barracks was so I could drop my stuff off and meet my squad. A grin suddenly reappeared on his face, and he just laughed out, "New kid, your barracks is that rucksack in your hand!" He pointed at the pile by my feet covering the rucksack. "That's your barracks and locker! You'll find out pretty quick that there's no rush to get out to the field. Whenever you get a chance to spend some time in the rear, take full advantage of it, because it's one less day that Charlie can hurt you." I nodded my understanding, because it certainly made good sense to me. Sage advice by a guy who had just survived eleven months in-country; but being that my company was there at Evans and not in the field, I thought it would be wiser to learn as much about my new life as possible in the event I ever did have to go into the field. He just shrugged, saying, "Don't say I

didn't warn you." and gave me directions to the company's perimeter.

After some small talk, dos and don'ts, and more
tips, he helped me shoulder my ruck and asked if I
could do him a favor by carrying a few things out to
the company. He explained that if there was something
I needed later, I could order it, and he gave me a "line
number" to memorize that was unique to me for ordering stuff. So, I of course agreed to bring the "ordered"
things out to the company so he wouldn't have to do
it later. How could I refuse? He had helped me out, and
I would return the favor. He stood behind me, hanging some things on the frame of my rucksack while we
continued our conversation, before stepping around
me and handing me a few more pieces of gear to carry
with my free hand. I followed him out of the stifling
tent into the blinding, scorching heat as he thanked
me again for the help. "Listen to guys and you'll be al-
right." As if an afterthought he added, "Oh, and just
to make sure you don't get lost again." he pointed in
the direction of the company and wished me good luck.
We both got a chuckle out of that. While thanking him
for the coke and gear, I was surprised to see his smile
seem to melt away until his face went blank. I turned
and thought, *Poor guy probably doesn't get to talk to anyone
all day.* I called out over my shoulder, "See ya, Sarge."
Never saw him again.

After about fifteen grueling minutes, I reached what
I hoped was going to be my final destination. My back
and shoulders hurt, my feet were blistering, the red-hot
steel helmet on my head was like a personal-sized oven
baking my brains, and the metal clasp on the dangling
chin strap kept branding my neck with each step. I
stumbled into what looked like a hobo camp and was

greeted by silent stares, nods, and heads shaking in wide-eyed awe and disbelief. The first impression I was giving made me feel like a total idiot. Sergeant Walker had loaded me up with nine new two-quart water canteens strung together with twine. They hung from each side of the rucksack like pails on an old vegetable wagon, bouncing and shifting with each step I made. Not a very good first impression, made worse by a filthy uniform far too big, streaked with gritty sweat stains, and I needed a shave. Embarrassed, I looked along a line of guys sitting on the barren ground or on air mattresses in front of what looked like small, sagging pup tents. Some of the flimsy shelters had mosquito netting hanging out of them, their long loose ends tangled into a ball and lying in the dirt. Other shelters just had shirtless guys lying in them, sleeping, reading, or writing. Depending on which way I turned my head, I could hear the Beach Boys, the Beatles, Otis Redding, the Doors, or Johnny Cash. In front of every other tent was a three by six-foot hole, dug down four to five-foot deep. Each hole was piled at the front and sides with the dirt that had been removed. Atop the red dirt were helmets and different types of firearms and munitions. Set up between the tents and holes were crude little blackened cans made from what looked to be opened and perforated tuna-fish cans. Balancing precariously on most was a flame-blackened aluminum canteen cup, stained a rich dark brown inside, their handles smeared with creosote-laced dirt.

As I neared the first set of small tents, or hooches, as I learned they were called, no one said a word to me; just pointed in the direction I should walk. *Nice meeting you guys too*, I thought. Stumbling onward, I at last found the CO and top sergeant, who just happened to be together discussing the new replacement troops that were supposed to be arriving any day. Talk about feeling like you're in the wrong place at the wrong time. I could only imagine the images of the troopers they were expecting and apologized in my thoughts: *Sorry, guys, what you see is what you get—all five feet six inches of sunburned, starving, filthy, smelly, unshaven, bewildered, blistered, and loaded-down-like-a-damn-mule me.*

Despite my slovenly appearance, they warmly welcomed me to Alpha Company, 5th Battalion, 7th Cavalry. None of that meant anything to me except the 7th Cavalry part. I had already learned back at An Khe, where we went through additional combat training, that the 7th Cavalry was George Armstrong Custer's ill-fated unit lost at the Little Big Horn River in Montana. *Not a good omen.* The CO started explaining some things, which were just passing through my ears without really registering in my brain. Top,[29] meanwhile, graciously relieved me of my rucksack and dropped it to the ground. While the CO droned on, the extra canteens, gas masks, air mattresses, and poncho liners that had been added to my ruck were removed. After some more pleasantries, he was ordered to bring me over to the 2nd Platoon, who had first dibs on replacements. We headed off, with few words exchanged between us, past a dozen or so hooches, with Top asking how each guy was doing, if everything was okay. We shortly reached our destination, where I was introduced to the sergeant of the 2nd Platoon, Marion Green, who was ordered by the company's top sergeant to set me up in a squad. I felt like I was being handed off like an unwanted pet who couldn't be paper trained.

---

29   Top—The company's 1st Sergeant, the highest-ranking NCO.

I immediately liked Sergeant Green because of his quiet demeanor, the way he talked, and gave advice, sort of fatherly instead of the kickass, yelling sergeants I had been exposed to during sixteen weeks of training. He was a tall, black, southern gentleman in his forties, old enough to be the father of every guy there except Top, who was only a couple of years younger than him. He rarely smiled and always sounded very serious when he spoke. "Son, you listens to me and those that been here awhile, and we'll try to git you through this thing so's you can git home to your family." He then called out, "Two-Three!" When he heard a grumble coming from one of the hooches, he ordered the sound to come to his hooch. While we waited for the unseen voice to appear, Sergeant Green explained that the numbers he was calling out were the designation for the squad leader of the 2nd Platoon's third squad. His own position's call sign was Two-Five, Top was Five, the CO was Six, and I was totally confused after being there only seven minutes, and now wondering if I was supposed to be adding all that up to give him an answer.

Two-Three turned out to be a guy named Sam Byrd, the acting squad leader while the actual one was away on R and R. He slowly approached us, suspiciously eyeing me and Sergeant Green as if a joke were going to be played on him. *No joke, Sam. I'm your new man*, I thought to myself. Like most of the others in the hobo camp, he was wearing only faded, baggy olive-green pants, and faded, unlaced olive-green jungle boots, the black dye scraped off the toes and heels to their natural light-brown leather color. His ensemble was accessorized with a threadbare sweat-saturated olive-green towel wrapped around his neck, and a well-used olive-green handkerchief wrapped around his left hand. I realized then why everyone had looked at me so suspiciously earlier: I was obviously overdressed for the occasion.

Introductions were made, and Sam turned out to be a regular guy from Philadelphia. A "brother," about twenty-two years old, who had been drafted, like so many of us who didn't want to be there. It was very obvious he didn't want to be with me at that moment. I was taking away some of his beauty rest, and he certainly wasn't too thrilled about walking me around in the sun trying introduce me to my new squad and platoon while having a great deal of difficulty pronouncing my last name. Couldn't blame him for that. Most of the guys just looked up at me and nodded when their name was mentioned. Sam told a big guy named Joe to get me set up and settled in. Over the next few days, I got to know everyone a little better and started to feel like one of the guys, though I knew I still had a lot to learn before I could earn their trust.

Joe was lifting weights and health conscious long before it came into vogue. He was twenty-four years old and also from Philly, like Sam. Originally, he had been planning to make the army a career and had requested a transfer to Vietnam from Alaska less than a month before. He possessed rugged good looks, something like James Garner, the actor, but he looked like a fifty's greaser with his black DA haircut slicked back. His arms were adorned with animal tattoos, from flying black swallows, to a black panther clawing its way down Joe's huge right forearm. The man looked ominous but was, I would find out, a really gentle person. Joe was about five feet, ten inches tall and very wide. I was to find out later he was also very strong when he, Jackie Teakle, and I went to fetch water in five-gallon Jerry cans. While I dragged one full can of water on the ground between my legs with both hands, Jackie labored with two, stopping every twenty feet or so to rest his arms and fingers. Joe also carried two full cans—in each hand! Always friendly, with a shy smile and helping hand, Joe was liked by everyone who ever met him. Yet, despite his mannerisms, in case of a fight, I would learn to want him on my side.

Jackie was the machine gunner in the squad. He, too, had only been in-country for about a month. A six-foot-tall, lanky Texan with sandy-colored hair, he was always smiling or laughing and fun to be around; had that long, slow, twangy drawl that sort of put you at ease. "Sheeeit, don' worry about it. We'll jis watch each other's backs an' everything'll be okay." Took him about a minute and a half to say that. We became close over the ensuing months, often sharing a hooch and always walking next to each other in the field. I was assigned to be the assistant machine gunner or, more realistically, the machine gunner's ammo bearer.

There were two guys who were always together and seemed to be a perfect match because of their appearance. Lee Tolley was very tall, with a slow gait that always made him look like he was laboring just to walk. Having been in-country longer than most, Lee was a little more serious and definitely less tolerant of new guys. He had already paid his dues in combat and didn't want to get too close to anyone. His sidekick, Gary Ratcliff, or Rat, as he was called, was the complete opposite, standing five feet, four inches tall and always giggling or messing around. Lee was a rifleman; Gary would eventually carry the grenade launcher. The reason they looked perfect together was because they were always a mess! It wasn't easy staying neat, but you tried. Those two guys always looked like they were caked with dirt or smudged with charcoal, hair never combed, nasty teeth, misaligned buttons on their fatigue shirts, a bootlace untied and dragging behind them, one sleeve rolled up above the elbow, one hanging down around the knuckles, empty C-ration cans and wrappers around and in their hooch. They never seemed to notice.

Sam Morris was another tall, lanky guy, about six foot one. Walked sort of stooped over, like he had a bad back from plowing fields behind a mule for too long. In fact, he looked like one of the displaced people in the realistic *Grapes of Wrath* movie starring Henry Fonda. Sam, too, was a nice guy and hailed from California but just wasn't a very talkative person. He would share in conversations, even a little humor, but would rarely initiate either. He had been in the Nam for a few months like Lee and Rat, Sam Byrd, and our absent squad leader.

Sam Morris

Three other FNGs joined the squad that week while we were still in Camp Evans. Jim Meade was a small guy like me. He had a very friendly smile and air about him, probably from being a bartender in New York City. Jim would become the new RTO and relieve Rat of the chore so he could carry the M-79 grenade launcher. Jim had the intelligence and small size perfect for a radio operator.

Arriving with Jim was one Harold Gottesman, Rabbi, as he was fondly called. Harold was an honest-to-goodness Jewish guy from Long Island, NY who had not tried to avoid the draft. He was a good guy, but you just had a feeling that someone in a headquarters unit had screwed up when they put him in the infantry. Harold was short, stocky, balding, out of shape, and terrified of everything from bugs to dirt. Covering someone's ass is one thing; carrying it is something else. I felt Harold would definitely have to prove himself to the others more so than Jim and me.

Arriving a few days before me was Carlos Gomez. No one ever knew much about Carlos because he either could not or would not speak to anyone. All anyone knew about him was what could be seen. He appeared to be Mexican, was of medium height and stocky, had a big space between his two front teeth, had bushy black hair and a thick black mustache. His most prominent features were his piercing black eyes, and a mouth that was always shaped in a sneer. This guy was scary looking, but he was a grunt like the rest of us. Or so we thought. No matter who approached him, for whatever reason— "Carlos, do you want to split this C-ration meal?" "Hey, Carlos, do you want to put up a hooch together?" (You need two ponchos snapped together to build one hooch.) "Do you want help digging that foxhole, Carlos?"—neither the question nor the manner in which it was asked mattered. His answer was always the same: "Fock you." Either these were the only words he knew in English, or he was a very ornery and stupid fellow. I even tried speaking to him in his own language, having already mastered conversational Spanish in high school during my four years of Spanish 1. Didn't matter at all. It was always the same two-word answer, given like he was spitting at you. You know, like the 1948 movie, *The Treasure of the Sierra Madre*. After a challenge from Bogie for identification, the bad guy spits out the words, "Badges? We don' need no stinkin' badges!" Of course Carlos would have finished the sentence with, "Fock you." Within two weeks, everyone stopped trying to initiate a conversation or offer him a helping hand. He refused to pull guard duty, joined no one for meals, and built no shelters, preferring instead to sleep sitting up with a poncho draped over his head, like a serape—and always away from the rest of us. The guy was definitely a weak link and a loose wire. Not someone you'd want to be in a foxhole with under fire. After a while, although we were pulling guard duty every night to protect ourselves from Charlie, we always kept an eye out for Carlos as well. He too was armed.

I spent my first week getting to know the guys while picking up survival, cooking, and hygiene tips. Some of the old-timers hinted at some of the combat action they had experienced but never really elaborated on anything, instead always ending a conversation with "You'll get to see for yourself, new kid, when the shit hits the fan. Just don't get too comfortable here in camp. One of these days, the choppers will pick us up and drop us off in some godforsaken boonies, in the middle of nowhere."

As the next days passed, a thickening cloud cover seemed to drop lower and lower, making the temperatures more bearable. Slowly the sweltering days and nights were replaced with damp, chilling breezes and a smell of rain in the air. On January 31, six days after I had joined my squad, and only two and a half weeks after landing in-country, the tranquility and security of Vietnam was shattered. Cities throughout the country, including the Imperial City of Hue, had been attacked by thousands of NVA and VC forces during the Vietnamese Lunar New Year celebration of Tet.

It was hard for me to believe that the beautiful, peaceful city I had just passed through, riding in a long line of trucks, sitting completely exposed atop a storage container, and watching guys throwing candy bars to kids, was now in the grips of an enemy intent, we would learn, on brutally murdering men, women, and children just to prove a political point. So, on the foggy, misty morning of February 4, 1968, our company boarded rows of idling helicopters, and my first combat air assault. Like many things you do as a teenager for the first time, it was an exciting, scary, and an adrenaline-pumping rush. The choppers took off in a massed formation and sped-off headed southeast into a dark, threatening sky. I watched the scenery scream by just below the Huey's skids, skimming the treetops that separated acres of barren rice paddies into individual square fields of every size. *I just came through here and everything looks so different now.* I thought. *Maybe it's the weather.* It had changed so fast in less than two weeks; each day we saw less and less of the sun until it eventually disappeared behind thickening clouds. The daily temperatures steadily dropped through the nineties, eighties, and seventies, and a fine mist replaced sunshine. As if a switch had been flipped somewhere, we had instantly gone from hot and sunny to cold and rainy. Below my feet was the same picturesque country-side I had seen and photographed earlier. But this time, everything I saw looked gloomy. The dry, sunbaked paddies were already soaking up every drop of moisture the oncoming rainy season would deliver. We wouldn't see the sun again for three weeks, and then only briefly one day. Other than that, we would be in some form of moisture: heavy rain to light drizzle, thick mist to dense fog, every day in the month of February; a leap year no less. One extra day in Nam.

It didn't take very long to figure out who you could trust or depend on in case of trouble. My early days as a kid had prepared me very well for military service. I knew I could survive the elements, shoot a running rabbit with a gun or a bow, and carry my weight in the field. But for many other guys, military service was their first exposure to the great outdoors and the survival game. It would take about three minutes after the choppers touched down in a muddy rice paddy to recognize the guys who might have problems.

The twenty-minute ride ended when the door gunners alerted us to get ready. Moments later the choppers flared to slow down and hovered about two feet above the softening paddy. For a few of us, it was our first "combat assault." Thanks to earlier training, we knew what to do and scrambled to jump off as quickly as possible. In a matter of seconds, it was over as the choppers tilted slightly, gathered forward momentum, and pulled away. The roar and commotion of our ride were instantly replaced by the sucking sounds of jungle boots running across an increasingly muddy two-foot-wide raised berm separating two fields. We had landed "heavy" with our backpacks due to the possibility of deteriorating weather conditions preventing any helicopter flights later. For us new kids, the shifting backpacks continually changed our center of balance. It was so bad that the push-pull weight-shifting would have made it difficult to run on a paved road, let alone a slippery berm. As more grunts headed towards a wood line, trampling the grass-covered dirt berm in the process, clods of ground started to break away, making the muddy little path even narrower. Shuffling my feet as fast as I could to get out of the open, and glancing up ahead at wood line, it looked like it was a half mile away, but was probably only a few hundred yards. Funny how our sense of distance and time changes when exposed to danger.

Harold, or Rabbi as he was now known, was about twenty yards in front of me and waddling as fast as he could, flailing his left arm and trying to use his M-16 in his right hand to maintain his balance. I kept my head down to watch my footing and tried to keep up with the old-timer's boot heels just ahead of me. When I looked up to get my bearings, I saw the Rabbi off to my left, lying on his back in the paddy, wallowing in the mud like a turtle trying to right itself. I don't know if he slipped or someone had shoved him out of the way from behind, but he was there, nonetheless. The weight, width, and position of his backpack kept him face up as he frantically tried to roll from side to side. As guys ran past him, he held out his arm, pleading for someone to help him up. We were not taking any incoming fire, so there didn't appear to be any urgency on the part of anyone to help him. None of the old guys would stop, so I just followed their example. Guys became old-timers because they were doing something right, and I wanted to become an old-timer myself. If I stopped to help him, the column of guys behind us would have to stop or slow down. Not good if we came under fire. That would be a whole different story.

About five minutes after we had reached the safety of the tree line, Harold slogged in looking like he had competed in the World Mud Wrestling Championships and had gotten annihilated. Not to be lost in Harold's escapades, however, was Carlos who had taken his time walking on a different berm far to our right, on the other side of the paddy. He had remained exposed, alone in the open for a very long time, and showed up a few minutes after Harold. Sam checked if everyone was okay, especially Harold and Carlos. Though shaking from fear, cold, wet clothes, and terribly out of breath, Rabbi was fine. Carlos of course quickly replied, "Fock you."

We spent the next week walking through hamlets located within small, forested sections of land in the middle of the barren rice paddy fields. Each day we received a few rounds of incoming sniper fire or mortar rounds, whenever a helicopter landed and remained on the ground. Through all of the walking, searching, and engaging the enemy, Carlos never changed his ways. He continued as a complete loner, always walking thirty yards to our left or right flank, completely exposed when the rest of us were walking in a column. If you were not the grenadier, machine gunner, or RTO in our company, you carried a can of ammo for the machine gun, in addition to your own munitions. After a few days, Carlos got tired of carrying his can and just dropped it in a muddy brook as we crossed over a small bridge. Yelling, threats, orders fell on deaf ears. He was becoming a real liability by not pulling his fair share. The new guys, including myself, had to pick up his slack—stay awake longer on guard duty, carry extra weight, and cover more ground. The old-timers would get on him and say he'd better straighten out or he'd be in deep shit soon. Nothing seemed to work, and the same sneer and answer was always his response. He'd look right through you with his piercing black eyes and spit out his favorite phrase. The old-timers figured he'd come around in a few weeks when he got tired of digging holes alone, getting last choice of the C rations, and sleeping out in the rain.

On February 3, a lot of things had started to change for a lot of guys in the Cav. Grunts never know what's really happening; the strategies and tactics made behind the scenes in some tent determined their movements in the field. We just kept saddling up and moving toward Hue. What we would eventually learn was that the 3rd Brigade of the 1st Cavalry Division, of which we were a part, had been called upon to move across miles of occupied territory and take up positions to block and engage any and all enemy soldiers and supplies going to or coming from the northwest quadrant of Hue. It had to be accomplished despite a low cloud cover that would keep our helicopters socked in at Camp Evans, and much of our artillery support not yet available due to the 1st Cavalry's ongoing relocation from An Khe. So, it made Charlie and us pretty even at the worst time.

By February 11, we had already made contact a few times, and maneuvered into a position to sweep a hamlet called Thon La Chu. The objective was another of the forested "islands" surrounded by open rice paddies. Elements of the 2/12 had been engaged in heavy fighting there for days and had dubbed it Tee-Tee Woods. The hamlet turned out to be a real beehive because, as we would soon find out and as the 2/12 already knew, it was hiding a very large force of North Vietnamese regulars and Viet Cong supporters. Intelligence-gathering and NVA POW interrogations estimated the village of Thon La Chu to be occupied by anywhere from one thousand to three thousand North Vietnamese regulars. The hamlet was, in fact, the headquarters location, main supply distribution point, and replacement center for all enemy operations during their Hue campaign.

Our initial ground assault toward the hamlet resulted in very heavy casualties, stopping our advance and pushing us back across the open paddies. It could have been worse—the entire perimeter of the wood line was ringed with Chinese-made Claymore-type antipersonnel mines and a web of interconnected trenches and tunnels. Napalm that had been dropped prepping the area in the early morning hours had saved us by melting the electrical wires needed to detonate the mines. We retreated into an empty village to regroup and lick our wounds, hoping Charlie wouldn't try to sneak out of hiding. The only casualty in our squad was Rabbi, who had his left earlobe pierced by an AK round. His medevac departure meant I would probably never see him again. It also meant longer guard duty each night for the remainder of us. One of our platoons was not so lucky, so its remaining members temporarily became part of our 2nd Platoon.

Each day for nine days, squads would take turns returning to the edge of the rice paddies and watch across the open expanse into the tree line for any signs of an enemy withdrawal. What we did see was a constant land, air, and sea bombardment of the enemy positions. When we weren't assigned to watch, we were either patrolling the surrounding villages for additional enemy concentrations or staying in the village we were occupying. Those days or hours off-duty while in a reserve capacity were spent catching up on letter writing, giving each other haircuts, or playing cards. One day, we actually received our monthly pay. *Gee, all this fun and we get paid too!* For me, it meant ten dollars. When you mix together boredom, money, young guys, and cards, it can lead to only one thing: poker. Within three days one guy would have all the money in the company, which he'd then wire home. Guys who didn't play poker were constantly being hounded by the losers begging for a loan. They were usually granted by the new guys, but never the old-timers. We thought they just weren't as trusting as us, but they had a different reason. The guy you loaned money to today, might not be there tomorrow to repay you.

Despite everything we had just been through during the firefight and the close bonds that were developing between everyone, Carlos never changed. He maintained his lone wolf demeanor, and continued to respond to questions, and orders with "Fock you." For the rest of us, communications were getting better as we got to know each other. Even with the constant drizzle, and being in a war, days "off" could still be fun—C rations were plentiful; instead of poker, because we had no money, the game was changed to gin or hearts; and it always felt good to crawl onto an air mattress in a dry hooch. Carlos, on the other hand, shared in none of this. Having opted to remain alone, he took up residence in a partially destroyed thatched hut, and dined on fresh chicken and duck he had dispatched with a machete he had found, and was becoming very fond of.

All good things came to an end when we were ordered to prepare for another frontal assault on Tee-Tee

Woods, the morning of February 21. We would again surround Thon La Chu in full battalion strength. Alpha Company, to which I was assigned, was to pour all the small-arms and machine-gun fire we could muster into the tree line to keep Charlie's head down, prevent him from peeking while our three other companies of the 5th Battalion worked their way into assigned positions for the actual assault.

We weren't very confident in how much our firing would intimidate our determined adversary. After all, we'd watched the enemy's position being pounded for nine straight days and nights. The wooded area had been so thoroughly mutilated by artillery fire from not only our firebase at PK-17, and the navy's five-inch guns off the deck of the USS *Lofberg* out in the South China Sea, but also from sorties of USAF F-100s doing high- and low-level bombing runs, dropping high explosives and napalm. No sooner did their bombs detonate, we could hear Charlie shooting at the departing jets with automatic weapons. Some minutes later, when the sortie returned to strafe the encampment with twenty-millimeter cannon fire, the same thing could be heard as the jet's afterburners roared. We were amazed anything could survive the constant bombardment day after day, but we were even more amazed at Charlie's tenacity. We couldn't help but wonder what we would run into when we finally broke through their lines.

While under the cover of darkness on the chilled misty morning of February 21, we quietly made our way from our perimeter on trails we had created and crawled into the familiar tall grass at the edge of the rice paddies surrounding our treed objective. Our company spread out along a line parallel to the wood line, ready to support the assault. Jackie positioned the machine

gun on a small knoll for a better vantage point above
the otherwise flat terrain. While he started to set up, I
crawled along our line and collected the extra ammo
for the M-60, returning with five ammo cans containing one thousand rounds. Four of the metal containers
were opened and placed within arm's reach behind our
position for instant availability. Three of the cans were
emptied immediately, each cardboard box containing
one hundred rounds was ripped open for easy access
to the linked machine-gun ammo. Once set up and the
shooting started, I wanted to be able to connect the end
of the belt already being fed into the gun with a fresh
belt for continuous fire. In that way, Jackie could concentrate on targets without ever having to stop the firing to reload.

Big Joe, about ten yards to our right and holding
a ninety-millimeter recoilless rifle for knocking down
any bunkers or suspected machine-gun positions,
looked totally perplexed. I have no idea where he got
it from or how he knew how to fire it, but there it was
ready to spit out some rounds. We never heard it fire
and found out later there was no ammunition for the
rifle. Five yards to our left was Rat with the grenade
launcher. To his left were Sam and Jim with the radio.
For twenty minutes each man along the entire assault
line lay quietly in the dark with his own thoughts, waiting for the word that would shatter the peaceful stillness. I was thinking about what the day would bring
once we stopped firing; once we had to leave the safety
of our positions; once we were exposed and started to
run across the two-hundred-fifty-yard- expanse of open
paddy to reach the well defended wood line.

I felt rather than saw a presence just to my right.
Turning, I realized it was Carlos lying with his head

only three feet away from my elbow. He had crawled up
without either Jackie or me noticing him. We looked at
each other, and Jackie whispered, "Get him away from
us!" Looking out for his safety, I slid back to my right
and told Carlos to move away because we had a large
concentration of firepower that was sure to draw enemy fire. Of course his response was "Fock you." No
matter what I said, in both languages, he responded the
same: "Fock you." I was getting pissed off, so I crawled
back up to my position and told Jackie to shoot the
son of a bitch a few hundred times, maybe then he'd
understand when people were trying to be nice to him.
Unfortunately, it was too late to reposition the gun,
because the order to 'Open Fire!' was given. In an instant, the quiet Vietnamese farming area was shattered
by automatic small-arms fire of almost one hundred
American troopers of the 1st Cavalry Division. Joining
in the fireworks display were the explosions from the
unseen artillery batteries that already had the target coordinates.

I hadn't noticed with all of the commotion that Carlos had moved away from us. Maybe he didn't like being pelted with hot brass from the M-60's ejected shell
casings. Over the roar of the machine-gun, while keeping his finger depressed on the trigger, Jackie yelled, "Do
you smell something burning?" I looked around while
snapping on another belt of ammo, saw smoke rising
from the opposite side of the gun barrel, and pointed.
He was putting so many rounds through the 60, that
the canvas strap used to carry it was smoldering, just
from touching the barrel. My index fingers and thumbs
were starting to bleed from snapping the metal links
of the ammo belts together as fast as I could. The hot,
ejecting rounds were flying in an arc and piling up right

where Carlos had been lying. It was too late to worry
about him by then anyway. We continued to fire along
with everyone else when suddenly, with a loud roar the
ground started shaking from explosions behind us.

Through the misty fog and smoke I could barely
make out the shape of something that looked like one
of the steel shipping containers with tank tracks on it.
Being an FNG, I had no idea what it was. Again, without stopping the gun, Jackie glanced over his shoulder
to see what had caused the explosion and yelled over
the ear-shattering gun fire that it was a Duster. The olive-green apparition was a light tank topped with forty-millimeter cannons mounted high up in its front. As
its crew started rapid firing again, I watched for a moment as the right barrel recoiled while the left barrel
traveled forward to its original starting position. Then
the left barrel recoiled when fired while the right returned forward. The barrels repeated their in-and-out
pumping motion every four seconds, easily drowning
out the sound of the M-60. All I really cared about was
the Duster being on our side.

Each time it fired, we could see and feel ground debris being kicked up and thrown forward by the shock
waves from its muzzle blasts. We also noticed that Carlos had decided to take himself off the shooting line
entirely and was lying between the Duster and us. A
look over at Sam and Rat brought the same disbelieving, head-shaking reaction that Jackie and I had. We
couldn't worry about Carlos or the Duster and turned
back to concentrate on where we were firing. Over the
deafening blasts from LAWs (a shoulder-fired rocket
launcher), numerous machine guns, grenade launch-
ers, M-16s, and the twin cannon fire of the Duster, we
heard from behind us the terrified screams of "Medic!

I'm hit, I'm hit! Medic!" We all spun our heads around and saw Carlos holding his butt with a bloody hand. Simultaneously and without any premeditation, Jackie, Rat, Joe, Sam, Jim, and I instantly yelled, "Fock you!"

We found out later in the day that he had been hit in the butt with a small stone thrown up from the Duster's muzzle blasts. I saw Carlos again months later on a hot day in late April when I had to leave the field. He was living in an empty wooden shipping crate behind the supply tent. He looked a mess, probably hadn't had a haircut since he arrived in-country, and wore creosote-laced, dirt-covered, threadbare jungle fatigues. Hanging around his neck was an army-issue olive-green towel, and in his hand, wrapped with an olive-green handkerchief, was a machete. He looked like a mean dog chained to a fence pole that no one would go near. I said hi to him, but I'm not sure if he recognized me. I knew there was no sense in trying to reach him or start a conversation. I later learned no one would even go near him because they didn't trust his sanity. I know that for a fact because Rabbi had returned from his wound and was working in supply.

Chapter II
In the Beginning . . .

I remember back in the early fifties when I was probably six or seven years old, my father told me war stories at my insistence. My pleas were sometimes granted just to shut me up. He was probably ad-libbing some Hollywood movie he'd seen, but how would I know. Usually it was just a way of passing time while we sat in our '47 Dodge in front of the food mart. Seems like mom was always picking up a quart of milk and loaf of bread. I always sat mesmerized while one of his yarns built to a dramatic climax—the good guys, always American, would beat the bad guys, either Nazis or Japanese fanatics. The GI was always faster, smarter, and better prepared, equipped, or positioned. The incredible heroic deeds of the characters in the stories, good guy or bad guy, left me wondering how and if I would ever be able to do those things if in the same situations.

The sequence of events never changed. My mother would open the car door while he was trying to calm us kids down, and she'd put the groceries on the seat between them. She'd slide in, then jab him in the arm, telling him to stop scaring us. "What's the matter with you?" she'd admonish him. "You could give them night-mares and they'll wet their beds!" Hmm, there were times when I almost did, but I was twenty years old in my own Hollywood movie.

I can't tell you how many times I've heard someone say they were cleaning out an old bedroom bureau and found some medals, an old picture or two, and some tarnished bullets in the bottom drawer. They'd ask me what the medals were for, saying they never knew their father—uncle—brother was in the. . . I was fortunate to be contacted one day by Linda Thomasa, a wom-an in Michigan who was doing just that. The medals and pictures she found were of guys in the field and her brother, Bill Ebel, one of our fallen troopers in '68. She was very young when he left for Vietnam and really didn't know much about him. Being that her brother and I were in the same squad, I was more than willing to share some stories and give her some details about our short time together. She was very grateful for our telephone conversations over the following week, and now, because of her call, those pictures are part of our 5th Battalion, 7th Cavalry Association's website, as well as a few in this book.

I would think that the vast majority of us have nev-er told our kids anything about our military service. Writing down those memories has sure helped me put things in perspective and made me recall our band of brothers, the good times and bad, the laughs and the tears. It's the good times I remember best and share with someone who wants to know what it was like. Well, our kids aren't kids anymore. In fact, our grandkids aren't kids anymore. Maybe it's time to tell them something about your service in your own way. The short stories in this book might break the ice and raise a question from them if they read it.

I was glad to have lived with my father his last couple of years and finally hear about his younger days and WWII experiences. We didn't talk about the ugly side of war; we didn't have to. He was a combat medic, me a grunt. I like to think he enjoyed our talks, however short and few they were. As it turned out, we both felt bad for never asking or telling. Unfortunately, most find out about their parents' military service after they pass away, often when cleaning out their belongings and opening a bottom drawer in a bureau.

I think back on my days in the military so long ago, and although I remember the horrors and the terror, I remember the guys and the laughs we had much more clearly. The more I think back on it, the bigger my smile gets, and the better I feel. Perhaps something in this book might make you recall a similar incident, sure to bring a smile to your face too. Why not tell them about it? It might even explain some of your behavior over their lifetime, let them know that it wasn't necessarily something they did that prompted your actions, but something in you. Probably something we lost inside is more like it. As far as the combat stuff goes, many of us saw a lot, many more saw none. We should all be proud of our service, and remember and honor our fallen comrades until the day we get our final orders. To ease into the subject with your kids, ask if they're curious. I see something funny, and I can't help but relate it to something I experienced. You can start telling your story with how you got there.

Frequent Flyer

We boarded a commercial Continental Airlines Boeing 707 in Oakland, California, on January 12, 1968, after a week of additional personnel processing and vaccinations, returning earlier-issued cold-weather clothes, and getting new stuff for hot climates. I sat with a bunch of guys I had been through Basic and Advanced Infantry Training with who would make the flight fun at times. We had twenty-one hours to do whatever we wanted to do before reaching our destination of Bien Hoa, a city just northeast of Saigon in the Republic of Vietnam.

During the long flight, my mind ebbed and flowed between the past, present, and what the future might bring. Thoughts of the parties, friends, and loved ones I had left behind in New Jersey kept running through my head. I remember thinking about the advice my uncles and other veterans at work gave me: "Keep your head down. Don't volunteer for anything. Stay out of the Tank Corps." Though good advice, their words didn't mean as much to me personally as did my father's a week earlier, just before I headed for the staircase of the departing jet at Newark Airport. He was a man of few words, so I didn't expect to hear much. "What can

I say?" he said with a shrug. "Come back." I still get choked up when I think back to that moment.

From the instant we took off from California and headed west toward our first stop in Hawaii, the trip was strange and at times confusing. I could swear I heard Rod Serling saying, "You're about to enter…the Twilight Zone." For months we had trained for, been informed of, and read about the war in Vietnam—men were dying, trucks were blowing up, there was no front line, and the enemy was everywhere. And yet, we were flying on a commercial airliner equipped with everything, including pretty, young stewardesses, plus equipment and replacement troops headed for a combat zone. "How bad could this Vietnam place really be?" was the question. We collectively decided that they would drop off the flight attendants in Hawaii and replace them with combat guys so we would be able to fight our way off the jet when it landed. At times, it felt as if we were sheep being led to slaughter. The civilian employees of Continental Airlines seemed *too* friendly. We suspicious Easterners thought something must be up, there must be a catch, and although we asked the returning veterans on the plane what to expect, they would not tell us. "Just wait, you'll see," they said at first. Later in the flight, they either ignored us or just shook their heads at our naive speculations.

After the two-thousand-plus-mile first leg of our flight, we landed in Hawaii at three o'clock in the morning. We were allowed to leave the plane and enjoy the beautiful confines of the terminal for about two hours before boarding. The next leg took us to Wake Island another two thousand miles away, and just as we had suspected, the plane's crew had been changed. But much to our confusion, the new crew was not combat guys but civilian people just as nice and friendly as those who had left. Just the same, suspicions were raised because many felt the new stewardesses were not as pretty as those on the first leg. *Hmmm*...Hey, you notice these little things when headed for a war zone.

More guys boarded in Hawaii; some returning and others were replacements troops like us. One of the new passengers sitting diagonally across the aisle from us was a Huey pilot returning from R and R. He sounded like a regular guy, a warrant officer, but looked to be a little forlorn. Maybe just tired after spending a week on the beach in Honolulu with his wife. During the course of conversation, we naturally tried to pick his brain about Vietnam, but after a short time we could sense he really didn't want to talk. So, we all just settled back into our seats.

Our body clock started to malfunction somewhere over the Pacific. No matter how many hours we flew, it always looked like early sunrise outside of the small cabin windows. Between the time zone changes and crossing the International Date Line, we didn't know the time or even the day! Should we sleep, wake up, play cards, what? Combining that with the engines constant hum, sleep deprivation and boredom, it was just a matter of time before nerves started to fray. Loud heated arguments started flaring up on both sides of the aisle. With the noise they were making and the sudden "jump out of your seat" blaring intercom-"This is your captain speaking,"- sleeping was almost impossible. Nonetheless, some guys tried to doze off in the continuing state of "sunrise." Eventually, order was restored, most of the window shades were pulled down, the overhead lights turned off, and it wasn't long before the plane became much quieter, except for the snoring that drowned out the jet engines and the occasional useless message from the cockpit.

I was playing cards with Jim Mello, a rugged-looking guy from Connecticut who had gone through training with me, and Donny Miller, my best friend from Pompton Lakes where we had grown up. None of us could sleep, so we tried to kill the time as best we could. While most of the plane's passengers and crew slept, we noticed over our cards that the warrant officer was getting really restless. It seemed the closer we got to our destination, the paler he looked. As the time slowly passed, he started mumbling to himself incoherently, and it appeared he was breaking into a cold sweat. The three of us questioned whether one of us should approach him, but because the guys in the seats next to him didn't seem too bothered by his actions, we shrugged it off. We reasoned he was probably upset about having just left his wife in Hawaii.

Donny Miller and the author

His condition only seemed to worsen. He'd twist around in his seat to look toward the rear of the plane a few rows behind us, then quickly jerk back around to the front. That was immediately followed by pressing his head back into the headrest and holding onto the armrests with a white-knuckle grip. We at first tried to ignore him thinking he needed the rest room but didn't want to walk to the back. Try as we might, though, it was obvious he was having some type of serious issue. Feeling we should do something for him, Mello leaned across the aisle and asked if he was okay, if he wanted water or something he could get for him. The pilot tried to assure Jim he was okay, maybe just overtired. We went back to playing cards but kept glancing up at him just to make sure.

For the next hour the only thing that was constant was the drone of the four jet engines. Guys were sprawled all over the seats in the long cigarette-smoke-filled cabin, arms and legs dangling over armrests and splayed into the darkened aisles. Donny and I decided to try to get some sleep and reached up to shut off our overhead lights, while Jim said he would continue reading *The Source* and keep an eye on the Warrant Officer's condition. After what felt like only a few minutes of shallow sleep, the silence of the plane's interior was shattered by a blood-curdling scream.

The Warrant Officer was trembling and pointing to the rear of the plane, yelling, "There's a dead woman back there. Oh my God, she's dead, she's dead!" Mello jumped out of his seat and tried to calm him down, while I spun around the last two rows of seats in the cabin to look into the back of the plane. The "dead woman" turned out to be one of the stewardesses, who was also trying to get some sleep and was by then jumping up herself. As she jumped up, we met face to face in the dimly lit corner of the aft cabin section and scared the hell out of each other—she probably thinking I was about to molest her, me thinking she was rising from the dead.

We both stopped screaming, and she peeled herself off the window when I lifted my hands in a gesture of surrender to prove I wasn't a threat. I calmed her down somewhat by explaining that the Warrant Officer was having a breakdown, believing she was dead. Hearing him yelling in the background and knowing my intentions were innocent, we headed up to his seat. By the time we got there, Jim had calmed him down a little, though he still looked terrified. Then again, if you met Mello with a two-day growth of beard in a dark cabin, you'd probably be terrified too.

Anyway, the flight attendant tried to assure him in a soft, gentle voice that everything was okay, that she had only been sleeping. Her demeanor in helping the poor soul had little effect as he continued to shiver uncontrollably. Feeling we had handled the situation okay, or at least appeared to have had some compassion for his state of mind, the flight attendant asked if we would stay with him, keep him calm while she went forward to speak to the captain. Donny complied and changed seats with him, allowing Jim and me to keep him occupied with cards. He tried to appear calm during the seat changes, apologizing profusely to everyone, saying repeatedly that he must have been dreaming. He was really struggling with the situation, both as a man embarrassed by his actions and as an officer. As our flight continued toward our final destination, his reassuring words were directed as much to himself as to the replacements on the plane. We tried to humor

him and occupy his mind with thought-provoking discussions, but nothing seemed to work, and his condition didn't improve much. Eventually our flight made
an emergency landing on Guam, where he stayed for
immediate medical attention. The entire episode wasn't
a very good omen and did wonders to our own nerves.
Maybe this Vietnam place is bad.

We again took off after a short layover and continued the never-ending flight over water, chasing the sun.
The twenty hours it had taken to fly eight thousand
miles was becoming an eternity to us. The big jet's cabin space felt smaller as cigarette smoke got thicker and
nerves got tighter. Almost hypnotized by the monotony
and eerie quiet, everyone about jumped out of their skin
when the stillness was again suddenly shattered. Our
dream state had been interrupted by an exceptionally
loud intercom message from the captain in the cockpit.
"Good morning, gentlemen. I trust you've had a good
night's sleep by now. If you look out of the left side of
the plane in a few minutes, you'll be able to see Vietnam
through the clouds."

One side of the plane's interior erupted as if every seat
had suddenly received an electric shock. Almost everyone on the right side jumped from their seats and started
to climb, lean, and hang over seats on our side, trying to
position themselves for a first view of their soon-to-be
new home. We too leaned and looked down from our
window and waited. In a few minutes, the plane started
its approach, and we were staring down at a soft yellowish green landscape outlined by the beautiful, dark
blue South China Sea. Far below us the checkered terrain looked like an enormous quilt of every imaginable
shade of green. Dark-brown rivers shaped like multifac-
eted lightning strikes separated the fragile surface, as if
the ground had been split apart by earthquakes. Small-

er tears extended from the gaping openings, leaving a frayed web of light-brown tributaries and islands. The peaceful green continuum gave way to a pockmarked surface where in all directions columns of dense black smoke billowed up. We stared dumbfounded, thinking they were about to land a commercial jet while the entire countryside was under heavy mortar attack and us without even having any weapons or helmets on the plane.

The speculation about how we were going to get off the jet continued in earnest while it was actually taxiing down the runway. After all, we still had stewardesses on board, even if they were much older than and not as pretty as the first two crews we'd had on earlier flights. Everyone was grappling to get a better view, starting to debate our chances of survival—whether the rising smoke was from mortar rounds or rockets, whether there was a ground attack in progress at the airport, whether the war had suddenly escalated while we were enroute, whether they were going to hand out rifles as we ran off the plane.

"Man, no wonder that Warrant Officer cracked up," someone said amid the arms and bodies.

"Yeah, this is going to be tougher than we thought."

We were finally told what was happening when a returning grunt sitting near us turned and said with a scowl, "Dumb fucking cherries, that's diesel fuel smoke coming up from burning cans of shit! Now *sit down!*" That would have probably been my next guess anyway. So much for fighting our way off the plane.

Thankfully, the plane landed without incident. The first thing we noticed when the doors opened to accept the staircases being rolled into position was an incredible blast of heat. After sitting in air-conditioned comfort for twenty-one hours, our breath was sucked right out of our lungs. As we walked down the stairs under a bright, blazing sun, our khaki dress uniforms were soaked with sweat by the time we reached the bottom step. When we finally stepped onto the tarmac on Vietnamese soil, our feet instantly started to burn. The next thing that assailed our senses was the unforgettable, putrid odor of burning human waste and diesel fuel. What a welcome. I couldn't imagine what my departure was going to be like.

We were escorted from the runway in Bien Hoa, which is about fifteen miles northeast of Saigon, to a fleet of awaiting olive-green air-conditioned army buses. All of their windows were covered with a heavy-gauge wire mesh that prevented anyone one from escaping, or more likely to keep bad, noisy, explosive things from being thrown through the windows. For most of us, it was the first time we had been out of the United States and were shocked by the living conditions of the Vietnamese peasants passed in route to the replacement-processing base camp. The bus became quieter when we passed small, dilapidated shanties that lined the streets, some built of concrete, streaked with dark mold, sagging roofs of saplings covered with dry brown grass. Other less fortunate folks lived in huts of old wood, using uncut metal sheets of preprinted Coca-Cola cans for roofs or siding.

We noticed an occasional pull-cart stacked with sundry items parked in the gutter away from traffic. Small children wearing only a shirt, nude from the waist down, chased chickens in the littered dirt streets. Old men who looked like Confucius with small, pointed beards sat at rickety tables playing card games or checkers, sipping tea from delicate little hand-painted porcelain cups. A skinny dog or pig rummaging around a building was spotted from time to time. Bicycles, seemingly by the hundreds, and a steady flow of mopeds filled both sides of a narrow road shared with hulking American trucks and Vietnamese taxis. We figured these were the people we were sent to defend against the Communist threat, and it looked like they needed it.

Formula for Friendship

After an eye-opening bumpy ride, the buses passed through rows of barbed concertina wire[30] and a detail of armed Military Police sentries who checked all who entered or left the camp. It was here that we would spend more days for additional processing to determine where every one of the replacement troops would be assigned. Oh, lest I forget, if our arms hadn't already been abused enough back in California, we would receive even more shots to protect us from any other potential diseases we might contract that they hadn't remembered to vaccinate us against twice before. Ironically, I don't remember ever getting one for the Asian flu. Go figure.

The base camp looked like most I had seen in all of the black-and-white WWII movies. In color, though, it was slightly different. The bright sandy soil was offset by hundreds of bleached-out gray buildings connected by raised wooden walkways. In every direction there were hordes of olive-green-attired GIs moping about,

---

30   Concertina wire—Coils of barbed or razor wire stretched out like a slinky, and used for defensive purposes.

as well as parked or moving motor vehicles kicking up plumes of untreated ground. And everywhere one looked in the open common areas, between the faded barracks and the outlying buildings, were stacked faded green sandbags encircling large corrugated-steel drain-pipe sections, to be used as emergency shelters in the event of a mortar or rocket attack. Now that wouldn't be a very nice way to welcome visitors to a country they were sent to protect and save, would it? That was the first indicator something wasn't right here. *Wait, isn't this supposed to be the safe rear area where there is no fighting?*

The loose sandy roads throughout the base were black, the result of them being covered by a fragrant petrol chemical sheen of creosote oil. This goo, which stuck to the boots and pant cuffs of everyone coming in contact with it, was necessary to minimize potential dust storms created by all of the passing jeeps, deuce and a half's, and ubiquitous tanker trucks carrying water or fuel or more creosote. Contrasting with the black roads was a white-hot sun overhead and a blue sky streaked with tall columns of billowing black smoke from burning untold gallons of multipurpose diesel fuel. It was a convenient fuel for sanitation control when poured into two-foot-diameter-by-one-foot-high metal drums and ignited to "process" human waste. Each blackened drum was collected daily, pulled out from behind a horizontal door flap opening under multiple outhouses throughout the base. I don't think it's necessary to describe the rather unpleasant aroma. The only real colors on the base, other than black, green, and sand, came from Old Glory waving from flagpoles around the grounds.

We were assigned bunks in long single-level wood barracks. All of the side walls were basically open, having only angled, horizontal wood slats that gave the siding the appearance of opened jalousie windows. All of the building's openings, including doors at either end, were sealed with mosquito screening, which unfortunately also served to limit any air circulation inside. Bright shiny silver corrugated-metal panels served for the roofing that enabled the wood-planked floors to hold the heat in nicely. The combination helped to make our evening sleep just a bit more uncomfortable. It was another wonderful new and unique experience to wake up exhausted each morning, soaking wet as if having just taken a shower, yet still lying on one's damp, sagging, one-inch-thick mattress fitted nicely atop a metal bed frame with a broken spring here and there. There would be days in the future when we wished we had such luxuries. Outside our doors were raised wooden sidewalks traversing each building, giving the compound the look of an old Western movie set. The walkways were built, no doubt, to keep pedestrians above ground level to prevent kicking up dust in summer or mud during the cool rainy season. Based on the parched surroundings, we had apparently missed that wonderful time of the year. Our great fortune in missing the heavy monsoon rains allowed us to bask in searing temperatures radiating down from a glaring sun framed by cloudless but black smoke-laced skies. The unrelenting heat and humidity brutalized the thousands of newly arrived transient GIs, who shuffled trancelike through the glaring sun and rippling mirages looking like melting zombies, mindlessly waiting to be processed.

With all the anonymity and confusion in the camp, we wondered how we could ever be assigned to the same unit. We put our heads together to figure out what was going on, how the system worked to process and assign thousands of guys to so many different places in so little time. Of the nine of us who had gone through sixteen weeks of training, rooming, or bunking together, we had recently flown from the east coast to California and managed to still stay together to arrive in Vietnam as one. Seven of us had been drafted out of college because of numerous reasons and represented all kinds of disciplines: engineering, science, nuclear physics, business, and teaching. We reasoned that there had to be a simple formula or system used to move so many people every day because they just couldn't be assigning people by name. So it must have been by lot.

After only one day of waiting on lines, we figured it out. There were enormous speakers mounted atop tall telephone poles spaced throughout the camp. The hundreds or thousands of replacement troops roaming around lost, maybe reading, talking to or meeting new friends, filling sandbags, or, if unlucky enough, burning doo-doo while on a "special" detail would suddenly hear the speakers start blaring. Everyone would stop in place and look up as if there were subtitles beneath them. It could be an announcement to warn everyone of what was for dinner that night or, more importantly, calling for all replacement troops or maybe only a few to form up in lines at the parade ground. Or maybe just one guy to report to.

When the speakers came to life, almost instantly guys in every direction started to drown the message out by yelling, "What did he say?" "Did he just call my name?" "Quiet! Shut the fuck up!" You could tell by the look on everyone's face that they were straining to hear and understand the barely audible, static-filled, and feedback-shrieking voice of someone with a heavy southern drawl. Usually, the only understandable word was "parade." In a matter of minutes, the entire encampment looked like the movie set for *Soylent Green*. There were those awakening from overheated stupors joining the hundreds of dirty, sweaty, uniformed bodies shuffling from barracks or work details. No one was really sure of the announcement but walked nonetheless looking for one of the elevated platforms that had someone standing on it. That was probably the designated location, but you weren't sure if you were actually supposed to be there. A lot of guys who might have been on a faraway detail who were able to understand the distorted message would show up late anyway because it was hard to find the assigned area amid the hundreds of identical barracks and mazelike intersecting boardwalks.

We had been beating one system or another all through training, so why not here? Back in the states, our room was always more like a college dorm than a barracks. While guys in other rooms were going crazy trying to get ready for inspections, wearing socks over their boots so as to not scuff their freshly hand-waxed and machine-buffed floors, we were partying every night. For us it was simple: The last guy out of our room each morning would just throw a quick layer of Johnson's Clear, a liquid wax on the floor, swish it around with a mop, and we won "Best Room" every week. We never worried about taking a chance or doing something wrong, because our motto was, like most grunts, "What can they do to us, send us to Vietnam?" We already knew we were going.

Getting back to the formations, at some point everyone met at the designated location, usually two or
three times per day, and were ordered to form up in
one, two, three, four lines to await their fate while trying to remain standing under the intense sun. If anyone had had the good fortune of having a detail in one
of the clean air-conditioned Quonset huts where the
regular cadre performed their duties, these mandatory
outdoor lineups on the trampled parade grounds provided them the opportunity to sweat and get covered
with sand and creosote-laced dirt from passing trucks
and jeeps like the rest of us. They would then have the
opportunity to look very much the same as the rest of
their filthy brethren who had been assigned harsher details.

A sergeant standing behind a podium atop a raised
platform would order the long lines of replacements
to count off by twos, threes, fours, whatever. In other words, if we counted off by threes, the first guy in
line would be a one, the second two, the third three,
the fourth one again, and so on. After everyone had
counted off, we would be ordered to re-form lines where
all ones reported here, twos there, and threes another
place until all of us had shuffled into another line. A
piece of cake to beat.

Other than standing in lines under the sun and getting small work details, the three days of processing
were not without fun. On our first night in-country, we
were told that the EM Club, or enlisted men's club, was
pretty good, so a few of us headed there to cool off with
a couple of cold brews. The place was called the Jet Set
Club and looked no different than our barracks. It was
already packed with troops when we arrived around
six, and like other countless replacements before us, we

started firing back beers "celebrating" our safe arrival. There was nothing fancy about the club, just your basic GI beer hall, but it was far better than we had anticipated less than twelve hours earlier. I mean, we had originally thought we'd be spending our first night in a foxhole. If you remember, prior to our landing, we were speculating on our chances of surviving our first day in-country after having to fight our way off the runway—*stupid new kids.*

Well, the alcohol flowed that first night, and everyone's spirits soared. Then, amid raucous hoots and hollering, a five-piece Vietnamese band arrived with Beatles hairstyles. All of the newly arrived troops didn't know what to expect, what with all of the stereotyping we had been exposed to all of our lives. I don't know, I guess I expected to hear "Ruv Me Tendah," by Eris Presrey, maybe "Rock Aroun da Crock," by Beer Hairy and da Comet, or other such merodies, er, melodies. Instead, they started playing "Satisfaction," sounding exactly like the Rolling Stones, and after a few seconds of stunned silence, the place went nuts. For the remainder of the night, we were entertained by other top rock groups of the time, every song sounding exactly like the original, with British accent or American southern twang where needed. I'll never forget that bizarre evening.

Jim Mello was sitting next to me and just as stunned. I yelled to him, "Mello, are you shittin' me? We landed in a commercial jet, we're staying in aboveground barracks with beds, drinking cold beers from the 'world,' and listening to a good rock band. How bad can this place be?" We were partying with three guys at our table we didn't know but who looked just like us—soaked with sweat, needing a shave, and wearing dusty new jungle fatigues. Introductions were made, jokes were told, and we all proceeded to get drunk. A big redhead-ed guy from California asked us our unit. Figuring he had arrived in Vietnam before us and had already been processed, we said we hadn't been assigned yet. The smile on his face was immediately replaced with a look of sympathy. It turned out that he and his two buddies were grunts with the 25th Infantry Division and were processing out of country. Jeez, we still had 365 days left. Their attitude toward us changed, but they stayed, and we continued to party. They weren't willing to tell us any war stories, only tactfully saying to us that we would learn that things could get pretty bad at times. "Enjoy today, guys." *Maybe this Vietnam place was bad after all.*

After the first day of breaking the assigning code, those of us who wanted to remain together in Nam walked to the formations and waited at the end of the lines until the person in command announced the number to be counted off. We would then drop back a little out of line, count the backs of the people in front of us, cut back into lines at the right slots, and all be ones, twos, whatever. If any one of us miscalculated the position, we simply went to the new assembly area anyway to where our friends were. Names were taken and checked off lists, and as before, the rest would be dismissed and shuffle off until the next gathering.

Consequently, in late afternoon of the third day, all threes from a long line of dirty uniforms, including most of the guys from training were assigned to the 1st Cav-alry Division. Our orders read that we were to board transport planes bound for a place called An Khe the following morning, January 17. To everyone's relief, we had managed to stay together and now belonged to the same unit, a unit a few sergeants in the states had told us was really good but had seen a lot of action.

Top row: The author, Donny Miller; middle row: Jim Muskett, John Pocatelli, Wilbur Waslewski; bottom row: Jeff Hill, Jim Mellow, Jim Farrell, Don Davis

Like all replacement troops, we were curious as to where in-country our new home was located. Erected next to the parade grounds where all formations were held was a huge map of Vietnam, supported and framed by four-by-four wooden posts. Moments after everyone was dismissed, those who had received assignments naturally ran over to the map, searching to locate the area where they were to be stationed. We of course did the same on that hot dusty day, fully immersed in the tension and excitement, as were other guys crowding impatiently around us to find where they too might be spending their next twelve months.

Nine of us searched the strange names with eyes and fingertips, trying to find the one place that matched our orders. We naturally started to look around the Saigon area because most of the other guys were finding their reporting destinations there. We had studied the map for a good five minutes, straining our eyes, when Jim Farrell from South Jersey said with a rather flat, unexcited voice, "I found it." Jim was six feet two inches tall, so most had to stand on toes to see where he was pointing. An Khe was a good two feet northeast of Saigon, putting it hundreds miles north of our present location. That also meant we would be in the upper half of the country, very, very far from where we stood.

Final Destinations

The following morning we packed up our belongings and boarded a C-123 transport plane and headed north. The topographical map indicated we'd be going to the Central Highlands of Vietnam's mountainous II Corps region, home of the 1st Cavalry's base camp. As we flew north, the terrain below changed from wide, flat plains of rice paddies to rugged mountain peaks soaring thousands of feet high. Where Bien Hoa had been bright and hot, the mountainous area appeared to be cloudy and cold, evidenced by the large hardwood trees replacing the tropical growth.

During the long, cold flight, we sat in a silent and somewhat hungover atmosphere. The two-engine prop plane, having no stewardesses, landed without incident, taxied, and stopped in front of a small, gray wood building. It seemed out of place, because with everything around it being bare, it was surrounded by a white picket fence. No flowers. It too was topped with the same type of corrugated tin roof we had already become familiar with. The makeshift terminal, not much larger than a two-car garage, was sparsely decorated. A couple of large wooden signs painted with black lettering on a white background hung from the building's facade above the doorway. On the smaller sign was an inscription wrapped around a bright yellow-and-black 1st Cavalry Division patch that proclaimed, "This is Cav Country. Be Sharp. Be Alert. Heads High. Salute. Stay On The First Team." The larger sign directly below it simply stated, "Welcome To An Khe Army Airfield, Passenger Terminal." It too had a painted 1st Cavalry Division patch at its center.

We boarded waiting open-bed trucks and headed for what we thought would be our new home. A short time later, we passed through the entrance of the base, it too lined with barbed wire and manned by armed guards. Just as the terminal was smaller than the huge, modern building in Bien Hoa, the base camp itself was much smaller than the one we had departed from that morning. The war must be closer to here, we thought aloud, because instead of seeing troops and trucks, everywhere we looked, there were olive-green helicopters with gold crossed sabers painted on their fronts—in the air or lined up on the ground surrounded by sand-bagged protective barriers, others in hangars or out in the open while being repaired by mechanics.

The airfield itself and the dirt roads crossing the base were also covered with creosote, but here a thicker coat of the oil-based liquid normally used as a wood preservative on telephone poles was laid to hold down dust and debris from the hovering helicopters' large rotor blades. The air felt cooler than at Bien Hoa and smelled much worse, irritating skin, eyes, and lungs. Like every base in Vietnam, plumes of dense black smoke rose in all directions from the burning metal pails of human waste doused with diesel fuel. But here, the gaseous odors were combined with the vapors from aviation fuels, grease, oil, hydraulic fluids, chemical defoliants, diesel exhaust from trucks and heavy equipment, and naturally the evaporating creosote, which coated not only all of the loose dirt on the base but tires and boots as well. The entire volatile mixture cast over the base a petrochemical dome the likes of which none of us had ever experienced.

In the distance behind the huge flat airfield was a hill rising a few hundred feet high. Squinting up through the haze and smog, we could see a huge bright-yellow shield with a black horse head in the upper right corner and a diagonal black slash bisecting it from the top left to the bottom right. It was the 1st Cavalry's unique insignia, painted on the highest outcropping of bedrock called Hon Cong Mountain, overlooking the base like a guardian for all to see. We followed our guide through a wood-beam-framed opening topped with another Cavalry sign nailed to its crossbeam. Somewhat like entering a ranch back in the world where you enter the driveway entrance. It too had the Cav insignia front and center, with the names of battles it had fought. One sentence really caught my eye and made my shorts get a little tight: "Home of the 7th Cavalry," and listed battles from the Old West right up through the Philippines, Japan, and Korea. *Holy crap, it is Custer's unit!*

We were eventually brought to another processing area where the lineups and formations started again for the third time. More equipment was issued, and what seemed like hundreds of government forms were signed: finance records for salary disbursements, savings bonds, beneficiary forms, next of kin, on and on for days. It was explained to us that because we would be going into the field, we really didn't need much money, unless we liked to play cards or needed to buy cigarettes. I elected to keep ten dollars a month and had the rest sent home. Though our days were pretty busy, our nights were the same as in Bien Hoa—we found the EM club and partied most of the time, though not as hard as at the Jet Set Club.

The guys at An Khe seemed to be more serious than those we had first met down south, so we thought it wiser to listen and learn as much as possible. Speaking of which, we also went through a week of specialized training that was quite different from stateside. We were taught a great deal in a very short amount of time. We were told about and handled the many types of booby traps that could be encountered, and we learned the dos and don'ts of walking in a jungle or on a trail, even along a road. We were instructed on the use and care of the new Soviet and Chinese weapons we would probably find, as well as numerous old WWII weapons resulting from the French, Japanese, English, and American occupations of Vietnam. We were taught how to set trip flares for security in the field, the importance of jungle hygiene, potential diseases and treatments for wounds, Claymore and land-mine demonstrations, attack helicopters firing mini guns and rockets, a napalm detonation, and even the difference in the sound from our weapons and those of the North Vietnamese Army. Eventually we were issued and fired our personal M-16, adjusted its sights, accordingly, received a steel helmet, and other goodies we would carry for a year. We learned to use different types of radiotelephone systems, how to board and jump from helicopters, and how to do all kinds of new stuff we never learned about in the states. The fun part was to learn rappelling, jumping from high towers and sliding down long ropes in the event we had to do it from a helicopter one day. It was intensive training from real grunts, using real stuff, and they got us as ready as new guys could get.

Throughout all of the processing, we continued with the same system we had used in Bien Hoa: Hang back, find out the count, adjust accordingly, and climb back into line. But the system finally let us down on the last day. Nine of us had managed to stay together throughout the two weeks of processing in California and Vietnam. We were the only ones left on a short line outside of a Quonset hut, waiting to receive unit assignments. Inside the hut were four desks with guys doing more paperwork, so when one guy walked out of the building, the next guy in line walked in and sat at vacated desk for his assignment. Before being given assignments, we were offered other specialized duties if we were interested: Long Range Reconnaissance Patrols (LRRPs), tracker teams using specially trained dogs, helicopter door gunner, even the option of enlisting in the army for a full six-year obligation to get out of the infantry. All of the assignments required more time, training, and risk. We realized there might not be anything more we could do to stay together. There was no recourse left to us unless we could convince the guys inside to change our destinations.

Comparing orders as we left the building, we were disappointed to see we were being divided for the first time in three months. Donny Miller and I were being separated for the first time since we were ten years old. The group was being scattered to the 1st and 5th Battalions of the 7th Cavalry, and two others to the 2nd Battalion of the 12th Cav. We all talked about maybe being able to run into each other at a base camp or something like that, but I don't think any of us really believed that would happen. It was then that some guys went back into the building for reassignment. Donny and two others joined the LRRPs, pronounced "Lurps"; one guy signed up for the K-9 teams; and one went so far as enlisting for two more years to become a typist. For some, they hoped to be able to see the rest of us over the course of a year. Because of their specialized units, they would now have more opportunities to cross our paths.

With all of us still standing in front of the Quonset hut and staring at the orders in our hands, we knew things were getting serious—no more games, no more beating the system, no more depending on each other for support. That night we all partied together for the last time, not knowing if we would ever see each other again. The beers were just as cold and the music just as good, but the atmosphere was not quite as festive. At the end of the night, we met in a circle outside our barracks and shook hands, wishing each other good luck and goodbye. My orders had me leaving before the others, who were scheduled to leave over the next couple of days, except the guys who had been reassigned. Some would remain for weeks of additional training both in Vietnam and Thailand. So, early on the following morning, I hitched a ride to the An Khe airport. The guy driving the jeep was so quiet you would have thought we were going to a funeral. When I boarded a C-123 cargo plane around nine, I started to wonder if I might have a special job requiring me to get there as soon as possible. After all, it was just me and a bunch of cargo traveling 175 miles farther north, this time to a place called Phu Bai, about forty miles north of Da Nang, a place we were told was really far north.

Chapter III
Decisions, Decisions

At some point in our lives, we've made a decision that we second-guessed. We're human; mistakes happen. Hopefully, we learn from the experience and become a little wiser. Unfortunately, there are times when someone else is affected by our decision or an error in our judgment. We feel terrible, sometimes not able to forgive ourselves, and can only hope the wronged individual understands. When choices are made in life-or-death situations, sometimes they are right, sometimes not. The end result could be unbridled euphoria or the worst possible outcome. If we could predict the future, we would never make a choice we will later regret.

The harsh reality of our circumstances many years ago, like so many young adults today in harm's way, dictated that potentially painful snap decisions sometimes had to be made by our very young, inexperienced minds; right or wrong, like it or not, good or bad—we had to make them. In battle the results of some of those decisions led to actual or apparent acts of bravery. Occasionally, some of those decisions led to actual or apparent acts of stupidity. Sometimes the decision exposed us to even greater danger or had dramatic long-term consequences. There are decisions we all wish we could have made differently, but as we all know by now, there aren't any do-overs in real life. Personally, deciding to do an embarrassing "John Wayne" on a machine-gun nest instantly comes to mind.

When the results were tallied at the end of a particularly bad day in combat, we always had a chance to sit down alone and reflect on the events. In fact, we couldn't get away from those private moments—it was called guard duty. Thinking about what we had just experienced or decisions we had made during some extremely anxious moments might have led to some very real emotional, spiritual, or physical trauma— sometimes fleeting, sometimes long lasting. It made no difference if the situation was dangerous or not, real or perceived. Somewhere deep within the convoluted folds of the brain, the mysterious region where we talk to our self, the question was often asked: "What the hell was I thinking?" Actual combat situations occasionally created a paradox whereby "bad" decisions sometimes resulted in safe passage or even medals of valor. Unfortunately, "good" decisions could sometimes result in the highest price a soldier can pay.

Just one day after the Carlos incident, we walked right into a terrible situation. The results of decisions made on that dreary afternoon long ago have, I am sure, affected thousands of people to this day and will likely continue to do so for the rest of their lives. Sometimes it's called PTSD. Personally, I thought I was making the right decisions, but actually they were mostly wrong. Luckily, it turned out to be okay. Other guys that day thought they were doing everything right, but the results weren't so good. In the days following the chaos in February 1968, there were many questionable decisions made by a lot of people.

You Go First

On the morning of February 22, 1968, during the Tet Offensive, after two weeks of horrific fighting, four companies of the 5th Battalion, 7th Cavalry, 1st Cavalry Division prepared to saddle up, move out, and continue their mission objective: the northwest quadrant leading to Hue. Specifically, a railroad bridge crossing over the moat beneath the NW corner of the Citadel wall. To get there, we would walk about nine miles to "conduct a movement to contact" toward Hue: locate and destroy any enemy that got in our way." [31] Easier said than done.

The day dawned with the same uninterrupted weather pattern we had experienced for the previous eighteen days: intermittent rain, a fine mist, pockets of dense fog, and ominous low cloud cover. Just one good day after another. Finishing a quick C-ration breakfast, the RTOs went about replacing the PRC-25 communications radio's battery, while the riflemen, grenadiers, and machine gunners cleaned their weapons to insure they were in good working order. Everyone topped off

---

31   Baker, *Gray Horse Troop*, 25.

their munitions—bullets, grenades, Claymore mines, trip flares, et cetera. Once the important things were out of the way, each guy gathered his belongings. Our hooches' or tents to most folks, made by snapping two ponchos together and draping them over a horizontal sapling, were disassembled. Our bedding and linens, consisting of a poncho liner, basically a nylon blanket, was rolled up, while our bed, an air mattress, was deflating. When completed, the two items were rolled within the poncho to form a semidry protected cylinder. Once all personal belongings were accounted for, they were stuffed, hung, or tied into or onto a rucksack. We threw empty cans, used batteries, spent ammo casings, and any other items no longer useful into the four-to-five-foot-deep foxhole that had been dug the previous night. The hole would then be refilled with the dirt that had been mounded around its perimeter, thus preventing anything that had been lying around from being of any further use. When each trooper finally completed his daily morning chores, he carried his personalized bulging olive-green rucksack to a central location where a large cargo net lay spread open on the ground and added his own pack to a growing pile of other nondescript olive-green rucksacks. The huge, tangled bundle would be airlifted to us at the end of the day. Well, most days, weather and situation permitting.

Having dispensed with our heavy packs, we saddled up "light" with just our fighting gear and headed out of our company's defensive perimeter, ready to join the three other companies that made up the 5th Battalion, 7th Cavalry. Everyone was relieved that we were finally going to leave the village of Thon La Chu, dubbed Tee-Tee Woods and what was left of the 5th NVA Regiment guarding the Tri Thien Front. It wasn't just an obstacle on the road to Hue but the hub of the entire enterprise,[32] the NVA HQ that ran all of the Hue operations for the Tet Offensive. Talk about a beehive. There were lots and lots of bad guys protecting it, but we didn't know that when we initially made contact. Based on intelligence gathered from NVA POWs from various units, some of which were thought to be at Khe Sahn, there were over one thousand dug-in NVA regulars protecting Tee-Tee Woods, and perhaps as many as three thousand.

We were finally leaving the hard-fought area after almost three weeks. Relieved, that is until a new order was given, which naturally brought on a cascade of grumbling. Every time it happened, we felt like we were being screwed. One could always hear from the ranks, "Stinkin' army, always messin' with our heads! Why can't they just leave us alone?" I believe that chant was started by a grunt when General George Washington said, "Men, I know it's Christmas Eve and we're caught in a snowstorm, but tonight we're going to cross the Delaware River in row boats!" A last-minute change had Bravo Company staying behind to secure a Duster (remember Carlos?) that had blown a clutch. Afterward they would be airlifted to join the rest of the battalion from a flanking direction. The remaining three airmobile companies would have to walk to Hue. *Huh?! I thought we were Airmobile.*

But before we even left our perimeter, we were ordered to make one last sweep through Tee-Tee Woods, a place where everyone involved had already seen too much action. Apparently, the sweep was warranted after Jim Meade, our squad's RTO, had been hit in the foot by either an accidental weapon discharge or a snip-

32   Bowden, *Hue 1968.*

er. Jim, who had been drafted, was a former bartender from New York, a nice guy, quiet and always smiling. He had joined the company with me as a replacement, and his tour of duty in Vietnam was over after three and a half weeks. God, it just felt like we would never leave that wicked place. But like the good troopers that we were, we took up the task and moved out to locate Charlie or any of his stuff that might still be in there again. One more time...

The wooded area had been mutilated during the six days of constant artillery fire, high- and low-level bombing runs, plus us shooting up the place during two frontal assaults. It was hard to believe anything could have survived, but the encampment was laced with bunkers and "spider holes," fighting positions sized for one person. And they were good, determined fighters, as we noticed when taking up positions around their encampment day and night, in case they tried to sneak out. So, as we had at the end of the previous day, we took it slow, acutely alert for any danger, slogged into water-filled bomb craters, climbed over piles of dirt, slid cautiously between stands of splintered bamboo, and worked our way over and through shattered hardwood trunks, limbs, and debris. Thousands of places for a sniper to hid. After an hour or so, we gladly completed the search, with only a few incidents, and were more than ready to get the hell out of there. When we finally cleared the carnage, we joined the other two companies on Highway 1 for the five-kilometer walk south toward Hue.

The order of the day was to march the troops quickly down Highway 1 to the Citadel. Seemed like a good idea because the roadway cut through wide-open rice paddies where it would be very difficult for Charlie to hide en-masse with large weaponry. Our battalion commander, Lt. Col. James B. Vought, and his Operations Officer, Maj. Charlie Baker, would also be marching with us that day. Having such high-ranking officers in the field eating dirt with the troops was not uncommon for the 1st Cavalry. If the shit hit the fan, officers witnessed firsthand the results of their decisions and were able to take control immediately. Knowing the top brass were willing to put their ass on the line provided no end of confidence to us grunts, knowing we weren't being used but led. Teamwork is necessary to survive tough situations, and the 1st Cavalry Division had it from top to bottom—well, except for Carlos.

As we walked smartly down the road, scanning our flanks for possible enemy movement, we were also constantly aware of possible defensive positions to get to in the event of incoming fire. We didn't have to look far that morning, because running parallel to the two-lane asphalt road about seventy-five yards or so to our right and elevated above the rice paddies were the rusted iron tracks of an old French railroad system. Standing between the tracks and road, like ancient sentries watching over their old friends, were the decaying remains of fifteen-foot-tall reinforced concrete telephone poles. Each column was about ten inches square at its base and tapered slightly as it stretched upward. Decades of neglect had left many with their rusting iron I-beam cores clearly visible where large chunks of cement had flaked off. Sagging down from narrow, rusted metal crossbars were thin bare wires, some that had broken hung from their insulators and lay across the ground. Add a shirt to the slumped crossbars and trousers on the pole and you would have had an old scarecrow.

After years of exposure to the harsh weather extremes, Mother Nature had painted the deteriorating survivors with a palette of sun-bleached colors in red, green, and brown. Some poles had dead twisted vines, their tendrils stretching up in an effort to completely envelop the thin spires. Jagged, deep-green grasses rose from the mud to encircle the bottoms, giving a false impression of a solid foundation. Where the concrete was still visible, streaks of mold and black sooty blotches hastened its demise, conjoined by thin veins of rust that had trickled down for years. The morning's rain washing across the exposed metal would eventually add more character to their profiles. Simply looking at the crumbling stanchions easily represented Vietnam's colonial past and remained a symbol of the contributions the vanquished French had made to the country's infrastructure years earlier.

Dips in the terrain along the way had required grading to maintain a continuous level surface. Where necessary, Highway 1 and the railroad tracks were elevated five or six feet above the muddy rice paddies that surrounded them, each mode of transportation supported by sloping, grass-covered dirt embankments. No piece of workable land in any direction went unused. Even the narrow space between the road and tracks held a paddy. We passed through the countryside spread out in two long columns, each one walking along a shoulder on both sides of the road. Together, the roadway and tracks formed a long corridor pointing directly at Hue. If you viewed the landscape from above, the parallel bands formed by the highway and tracks would look like a giant ladder, with small, abandoned hamlets being the rungs. The buildings were of typical bamboo and dark-brown dead-grass construction, and if there were five or six of them, they were sometimes bisected by the highway cutting between them. Each building encountered was searched for security reasons. If it wasn't a road or railroad track or house, it was usually a barren rice paddy of mud. Each dwelling had a court-yard, usually containing a small garden and a few ba-nana trees. Privet hedges served as fencing, with gates in place to contain the few farm animals the people might own. Larger hardwoods and shrubbery surrounding the entire perimeter of most hamlets provided shade and privacy.

No words were spoken aloud as we traveled that morning, and with the exception of each grunt's boot heels tapping on the asphalt, immediately followed by soggy socks squishing in a syncopated cadence, there were few other sounds. Click, squish. Click, squish. Click, squish. From time to time, we'd pass a low, mold-encrusted cement marker on the side of the road that broke up the monotony of the unchanging, mud-dy brown landscape. Each looked like a foot-tall head-stone rising out of the ground, helping each passing grunt who was still able to remember some basic math how far he had already walked. The deep-set numerals carved under the word "HUE" indicated the number of kilometers to our objective, reminding anyone who no-ticed it of the decreasing distance and increasing dan-ger. The nearer our destination, the more vigilant we became when approaching each successive hamlet.

All eyes continuously scanned the landscape, swing-ing back and forth like the pendulum on a cuckoo clock while also remaining alert for guys up ahead raising a bent arm, signaling those behind to stop. When we ap-proached to within three kilometers of the city, the sud-den stops began happening with more nerve-racking frequency. Always ready to respond to possible danger, every trooper up and down the line, when the halt signal was given, immediately spun ninety degrees left or right and dropped into a low kneeling position to defend our flanks. Everyone held their positions, scanning the fields and far-off tree lines for possible movement while the lead squad in the column cautiously advanced toward whatever had presented a danger or was deemed suspicious enough to investigate. Ten to twelve guys would check out the obstacle, ensuring the formation would not walk into an ambush. The rest of us waited, heartbeats increasing, and prayers made for continued silence. The march would resume only after the point squad returned from its sweep and reported their findings to the platoon leader. Then, relieved that no contact had been made, the point squad gladly headed to the rear of their platoon. The simple leapfrog maneuver graciously allowed each squad to rotate out of the intimidating point position and relax a little until their turn came again.

I could hardly recognize the area we were passing through as the same picturesque countryside I had enjoyed a little over a month before. Maybe it was because I was perched atop a bouncing deuce and a half on a sunny day. Unlike the first time, though, the scenery now seemed far more intimidating. Maybe because my boots were on the ground. The hot temperatures and bright sun had disappeared a few weeks ago, replaced by constant cool, wet weather. The colorful pagodas and brightly decorated burial mounds and monuments honoring the dead now seemed threatening to we the living. Gone from the roadsides were the smiling adults that had waved to the huge convoys delivering more troops and supplies to the area. No longer present were the stoic vendors pushing their colorful tricycle carts heaped with fruits and vegetables. Nowhere to be seen were the bare-bottomed kids, jumping, shouting, and stretching their hands up in hopes of snaring some thrown candy. Other than us, there was no traffic on the road—no bicycles, mopeds, or rickshaws. In fact, we had seen no signs of any life-form whatsoever.

Our pace had slowed considerably from the time we first started earlier that morning. One would think we'd have been relieved knowing we were no longer rushing to our destination and possible enemy contact. Instead we found our anxiety level increasing, probably because of a combination of things that had us spooked. Besides slowing down to study a monotonous landscape that was only partially broken up by little road markers and telephone poles, we found it hard to ignore the towering black columns of smoke above a distant tree line. The tops of the telltale funnel shapes appeared to be almost leaning against the dark gray clouds and were obviously coming from Hue, just down the road a bit. We knew that with every step we took, the smoldering city and enemy troops grew closer. The only comfort we could take was knowing there were less bad guys there after our two weeks of engagements. A hell of a lot less.

We had already been on the road well over two hours, and it was making our feet and our eyes a little tired. I had been so focused on detecting a possible ambush that I barely noticed the steady cool drizzle had slowly morphed into a thickening fog and fine mist. Not a good sign. We trudged on while the subtle weather change continued to reduce our visibility by the minute. Soon we could no longer see beyond a few hundred feet. Not being able to see very far ahead or to our flanks just did wonders for our nerves. We could sense danger ahead but feared we wouldn't be able to see it until it was too late.

Suddenly and without any warning, as if to validate our anxiety, groups of panicked elderly Vietnamese men, women, and small children seemed to just materialize out of the gray mist right before our eyes. They were heading directly toward us and traveling as fast as their age, load, and physical condition allowed. And regardless of age, most balanced on their shoulder a long bamboo pole whose ends flexed up and down with each quick step they took, each person seemingly unfazed by the weight of the large bundles of belongings that bounced at each end. Some people marched headlong, bent forward from the weight of a single sack slung over a shoulder; some women were pregnant and carrying a baby in their arms. I guess it was the richer ones who pushed a bike loaded with belongings, while some others pulled creaking wooden carts piled high. The sudden appearance had the same effect on both soldier and civilian as hearts stopped for an instant and weapons were raised, preparing for the worst.

As they should, our point squad stopped them before they could reach the formation. Almost immediately a few officers went forward for questioning, while a few grunts walked among them to check bundles for weapons or explosives. The order to stand down was soon passed over the communications radios, along with a warning to be especially alert while allowing the refugees safe passage. As we lowered our weapons, the Vietnamese grabbed their belongings and were soon walking quickly between our columns, many of them looking back over their shoulder in panic, pointing toward the besieged city, shouting an obvious warning in their native tongue. None of us could speak Vietnamese, but we understood the terror in their faces and the desperate alarm in their voices. Our responses in English were along the lines of "Thank you, Mama-san. Thank you, Papa-san. We think we're walking in the wrong direction too."

We restarted our trek even more jumpy than before now that we knew without a doubt what lay ahead. The routine remained the same: boot heels clicking, socks squishing, eyes scanning, nerves fraying. And then things started to turn for the better. The day had started out gray and rainy and had gotten progressively worse, but around eleven or so, the sky started to appear as if it was about to clear up. The fog slowly started to dissipate, and the temperature was rising. A short time later, as if to let us know all was not bad in the world, a glorious shaft of sunlight burst through the clouds and lit up the entire column of troops. Its effect was to instantly bring a smile to most of us, like an omen that the worst of the fighting was behind us. Glory to the heavens! The newly felt warmth was fantastic, and spirits rose even higher when our water-logged fatigues and boots started drying.

Soon after the sun appeared, so did more small family groups of black-pajama-clad Vietnamese refugees heading our way. Like those earlier, most wore the typical conical straw hat and were transporting what few belongings they still possessed. Not being very worldly myself as a freshly minted twenty-year-old, I was fascinated by the efficiency with which they carried their worldly possessions, simply dangling bulging burlap bags from each end of a bamboo pole. I watched amazed as the tattered rag-like bundles swayed and bounced in a steady rhythm with each step their owners took. Judging by how much the bamboo poles were bending, it was hard to believe that the mass of the entire weight was balanced on a frail shoulder and supported by only one thin bony arm and hand.

As before, the people seemed to be relieved to see us as they passed, some bowing their heads in thanks, others pressing their palms together in prayer. Many of them were crying, none smiling, but unlike the earlier crowd, these folks were relatively quiet, not talking much or giving warnings. Maj. Charlie Baker noticed a couple of refugees who had already passed the point squads. To say that they looked very much out of place among the shuffling mass would be an understatement. They carried no bundles, were the same age as us, and were wearing brown khakis. Alertly, he had them stopped. Yep, they were North Vietnamese regulars attempting to walk through the middle of our formation. So with an opportunity to extract some firsthand intelligence from prisoners, the formation came to a complete halt. There was no sense in walking into a bad situation before they were interrogated, so we waited for an interpreter to be flown out.

No sooner had the bad guys been plucked from the crowd than the rest of the people opened up big time. Same as earlier, the terrified mass ranted in Vietnamese something that was hard to ignore. I clearly remember a very frail old woman whose body was stooped over, probably from many years of toiling in a rice paddy. Like many of them, she was almost frantic to leave, but we were holding them back, to look for more impersonators as well as any civilians who were in need of medical attention. It took a lot of effort for her to turn her stiff body around, but she pointed back down the road she had just traveled, shouting, "Boo-coo VC, boo-coo VC." When she turned again, our eyes met, and I couldn't help but think, *That could be my grandmother standing there but for a lucky draw of the cards.* Maybe she was thinking the same thing when she clasped her hands together as if begging in prayer. Staring right at me, she had terror in her eyes, and I heard the desperation in her pleading voice as she kept repeating and jabbing her finger, "Boo-coo VC, boo-coo VC." None of us needed a translator for the phrase that was quickly learned by every grunt in-country. Used in this context, it roughly meant, "Please be careful, boys, there's a lot of bad guys ahead. And I mean a lot!" All I could do was nod my head in understanding and thanks.

We appreciated their warnings, but it was the urgency with which they were presenting them that definitely got our attention. As it turned out, this was one of those situations where someone was in the right place at the right time.

Believe it or not, we had a national TV news crew walking with us that morning—cameraman, sound man, and producer; today they would call it being embedded with the troops. They were just eating up the commotion—a road full of terrified refugees; nine prisoners of war, or enemy suspects, VCS as they were labeled, hands tied behind their backs and being interrogated; the gale-force downdraft of the rotors driven by the powerful two engines of a CH-47 Chinook helicopter about to land, kicking up dirt and debris; GIs helping some of the emaciated people to remain upright; lines of heavily armed, combat-hardened troopers of the 1st Cavalry Division about to march fearlessly toward Hue; dramatic shafts of sunlight breaking through the storm clouds. The scene was so dramatic it almost looked staged. The producer kept running around between our columns and shouting at the other two guys, "Get pictures of that old lady! Hey, Harry, come over here and record some of the yelling and crying! Come on, guys, move! Take a shot of those filthy kids. And get some GIs in there too, will ya! Harry, are you picking up the helicopter in the background? Then get closer! Mike, stop standing there like you're giving out candy on Halloween and get some long-range shots. There, the smoke columns coming up from Hue—over there!"

We loved it. Guys were wondering aloud if we would be in some history-making film. "Oh man! Just like the black-and-white films of GIs liberating a French village in WWII." "Yeah right, except we wouldn't have flowers thrown at us or hugs and kisses by attractive ladies from the local populace wearing dresses." Looking at the bent and frail bodies around us, I didn't think anyone would want to be filmed getting a hug or kiss from the local populace. We stayed with the refugees for a while until they could be loaded into the chopper. It was the best way to get the very old, very young and wounded out. The others would leave the area on foot if they chose.

Some of the people were so terrified we had difficulty keeping them there. For all we knew, they were reluctant to ride in a chopper because they were afraid to be separated from family members, or thought they were going to be held prisoner, or feared who was down the road behind them catching up. The language barrier often created problems. And in all honesty, we were usually uncertain when we met civilians, never sure if they were thanking us when bowing with clasped hands or begging for mercy. But seeing what they and their country were going through gave us reason to be there.

The entire parade of GIs had been marching in a military formation called "companies abreast," that is, aligned side by side into two separate columns. Alpha Company, to which I was assigned, was ordered to leave the main column on the road, move off to the right through a muddy rice paddy, and resume the march atop the elevated railroad-track embankment. As each of our squads climbed the small rise, they immediately spread out into a staggered formation and knelt down, ready to walk along both sides of the tracks when the order was given. So now, rather than being part of a large formation, we found our undermanned squad, now the size of a single fire team, the spearhead of the company. We could see forever from our new vantage point, but once standing up, we'd be silhouetted against a clearing-blue sky backdrop from any direction. Now we knew how pop-up silhouette targets felt during our rifle and machine-gun qualifications in Advanced Infantry Training.

Back on the road, Charlie Company would lead, while Delta was behind them in reserve. Both were re-forming, squads splitting to walk on each side of the road. Earlier in the day, a couple of guys from each company were assigned to walk farther out in the paddies, away from the main columns, to provide eyes and ears for the main unit for potential trouble. Never a fun job. Worse than walking point, because you were alone. Really alone. No one there if you got hit and needed help. A real spooky feeling. Fortunately, like walking point, the job was rotated within the squads, giving more guys a chance to feel alone. Because of the imminent danger, all those guys were pulled back into the main columns. If it was as bad down the road as Mama-san claimed, the guys in the flanks would only be able to alert the main unit when we heard them being shot.

The smallest improvements in our conditions always raised our spirits. After all of the mud and wet socks, and despite the potential danger, this day was starting to look better. We would be walking on a relatively hard railroad bed instead of mud, the scenery ahead looked better, and there was a distinct possibility that we might actually see more of the sun for the first time in over three weeks. The reality of the moment, though, was everyone kneeling up on the tracks or roadway was tense, silent, eyes searching in every direction. Or, if they were farther back in the columns, they might be heating up lunch or having a smoke. I'm sure that in the back of everyone's mind was what had transpired over the previous days and what might still lie ahead. We all knew US Marines were still fighting a determined enemy inside the city, and we were headed there to help out if needed, or to remain at the city's edge to engage the NVA soldiers trying to escape. A lot of those who had already left the city and headed up the road to where we had been weren't able to escape very far.

Our journey toward Hue continued after the civilians were evacuated, intelligence was provided from the nine VCS directly to the battalion commander and operations officer who were already on-site, and the guys were all in their new positions. When all was ready, an emphatic caution from the battalion commander to be especially alert was passed on to all company RTOs and spread through the ranks by word of mouth. He had been in the field with us all along, living through the same lousy weather, nights spent with no sleeping gear or shelter, wet socks, cold food, and firefights. The command group of Lieutenant Colonel Vaught, Battalion S-3 Major Charlie Baker, and their RTOs would fall in behind Delta Company's front platoon as Charlie Company headed toward Hue.

A short time after we restarted, another cluster of six or seven huts positioned between the elevated two-lane highway and tracks was searched without any problem. Like so many other hamlets, twenty or thirty feet past the last hut, the flat ground dropped sharply for a few feet, then leveled off to the terrain's natural level. The flat depression was about fifty yards wide and seventy-five yards long and nestled between the elevated highway and track embankments. On the far end, a berm, slightly higher than the planting area and about the width of a cart, formed a crossing between the highway and the tracks. The configuration created a natural boxed-in planting area. Beyond the pathway, the ground dropped again to the lower level for additional plantings.

I checked across the paddy to our left now to make sure we and Charlie Company were staying abreast of each other. They too were scanning the landscape ahead and to the left of the highway for danger. To our front lay another hamlet, followed by a dense tree line. Off to our front right and lower than the railroad embankment was a cemetery about 350 yards away that ran parallel to the tracks. It appeared to be much larger than those I had seen a month earlier on my ride up the highway but no different than others. Because of its size, it extended well out into the rice fields. Most of the individual burial sites consisted of a simple grass-covered mound, separated from an adjacent plot by low shrubbery. A few grave sites, probably holding the remains of more prominent citizens, were surrounded by a two-foot-high cinder-block enclosure. Some were usually adorned with stone lanterns decorated in reds and yellows that contrasted sharply with the whitewashed wall. This cemetery also had the vibrant deep-green trees on three sides. The sky finally cleared, and intense rays of sunlight glistened off water droplets that stubbornly clung to the grasses and cold cement. Even the old, rusted railroad tracks reflected a sparkle. The overall effect was exceptionally bright daylight that forced us to squint. After weeks of focusing through rain and darkened gray skies, the bright sunshine almost hurt.

After walking about another hundred yards, at 11:43 a.m. our quiet walk was shattered when we started taking an incredible amount of small-arms, mortar, and automatic-weapons fire from our front and sides. Surrounded by open rice paddy fields and standing tall on the elevated railroad bed, we were completely exposed as the point squad. Our RTO, Lee Tolley, was singled out almost instantly. Everyone's natural reaction was to dive from the elevated locations. I think my second thought was *Great. We finally dry off and feel the warmth of the sun and now we have to jump back into a muddy rice paddy.* Talk about hating your enemy! Both lead companies were pinned down for quite a while, trying to get the upper hand by returning fire, but because of the wide-open terrain and little ability to maneuver, casualties started mounting up fast.

Apparently the same eleven-ton Duster that had taught Carlos how to speak English the day before had had its clutch fixed and caught up to us, rumbling down the road past Delta Company. He immediately started firing the twin forty-millimeter cannons far out to our right at a small farm building in the middle of the rice paddy. I turned around just to make sure the noise was coming from something on our side because I didn't know the Duster was in working order. Ah, armor! He traversed the cannons toward the cemetery and fired a long stream over our heads, then another to our front, in an attempt to gain fire superiority. If he couldn't do it firing 240 explosive rounds per minute, we'd surely have trouble doing it with M-16s, 79s, and 60s. The Duster would at least be able to provide some covering fire for us to move around and try.

Like the other guys on the tracks, I had moved down the right side of the embankment alongside some high grass. On my stomach and nose pressed into the mud, I watched a small spider walk about a sixteenth of an inch away from my eyeball. Probably the first time I was glad to wear glasses. Making matters worse, I didn't think I could get up, because I could hear and feel the shock waves of the Duster firing directly overhead. The incredible noise and chaos had come on so suddenly that it was both numbing and motivating. And the unforgettable bullwhip "cracks" from AK-47 rounds emphasized the urgency of the moment. After what seemed like an eternity of automatic-weapons fire, shouts for medics, and orders being barked out to maneuver, not much changed as both sides returned and received fire.

I had the distinct impression that someone had me in their sights every time I lifted my head looking for a target. Or they could have been rounds meant for the Duster falling short. In the middle of a hail of bullets and the Duster firing, something exploded in the high grass to my right. *Was that a mortar round, or are guys behind me starting to throw grenades? Holy crap!* Despite my brain working on overload and my adrenaline pumping hard, trying to determine where Charlie was hiding, wondering how and where the rest of my squad was,

and saying prayers to be able to get those answers, I
suddenly became aware of a hot sensation on the back
of my left hand. Then I felt a slow trickle of something
warm. *Oh no*, I thought. *I can't even turn my head to see
how bad I'm hit. Doesn't hurt too much, but I can definitely
feel something warm and wet dripping down my wrist.* My
mind went into the pure logic mode to best calculate
my next critical move, all the while praying there was
not too much damage. *Should I try to turn my head to look,
just in case I have to stop the bleeding? And risk drawing
more enemy fire? Wiggle my fingers to make sure they work?*
When I heard the crack of another AK round whiz past
my head, I thought I'd better wait. When I asked myself
if I was going to wait for my hand to heal or the war to
end, or just lie here and get hit, I yelled at myself, *Do
something, dummy!*

Guys behind me were yelling we were ordered to
pull back. I got up the nerve to turn my head when the
spider was beyond my peripheral vision and glanced at
my hand. I was instantly confused when I didn't see red
as expected, but brown. Seems a rusty old wire hanging
from one of the dilapidated telephone poles had been
knocked down by the Duster and was lying across my
knuckles. My best guess was that the sun had heated
up the bare metal wire coated with rainwater. When it
fell, all of the collective heated drops ran down to my
hand. It was about that time I freaked out. *That's it, I'm
outta here. Spiders, wires, bullets, mortars, grenades, cannons—I'm gone.* I looked up ahead and saw Jack Teakle
crawling toward me. Just behind him was Big Joe Kochman, followed by Sam Morris, our acting squad leader.
At about that time there was another explosion to my
right but a little farther back. Word had been given to

pull back, and like good troopers, no one was about to disobey an order.

Jack volunteered to stay with the machine gun and lay down covering fire, while the rest worked their way back to a better-protected position. I looked behind me and realized Rat and the rest of our squad had already pulled back, leaving their full ammo cans for the M-60. Scared as I was, there was no way I was going to leave him there alone. I was the assistant gunner. He gets hit, I'm the gunner. I told the others I'd stay to help feed the 60 until they were well behind us. Once in position, they could cover our retreat. We all agreed with the plan and wished each other good luck as the AKs kept whizzing by. I started crawling around to gather the ammo cans and dragged them back, hoping no incoming rounds would find one of the cans or me or Jackie or the other guys or...

Soon Jack was spraying the area with long bursts from the 60 while I ripped the cans and boxes open and quickly linked each new belt to the one already being fed through the gun. Nonstop covering fire. We had done it to perfection the previous morning covering the last assault into Tee-Tee Woods. Our plan seemed to be working well. Executing "fire and maneuver" exactly as we had learned in training, coupled with the Duster's fire, and seemed to slow the incoming fire. The last two guys had left two more cans of ammo. It's a good thing they did, because we could suddenly hear the Duster's engine revving up while moving. Its outgoing rounds had slowed some of the incoming fire, so we thought the big piece of armor had run out of ammo. Otherwise, why move? Over the roar of the 60, Jack and I were having a conversation about the explosions. Jack yelled, slightly lifting his cheek off the gunstock, "Are the guys behind us throwing grenades, or do we have grenades being thrown at us?"

"Don't know." I yelled back. "The second one exploded farther back. Maybe they're small mortars." We stared at each other just long enough for me to pull my bag with ten frags and two smoke grenades closer. "Just in case." I yelled. The gun continued to roar, arcing red tracers toward suspected target areas while I continued to feed it belt after belt.

I don't know how much time passed, but with the guys behind us out of sight and the situation being what it was, Jackie told me to go, and he'd follow. I grabbed an unopened ammo can and suddenly heard someone yelling behind us. One of the guys from a different squad had crawled back toward us. Before we could understand him, another explosion erupted right where the Duster had been on the road. Right about where our command group was when we had started walking again. Charlie must have been correcting mortar fire, walking the rounds right to their target. Moments later the guy behind us shouted, "Three guys and the medic were hit!" Don't try to go back through the big pipe. It's a trap. The rest of us are going back through the high grass. We think it's safer than crawling along the berm."

Jack and I had a nice discussion since things got quieter—fewer incoming AK rounds, and the outgoing forty-millimeter explosive rounds had shifted more toward the roadway. So had incoming the mortars trying to hit it. We both came to the same conclusion. The mortar rounds were being walked back, trying to hit the Duster or maybe the small hamlet where they'd expect us to go. The last guys to go back had been hit in the same spot, so we didn't know if Charlie was hiding in the grass and covering the area we'd have to crawl past, and the guys behind us in the high grass were probably jumpy as hell and might think we were NVA. As dangerous as it was, we decided going up and over the tracks might be the best way. Element of surprise. The incoming fire seemed to be redirected to the Duster that was by then moving onto the road. Charlie would never expect it. No one could be that dumb.

We had both noticed the same thing before it got noisy: One of us could go over the tracks and drop down behind the big crossing berm and lay down covering fire for the other to follow. At that point we looked at each other and broke into big grins, which Jackie was prone to do. Almost simultaneously we said, "You go first!" We couldn't help but laugh in spite of the circumstances. We laughed again at the fact that we couldn't flip a coin, because neither one of us had one. We were paid with paper money, "Military Payment Certificates," MPC, as they are called. The bills looked exactly like Monopoly money—same size, a bunch of different colors, and just as "real" to us. Jack and I had a friendly discussion while ducking occasionally, and it came down to him being shorter, meaning he had less days left before going back to the world (home). Only a few weeks less than me, but he did have more time in-country, and that counted. So I was to go first. "Besides," Jack yelled, "you're a smaller target!" He giggled.

"Keep that in mind!" I replied. I hoped we knew what we were talking about, and I got ready for a mad dash up and over the tracks.

I was a fast runner, but not in sucking mud wearing jungle boots. Not to mention all of the extra weight I was carrying that would slow me down even more. I figured the incoming fire would give me plenty of in-

centive to step it up a few notches. I carried all of my
munitions in three bags, old Claymore bags to be exact. About the size of a fashionable Gucci bag except
without a gold clasp and made of olive-green canvas.
Matched well with my olive-green fatigues, though, and
coordinated with my two-tone boots. Each bag simply
hung down from a shoulder, each strap running crisscross over my flak vest. The one resting on my right hip
contained the assorted grenades, its strap crossing my
chest from my left shoulder to right hip. Another bag
was lying next to my left hip containing by then a lot
less than the twenty M-16 ammo magazines I had started out with earlier. It was slung the same way but crossing my chest from my right shoulder to down to my left
hip. I kept one can of machine-gun ammo and hung it
straight down from my left shoulder, allowing me to
drop it off quickly by Jackie when he crossed over. Oh,
and I also carried a "just in case" gas mask used the
previous week during a frontal assault, hanging from
my left shoulder to my right hip. Good thing we were
traveling "light" that day.

Jackie and I looked at each other, exchanged some
words of advice and encouragement, grinned, and nodded that we were ready. I got into sort of a push-up position to help with my takeoff, almost like getting into
the starting blocks at a track meet, while Jack turned
his head and immediately started laying down a wall of
fire directed at the areas we thought the heaviest enemy
fire was coming from. With every muscle in my body
completely tensed and my heart pumping full throttle,
I quickly glanced back over my left shoulder toward
my destination, ready to go from an almost prone position facing south to running upright heading north
in one single explosive move and gain the element of

surprise. I was all scrunched and tensed up like a jungle cat, ready to leap from the tall grass at some unsuspecting prey.

I took a couple of deep breaths, then screamed to myself, "Now!" I erupted from the ground by pushing my body up with both arms, planted the side of my right boot, and quickly spun counterclockwise, instantly launching my body into a perfect running position, head down, arms ready to start pumping. I executed the maneuver deftly using my superior dexterity and intelligence, and it would have worked out great, but I hadn't taken into consideration what might happen if all the weight from my heavy munitions' bags, hanging in different positions around my body, suddenly shifted. *Dummy.*

Well, no sooner had I gotten to my feet than a hail of bullets started flying our way. The AK-47 rounds breaking the sound barrier kicked up dirt and grass all around us. I had only taken a step or so while spinning up and hard to the left when I instantly felt the weight of ten grenades hanging next to my right hip. The moment they were yanked off the ground, the strap cut hard into the left side of my neck. At first, I just felt the weight and thought nothing of it until the centrifugal force created when I violently twisted my body started to make all of my gear swing wildly around me. I staggered instantly and found myself continuing to turn to the left without wanting to. Within a split second, I was wrenched and corkscrewed around like a wobbling top. It was as if I had just been snared by four Argentine bolos, yanked back, and spun to one side, lurching forward and spinning uncontrollably on one heel before I landed next to Jackie. My helmet was almost sideways, and the bags' straps were wrapped around my chest and neck like the mummy. Jackie glanced over in my direction, probably to check my progress, and was surprised to see me still there. He yelled over the roar of the 60, "I told you to go!" Coolly, I told him I had almost forgotten to take my can of ammo.

He shook his head and went back to hosing the cemetery and wood line, while away from his peripheral vision I thrashed around next to him. It felt like forever trying to untwist straps and loosen knots with my fingers and teeth, all the while cursing the uncooperative nature of army equipment as bullets whizzed overhead. When finally able to see the sun again, I was ready to try my great escape anew. This time I was able to turn around on my stomach toward the direction I wanted to go. I repositioned everything to keep the bags from shifting, having a good idea of what to expect the second time around. I tapped Jackie on the shoulder to give him a thumbs-up sign, and without taking his finger off the trigger, he turned to look at me. We nodded at each other again, and I was soon off, this time making it up to the railroad tracks. I did my best impression of Jim Brown, the NFL Hall of Fame running back, dodging would-be tacklers while a hail of enemy fire kicked up dirt and pinged off the metal rails. I crested the rise of the railroad bed at full speed and saw the duster leaving and an APC[33] moving on the road towards our position. Looking back down for the berm, I noticed one guy where we had thought there would be an entire company.

The lone mud-covered grunt was sitting in the small paddy between the tracks and roadway some forty yards away, the farthest diagonal corner from me. Without stopping my broken field running, I wondered

---

33   APC- Armored Personnel Carrier

where the hell everybody was holed up, while desperately looking for the higher berm we thought was there. The shocking realization that I wouldn't be able to stop to cover Jack as planned flashed through my mind. I understood immediately why none of the guys we had covered during their retreat were anywhere to be seen. It would be suicide to stop there, being exposed to so much enemy fire. And yet the guy on the far side seemed unfazed. Maybe it was a safe place.

I continued to serpentine along until able to jump down the opposite embankment into the paddy below. I slid, stumbled, crawled, slithered, swam, and clawed my way along a low berm, stopping occasionally to fire back while checking to see if Jack was coming. I moved as fast as possible through the soft, loose mud until I reached the other guy at the far side. I didn't know his name but recognized him from the processing center back in Bien Hoa, a little over a month before.

He was a new kid like me and had been assigned to Charlie Company. We were sitting in the mud, leaning against the oozing roadside embankment, trying to catch our breath and collect our wits. Not the best time and place to catch up on how things were going, but we weren't drawing fire. We had both been with the 1st Cav for almost four weeks and agreed the proposition that we'd make five weeks wasn't very promising. He asked if I had a cigarette because his were soaked, so I pulled out my waterproof pack and we lit up. I asked if he knew where everyone was, and he just shrugged, said he saw a bunch of guys he didn't recognize heading for the hamlet behind us. He said they might have been A Company, but then they could have been his too.

Moments later, a couple of rounds cracked nearby, and we naturally flinched, leaning one way or the other to get lower. Then the cracks of two more rounds spaced a second or two apart were so close I could swear I felt them splitting the air. At about that same time that we ducked, there was an explosion on the road above and slightly forward of our position. Unbeknownst to us, the APC had been hit with an RPG.[34] I leaned lower left, helmet toward the firing, while he leaned right. I don't know how much time passed with us in those positions, but the incoming rounds had stopped. I leaned back up and said something to the effect of "That was really close! Let's get the hell out of here!" It was then that I noticed the long unbroken ash lying on the back of his hand from the smoldering cigarette still held between his two fingers. It had burned close enough that he should have felt the heat. I didn't know if he'd been hit or was just paralyzed with fear. I repeated it was time for us to get out of there and nudged him while flicking the cigarette from his fingers, but he didn't move. I yelled to ask if he was hit, but he just sort of whimpered or mumbled. I realized why when I saw a drop of blood on his jaw.

I reasoned that Charlie had to have been firing from a distant tree line or somehow from between the road and tracks to be able get at us from where we sat.[35] The situation was deteriorating rapidly. I didn't know where the guy had been hit or whether by a round or shrapnel, but he was wounded, and I had to get him out. He was now my top priority, adding more urgency because Jackie still hadn't come over the tracks. I couldn't

34   RPG—Rocket Propelled Grenade; Soviet-made shoulder-fired forty-millimeter anti-armor weapon used by enemy troops and also known as a B-40; accurate up to 160 yards, with a maximum range 220 yards.

35   I was to learn many years later that there were in fact one-man spider holes dug into the sides of the road and railroad embankments.

see anyone around us because we were lower than the roadway, but I could hear the yelling and commotion above us. I yelled out for a medic and started crawling away from the incoming direction with the guy on my back in a fireman's carry. I hadn't gotten very far when someone standing on the roadway above me yelled, "Find me a radio! Get a radio!" I looked up in surprise because they had to see I had a wounded guy on my back. It was Lieutenant Colonel Vaught. The battalion commander. Not knowing what had happened, I thought it was strange. I thought all armored tracks had a radio in them. So I yelled back, "Get me a medic!"

He yelled again, "Find a radio!" I didn't know if the order was directed at me, but he was looking straight down at us.

I repeated, "Get a medic!" I didn't stop crawling, not knowing the extent of the guy's injury until his helmet fell off. He was alive and mumbling and his scalp was pretty wet near his left ear. But he was alive, and I desperately wanted to get him help. Surely, I couldn't be the only survivor available to look for a radio, and I wasn't about to leave him. I guess that's the main difference between an officer and a grunt. I was only focused on saving one trooper, maybe two. Hopefully three.

The guy was naturally bigger than me, so I had trouble making forward progress through the deep mud, using only one arm while on my knees and holding him with the other. Both of us were covered in mud, causing him to slip and slide down my back a couple of times. Ltc. Vaught must have called a medic, because eventually one jumped down, bandaged the guy's head, and asked where I was hit. It took a second or two before I realized it wasn't my blood he was seeing. Even together we had just as much trouble negotiating the mud, but the incoming rounds kept us motivated. After we had gone forty or fifty feet, a couple of guys on the road must have seen us and jumped down to help, and it was probably after one look at me that the three of them took over. I followed the guys carrying our weapons to the far end of the paddy. The two guys had trouble climbing up the lowest section of embankment where the roadway was about at eye level. But between them pulling the wounded guy while the medic and I lifted him, they got him up onto the road. One guy grabbed the medic's hand to pull him up while I threw their M-16s to the second guy. They all quickly ducked behind the smoldering track and disappeared into a hut. I was physically, mentally, and emotionally exhausted but still determined to find help for Jack. He was on the opposite side of the railroad tracks, alone, and might have also been wounded by then.

It felt like every one of my senses was being assaulted nonstop—eardrum-shattering sounds, lung-poisoning diesel fumes, horrific sights, mind-numbing anxiety. It is the chaos of combat—a cacophony of automatic weapons firing nonstop and the unmistakable cracks of AK rounds overhead; mortar and rocket explosions, followed immediately by the frightening whirring sounds of unseen chunks of shrapnel spinning through the air in search of an unlucky target; officers barking orders to position troops; shouts into communications radios calling for dust-offs;[36] screams coming from all directions calling out for medics; the din of aerial rocket artillery whooshing down from a circling Huey gunship, its powerful rotor blades slapping the air violently, their pitch changing with every maneu-

---

36   Dust-off—Medevac helicopter.

ver. And through it all, you have to keep your wits and make split-second, life-or-death decisions.

I don't know if anyone can really explain or paint or put into words the sound or smell of a battle. Maybe I haven't read enough books yet. How do you describe chaos, the taste, or feel of gritty mud? The sounds of combat are horrible, but the stench of combat is unforgettable: burnt gunpowder and chemicals from depleted munitions; the noxious diesel and aviation fuel exhaust fumes; burning grass, trees, magnesium, manmade materials like the APC's interior; methane gas leaching from the decaying food parcels thrown next to nearby houses; the smell of wet mud and the pervasive odor of unwashed humans, blood, and fear. All of the offensive ingredients are blended together by choppers flying in with ammo and out with the wounded. These smells are forever implanted into a soldier's memory, as much as the sweet aroma of cotton candy, popcorn, and caramel apples are to a kid at a county fair. The words, the definitions, are just that—words.

Despite the noise and confusion going on around me, I knew what I had to do to increase my chances of survival. I was ready to jump as high as a weighted-down five-foot-six exhausted man covered in thick wet mud was capable of jumping—hopefully high enough to get a firm handhold on the flat asphalt pavement above me. Once I got the leverage, I thought, I would be able to pull my way up while climbing the muddy bank with my lug-soled jungle boots. I couldn't leave my munitions behind because I was sure I would need them once I reached the top and started to draw Charlie's attention. With my heart pounding and praying for the best, I positioned my stuff securely, winced at another burst of AK fire raking air, and then jumped toward my hopeful escape route. My empty right hand and the left holding my M16 easily cleared the top. I stretched and reached for a handhold while trying dig the toes of my boots into the embankment.

As quick and calculated as the coordinated leap was, I started to slide back almost as fast. My hands and fingers could not dig into the road's shoulder near the macadam because it was compacted clay covered with a thin, slimy layer of mud. The result of slipping hands, a planted foot, and the weight of my munitions caused me to fall backward, landing on my back in the trampled paddy. Rolling over to get up without any hesitation, I made another, more frantic try and produced the same frustrating results. I quickly found out that with no one there to help, I couldn't get up and out. The churning jungle boots of the three guys getting up the hill while dragging the fourth had collapsed the grass-covered slope into a slurry of slick mud. The once-gentle slope had been reduced to a four-to-five-foot almost vertical rise of collapsing mud. The slick torn-up earth continued over the top to where the shoulder of the roadway lay.

I had been able to touch the macadam but no more and soon realized the bulkiness of my flak jacket prevented me from reaching any farther for the leverage I needed to scale the top. I found myself in one of those controlled panic situations when the world around you seems to be in slow motion, when seconds feel like minutes and minutes like hours. I knew I would be in deep trouble if I could not clear the embankment.

With my next lunge, I held my rifle with both hands, and as soon as I jumped, I speared the roadside shoulder with my rifle butt, using it like an ice climber's pick. As if running in place, my feet clawed to get more leverage on the collapsing embankment. I pulled on the rifle butt and pushed up with my legs. The maneuver allowed me to get high enough to quickly release the rifle with my right hand and stretch my arm out sideways for a handhold. I was so committed to making it on that attempt that it felt like my fingernails were digging into the highway pavement. Deafening cracks from the AK-47s were providing all the adrenaline and incentive I needed to succeed.

Finally able to drag myself up onto my stomach, I slithered forward to reach the roadway. Gasping for air while getting up on all fours, I lifted my head slightly to get my bearings and found myself staring directly into the barrel of a LAW (Light Antitank Weapon) less than fifteen feet in front of me. I was almost up, feet running in place, trying to get traction in the mud at the edge of the roadside, my mouth bone dry, heart pounding, eyes frozen in horror, hoping I wouldn't see a flash come out of the front of the launcher. All of this happening in a span of seconds while enemy fire raked the mud and asphalt, and bullets ricocheted with staccato-like pings off the burning APC to my right.

Once able to finally get up into a three-point stance on the roadway, I lifted my M-16 with my right hand, ready to flip the safety 180 degrees to "automatic" and spray the enemy position when I realized its barrel was square. Fortunately, my mind cleared enough to recognize it as the lens of the news camera, its crew hiding behind thick privet hedges along the roadside. As I dashed toward them, I heard the producer yelling over the sound of nearby grunts shooting at invisible targets. I don't remember his exact words, but they went something like, "God, that was great! Mike, did you get him coming over the road? Oh come on, Mike. All right, let's get the camera over there by that hut! Harry, set up the sound dish by those guys shooting over there! Hey, let's make sure we get those medevacs loading up! Mike, listen to me. When that gunship makes another pass, I want you to try to get it firing those rockets." He was like Cecil B. DeMille on a Hollywood set. I'll never forget his look as I passed a couple of feet from him and saw his eyes grow larger as he looked in a different direction. I continued toward a hut on the side of the road and couldn't believe my ears. "Holy mother of God, look at that! Get that big helicopter [Guns-a-Go-Go[37]] in the paddy before it completely burns up. God, I hope the crew got out." I neither saw nor heard the big gunship that was shot down while near the tracks.

Not waiting for him to ask me for a retake, I dove behind the hedges. My heart was beating as fast as a helicopter's miniguns were painting the wood line to our south. After a few deep breaths, I again stayed low and began running bent over at the waist, heading for a house where I thought I would be able to stay out of sight until I could catch my breath and maybe find some water. On the way there, I noticed a pasty-white, horrified sound man pleading, "Come on, Jim, we have enough stuff. Let's get the hell outta here!"

I was finally able to stagger into a hut lined with a bunch of guys I didn't recognize who, having just witnessed my mad dash, were both yelling and laughing at me for being so stupid and gung ho. I just shrugged as I started to go into shock. While I sat shaking from the horror I'd just survived, one of them recovered enough

---

37   Guns-a-Go-Go—One of two Chinook helicopters modified as a gunship, carrying weapons on all sides. Too slow for its purpose in Vietnam, the 1st Cavalry's second chopper was taken out of service. With improvements made over the years, Chinook gunships are still in use today.

to ask, "What the hell were you trying to do? You just gotta be a fuckin' new kid. Why didn't you just go *under* the tracks, through the drainpipe like some of your guys?" I knew the answer but decided to leave before they really got on my case. I needed to find a way to get Jackie back.

I wove my way through the small hamlet, trying to find anyone in my company, but no one seemed to know where A Company had gone. After five nerve-racking minutes, I finally located a guy from my platoon. Under the circumstances, he was the best guy I could have found. He was a long, lean Texan whose nickname was Pappy, so called because of his advanced age of twenty-two. He was well liked by anyone who met him, and with his slow drawl paired with a big red mustache; reminded me of Yosemite Sam. I found Pappy sitting on the ground, legs crossed, nonchalantly leaning back against the side of a hut, seemingly oblivious to battle raging around him. It was probably the tension in my face and my panicky rambling that prompted him to tell me to relax and sit down. "Don't worry, Bano. Things'll settle down soon an' we kin go back tah fightin' the war. But right now, I'm gonna have me some lunch." I asked if he had any water left, and he offered me his canteen, from which I gratefully took a few swallows to soothe my dry mouth and throat. From our vantage point looking north, we could see medevacs landing on the highway macadam and being loaded with the wounded. Pappy thought he saw some guys from our company on the opposite side of the road, the side from which I had come. While we talked, he slowly heated a can of beans, obviously in no hurry to join up with our other guys because he was "short" and didn't want to take any unnecessary chances.

I watched the news crew working their way toward us, or maybe the helicopter transportation dropping off munitions. While making their way, they were trying to solicit interviews from grunts who were trying to regain their strength. When the producer saw Pappy relaxing and having a late-afternoon snack in the midst of all of the chaos, he said something to the other two guys while pointing toward our position. I could tell by the way they suddenly ignored the other grunts that they had found their man. Sure to keep their heads down while running between the huts, the three men hurried over. Surprisingly, without even taking a breather, the moment they reached us and knelt down, the producer turned on a recorder hanging near his hip, lifted a microphone, and asked into it before pointing it at Pappy, "Where are you from, soldier?"

"Why, Ah come from the great state of Texas, an in about a week, Ah'll be back thar again."

The interviewer was elated that he had found a seasoned vet and glanced at his crew with an "I told you so" grin. "So your one-year tour of duty is almost over. Have you been assigned to the 1st Cavalry Division since you arrived in-country?" He aimed the mic back at Pappy while his two compadres operated their equipment. Perhaps a little more spooked than most, both searched the horizon for the arrival of another chopper, flinching with each explosion or stray bullet that whizzed by.

Pappy, taking his time as he always did, swallowed a plastic spoonful of beans and said proudly, "Yep. Best damned unit in Viet-nam!"

Pulling the mic back, the interviewer dropped the big question. "Tell me then—" a mortar round exploded nearby because of the incoming chopper, and I think we all flinched before he could finish the sentence. "Is this the worst action you've seen since you've been here in Vietnam?"

When the mic was pointed back at Pappy, he floored everyone within earshot—certainly the film crew and me—when he slowly replied, "Nah, this ain't nothin'. Just a few ole boys dug in somewhere causin' some trouble. Now Bong Son, that was a firefight. Knock-down, drag-out, worst fight you could imagine. Must've been a hundred of 'em!" Looking at the crew, I thought it seemed that the sound man, who was getting very antsy watching a chopper taking off, really didn't want to hear the whole story. "Oh, we'll git 'em tomorrah fer sure, if'n they ain't dade by tahnight. But yah know, if Charlie..." Pappy droned on and had us all hanging on his every word, as slow as they were in coming.

With the chaos in the background continuing, every head, except Pappy's, kept turning in every direction scanning for potential danger. I happened to notice the sound man nudging the producer who was kneeling while holding the mic for Pappy. When he finally got his attention, he bobbed his head a couple of times toward the incoming chopper as if to indicate they should go. "'Lessin' of course he tries somethin' else. Then we'll jest have tah..." For all Pappy knew, he was going to be on the evening news, yet he remained completely laid back while eating his beans between sentences. He had an audience and just loved spinning yarns.

The instant the reporter asked Pappy his name, thanked him, and shut off the mic, the sound man grabbed the reporter and pleaded, "Jim, let's get the hell out of here!" Five minutes later they were boarding a chopper heading back to Camp Evans along with a couple of combat photographers. By then, my breath-

ing wasn't so labored, and my heart rate had slowed
enough for me to try to find the others in my platoon.

Hearing shots fired from a hut on the opposite side
of the roadway, I left Pappy and was finally able to locate some guys from my platoon. As I made my way
behind the dense hedge row that surrounded the huts,
I wondered how Pappy wound up on the opposite side
of the road when he had also been walking along the
tracks on the opposite side of the road. I found a narrow opening between the hedges, took a deep breath,
and made another mad dash across the road. When I
jumped through another hedge, there were no guys in
my squad to be seen. In fact, there were very few guys
from my platoon. Sergeant Green, our platoon sergeant, probably sensed my condition and recognized
how distraught I was talking about getting Jackie and
came over to talk to me.

He was looking at me sort of cautiously and asked
how I was. I could only shake my head and shrug my
shoulders. He had a very caring way about him. Like
talking with your grandfather when you were young.
Soothing I guess is the word. We talked a bit, and I told
him where and approximately when I last saw Lee and
Jackie. He assured me he'd get some volunteers and
fetch them after it got dark. His expression seemed to
morph into one of concern as we talked, then one of
understanding. When he again asked if I was all right,
I nodded, and after a deep breath, answered, "I'll make
it, Sarge. Tough day at the office."

As he walked away, I overheard him say to Jim Robbins, one of our platoon's squad leaders, that I would
be in his squad now and to keep an eye on me. "We lost
the third squad today." Words I didn't want to hear.

About five minutes later, Jim came over and sat by me for some conversation, I'm sure to check on my mental state. Fortunately, we had had a few long conversations in the previous days, so he knew what to expect from me. Sergeant Greene had calmed me down somewhat, so our talk was ... normal. There was no doubt in either of our minds that I'd been shaken up but would still be able to function as a soldier. After that assurance, Jim told me what had happened to the guys in my squad after everyone had pulled back, after the retreat was called. Joe, Rat and Sam must have stayed together when they reached a big culvert under the tracks. Unfortunately, the escape route was targeted by Charlie, and they all had to be medevacked along with a medic. I was the only guy from my squad there, so Jackie must still be out there. That meant we were the only guys there from a squad of ten that had landed in a rice paddy eighteen days earlier. And for the time being, Jack was listed as MIA.

I listened in shock as Jim filled me in about the others. Big Joe had been shot through his left shoulder but was strong enough to drag a bunch of guys away from the kill zone, including the medic who was in serious condition. Sam had been hit in the hand or wrist, and Rat had been hit in the upper thigh. I had gotten really close to those guys and could only pray they would all be okay, pretty sure I'd never see any of them again. So, between the day's events and Pappy saying this was nothing, my next thoughts turned to the odds of me surviving unscathed for another 323 days in Nam as a grunt. It didn't take very long to come up with the answer. *Not likely, Johnny Boy*, I thought.

The action eventually subsided late in the day leaving plenty of time for the officers on both sides to come with the next day's plans on how to attack/defend the hamlet/cemetery. *Oh, the irony.* We'd be staying the night in the small hamlet that we'd passed before the fireworks began. Based on the day's activities and the proximity of the two forces, most of the guys, probably on both sides, had the same premonition: be prepared for incoming mortars. Charlie knew where we'd be, and he had a good idea of the coordinates —about fifty meters farther than the last round he fired at the duster. So, now assigned to the second squad with Pappy, we were preparing our defensive perimeter while occasional AK rounds whizzed overhead. As expected, the first mortar rounds landed just past our position, and gave us a little extra incentive to dig faster. There was always the possibility that we might have visitors later that night in addition to mortars.

We had no packs, and therefore no defensive Claymores or trip flares, meaning it was going to be a long night. And without food, bedding, or shelter, the night would be uncomfortable too, but not as much as for those who'd been medevacked. At about an hour after sunset while rummaging around to find something dry to sleep on, we heard a loud whisper from the other side of the thick privet hedge surrounding the small courtyard. The voice had an unmistakable Texas drawl, saying, "Hey, guys. Don't shoot, it's me. I'm comin' in. It's me, Jackie, from A Company. Don't shoot." A couple of us scrambled to the barrier and helped him crawl through a tight opening between two plants. He was covered with mud from head to toe. Above his big grin, he had thin lines of dried blood that had trickled down on each side of his forehead. To say I was relieved to see him would be an understatement. When asked what took him so long to get back, his ever-present smile grew wider as he replied, "When Ah saw Bano go over those tracks, an' heard all that shootin', Ah figured Ah was safer where Ah was. An' then when Ah ran outta ammo, Ah didn't wanna leave mah gun out there alone. So Ah figured Ah'd jes wait in the grass for it to git dark."

I guess that was the right thing for him to do. The others thought they had made the right decision to crawl through a culvert and had been medevacked. I made a stupid decision and don't have a Purple Heart.

Hunger Pains

Because of the heavy fighting and the worsening weather conditions late in the day, our backpacks were not brought out to us. Other than seeing the sun for an hour, it had not been a good day, and it appeared the night would be no different. We stayed as safe, warm, and as dry as possible, and ate whatever was lying around. It wouldn't be the first night we slept in the rain that month, nor would it be the last, not that it mattered because most of us had wet fatigues covered with mud that wouldn't dry even if it didn't rain. Its why guys join the navy or air force.

We didn't dare sleep in or near the huts. Too obvious a target. Instead, we slept by our fox holes alongside a three-foot-deep drainage ditch of stagnant water that surrounded the hamlet. Guys covered themselves with piles of straw that were lying around because the temperature started to drop; it was worth a try. About the only thing that gave us any solace that very long, wet, cold night was talking about the poor grunts of WWII and Korea who had to endure much worse, much longer.

The following morning found everyone chilled to the bone and shivering because the temperature had dropped into the fifties. A constant light rain had also returned during the night and prevented our mud-soaked fatigues, boots, and socks from drying. No packs meant no hot coffee to warm us up and no food to quiet our groaning stomachs. The increasing daylight revealed an eerie atmosphere with fog so dense that our world was confined to a twenty-foot radius. After a time, the fog dissipated somewhat but a low cloud cover still limited our ability to see very far up or down Highway 1, nor into the rice paddies surrounding us. The possibility that the NVA could be setting another ambush in any direction put many of us on edge. The worst view of all for us was the fog shrouded cemetery bordering the tracks that we had seen the day before. It was just a matter of time before we'd have to go back out and work our way through the gray light to find the enemy's whereabouts.

In our case, in addition to the dismal weather, tall grass, and treed areas, our field of vision would be further obstructed by low cement walls, mounded burial sites and headstones while at the same time offering Charlie great cover. The colorfully painted shrines in the threatening terrain now seemed bizarre and out of place given the carnage that had taken place the day before and might possibly happen again on this day. As one might imagine, between the graves, drizzle, fog, and vegetation, not to mention Charlie lurking out there somewhere, the place had us spooked. Our first objective, a blown-out concrete building behind a long wall of thick bamboo, was about four hundred yards from where we spent the night. Everyone knew that all hell could break loose at any second, but our cold, hungry, frustrated bodies definitely wanted to finish the fight so we could just get the hell out of there.

Because of the heavy losses we had taken over the past two weeks, we had just enough guys for two complete squads in our 2nd Platoon. The other platoons weren't faring much better, thus making our company pretty thin. Heck, our whole battalion was getting smaller. Back on February 5, when we had started out, the battalion had 481 men, including the six HQ people. By the twelfth we were down to 376. Even after getting more replacements, by the twenty-first we still only had 382. All I could think about, as we started our crouched stalk through the high grass toward the enemy's last known position, was that I didn't think I'd be able to remain unscathed eleven more months as a grunt, certainly not with the attrition rate we were experiencing. I mean, each day seemed to be worse than the one before. I wondered what Donny, Mello, and the rest of the guys were doing, if they had seen a lot of action too, if they were okay. I reflected on the day before when my nose was in the mud, the bullets were flying, and a spider was terrorizing me. I decided at that precise moment that war was not to be wished on anyone, not even an enemy.

Charlie and Delta Companies were again trying to work their way south along the highway and open fields, while what was left of our company was doing a flanking maneuver to the west away from the tracks. Everything was quiet at first, but after only a short distance, enemy mortar rounds started falling behind us into Delta Company's area. It appeared as if NVA were splitting our flock, herding only our portion of the spread-out formation toward the area where most of the intense fire had come from the day before.

Our lessening band of brothers in Alpha Company continued on through the tall grass and slippery mud, listening as the medevacs flew in and out of a staging area behind us. There was no place for us to go but forward, get this thing over with, and move on toward Hue. Within half an hour, we neared our objective with few casualties but started taking small-arms fire again. I made my way into the old block building with Randy Comegys, a surfer-type dude from Maryland whom I had met earlier. As terrifying and chaotic as the world was outside the building, I felt safe and almost giddy inside. Randy, searching the surroundings for enemy fire, was keeping me sane just by the way he looked. He wore his mud-caked pants rolled up to his calves as if ready to go wading. His olive-green, army-issue socks were pulled up above his boot tops and secured in place with red elastic bands. The half-laced black-toed jungle boots, scraped and worn down to bare brown leather, were rolled down, taking on the appearance of "high blacks," the old US Keds we all wore as kids. Randy always seemed to have a big smile that looked even friendlier because of a space between his two front teeth, framed by a droopy Fu Manchu mustache. Long, dirty blond hair poked out from beneath a camouflaged helmet cover that had been shredded over the past eleven months. Hanging out from the open neck of his fatigue shirt was a leather necklace holding a peace sign. As usual, he was goofing around as only an eighteen-year-old could under the circumstances.

While we peeked around the walls to look into the cemetery, Randy said, "I see one! Watch this." He leaned out and fired a burst with his '16, then quickly spun back inside. No sooner was he back inside against the wall when a returning burst of AK fire raked the outside wall where he had just fired from. "Cool, huh? Just like a John Wayne movie!" he said with a huge grin.

"Yeah, groovy, Randy," I said, amazed by his care-free attitude. "But I've had enough of John Wayne this week! Cut the shit before Charlie decides to use an RPG on our asses!"

He started breaking my chops a little, having heard about my previous day's exploits. A friend from Delta Company who had witnessed my touchdown run had filled him in. "No really, this is cool. He's in a hole on top of a grave mound." he grinned again, eyebrows arching up even higher. He leaned out again and fired at the enemy position. He was loving it, and I was cringing every time the outside wall was hit. The exchange of fire between the two of them happened the same way three or four times until Randy leaned out and was greeted by a long burst of AK rounds coming from a different direction. The bullets raked the building, throwing bits of concrete all over him and past the door opening. He instantly twisted back in, his grin just as big but a little crooked, and said, "Whoa, that was close! You wanna try it?" I wondered how he had made it through eleven and a half months unscathed. His antics and good fortune actually relieved a lot of my anxiety about my own future. After what I had experienced over the past two days, I had learned an important combat lesson: If you're going to get hit, you're going to get hit. I had to get back on the horse.

My new squad eventually completed a flanking maneuver, working our way around the edge of the cemetery bypassing the wide-open area. Instead, we remained on the side of a slow rise of trees leading down to the cemetery that provided some concealment and protection while we waited for orders. What transpired was really pretty funny, or shocking, depending on your rank, considering the incredible tension and frustration we were all feeling. I was lying within hearing distance and wasn't thrilled when I heard our RTO inform Jim Robbins, my new squad leader, that the CO, who we hadn't met, wanted the squad to move into the enemy's position. I was thinking, *Oh crap, not again*. Jim stared at the cemetery and said something to the effect that he didn't think it was a good idea and took the radio handset from the RTO. Jim was a very sharp, intelligent guy who had gone through Officer Candidate School for almost the full term when he came down with pneumonia two weeks before graduation. Rather than yield to the politics and start the whole cycle over, he decided to chuck a commission and come to Vietnam as a sergeant. He knew what he was doing, and based on his guys, they trusted his abilities.

Well, if you remember the numbers that were used for call signs mentioned earlier, I assumed he was talking to our platoon sergeant. For me, when I heard Jim's responses, it seemed worse than me yelling at a battalion commander to get me a medic. In any case, it was a great exchange up and down the chain of command. The company commander, who was designated County Line Six, ordered the top sergeant to tell the lead element to engage. Top, whose designation was County Line Five, or Line Five for short, ordered the 2nd Platoon's sergeant to engage. Sergeant Green, whose sign was Line Two-Five, then passed the order down to Line Two-Two, the second squad leader of the 2nd Platoon, to attack. For the record, the 2nd Platoon didn't have a lieutenant platoon leader, or else he would have been on the horn before Sergeant Green as Line Two-Six. Come to think of it, we didn't have a CO either until a few days before. And just to make things a little more confusing during the communication transmissions, the designation of the RTO who was relaying the messages would have been India, as in County Line Two-Two, India.

Anyway, being that most of our "leaders" were far to our rear and had no idea what we were actually up against, the RTO and I watched and listened to Jim mumbling something before replying. "Line Two-Five, this is Line Two-Two. Tell Six to go to hell, over." The RTO's and my eyes must have looked like those of a deer in a car's headlights. By Jim taking the responsibility to say that, after analyzing the situation for himself, he saved a lot of us that day. Over the next few minutes, the conversation must have sounded like this in return:

"Line Five, dis is Two-Five. Two-Two sez go to hell, over."

"Ah, roger that, Two-Five. Your Two-Two sez go to hell."

Top knew and trusted Jim's ability. He did not know the new CO, nor did he believe in giving an order without thoroughly assessing the situation. At that point, all he knew was that a darn good squad leader did not think a frontal assault with a squad on an enemy position that held a battalion at bay for an entire day was a good idea. I would think Top replied to the new CO, "County Line Six, this is Line Five. My Two-Five informs me that his Two-Two believes it's too risky, over." Being that it was the CO's RTO on the phone, he had heard all of the messages, meaning the CO never heard the "Go to hell" response. The radio operator probably handed the phone to the CO saying, "Here, it's for you" after saying there's a problem.

"Yeah, copy that, Five. What's the problem up there? Get your people in there to engage, out."

"Roger that, Six. Two-Five, this is Five. Do you copy? Over."

"Five, this is Two-Five. Ah copy. Two-Two, you copy?"

"Affirmative. I say again, tell Six to go to hell, out!" Well, that went back and forth a few times as an occasional bullet or two continued to whiz over our heads. Six must have asked how he could help. Jim requested a gunship or artillery support that could be directed from his position. The CO said he would see what he could get. That's all a grunt ever asks, at least try. Unfortunately, if it were the marines in our position, they'd be moving into a killing field, a senior officer would get a medal, and someone would be writing letters to the next of kin.

We were spread out during the exchange, eating the last of our crackers or candy bars, having a smoke, telling jokes, and generally waiting for the support. One of the guys in the squad was a brother by the name of William Phifer, who eventually asked for a .45 pistol because he saw where a sniper was hiding. His plan of action seemed unbelievable. He would have to crawl slightly downhill to a berm, slide over it, and crawl another twenty feet completely exposed into the cemetery before being close enough to throw a hand grenade at an enemy position dug down into a raised burial mound. Phifer was real good people but the last guy anyone would expect to do something like that. He was a quiet, highly intelligent, introverted person, preferring museums to parties, reading a good book to playing cards, political discussions to jokes—not exactly the usual stereotypical inner-city black kid from

Manhattan. The main reason no one would ever expect him to do something like that was not because of his intelligence, gentle nature, or color, but the fact that Bill was overweight and about the clumsiest guy in Vietnam—always tripping over his boots because of a severe pigeon-toed condition.

After having an entire battalion pinned down for almost a full day, something was about to happen. Phifer would need someone to cover him when he went into the cemetery, so two guys volunteered. One was a guy named Jason Edwards, whom I did not know very well, being I was new to the squad. I knew I was the smallest guy there and the berm was really low, so it was my chance to "get back up on that horse" so to speak. We three crawled down and had almost reached the berm when an unrecognizable helicopter came into view at the far end of the cemetery. We were at first shocked and reluctant to move because it was the first time any of us had ever seen that type of helicopter, and we weren't sure whose side it belonged to. It didn't have any markings painted on the nose, certainly no 1st Cavalry gold crossed sabers that we were used to seeing. It looked something like a small jet, not a helicopter. Same sleek shape, a bubble canopy, short wings on the sides, and just wide enough for a human.

Having already received incoming machine-gun fire the previous week from a nervous Huey door gunner, we were naturally concerned with having a similar mishap. But this was no door gunner with an M-60 hanging out of a Huey coming at us. This thing carried two rocket pods off each small wing and a minigun in a chin turret. What had us most concerned, was when the ship rolled in at the far side of the cemetery and straightened out, the minigun lit up while flying straight at us.

There was not enough time for us to panic, because you can't get out of the way of a minigun. All we could do was just watch and wait our fate. In a matter of seconds, it screamed past us and rose at the far end of the cemetery. After it took a couple of runs, we realized the minigun in a circular pod hanging beneath the front of the new contraption could move, and there were two guys in the chopper, one in front of the other, like in a fighter jet. Fire was directed by the gunner in the front seat, with the pilot sitting a little higher behind him. With the six-barreled gun firing four thousand rounds per minute, the ship sounded and looked like a giant buzzing bee. To say we were relieved it was on our side would be a great understatement. We would eventually learn it was a newly arrived gunship the CO had called in. An AH-1 Cobra attack helicopter. *Thanks, Boss.*

We all three adjusted our pants and commenced to crawl, Jason and I going to provide some covering fire for Bill. The other guys behind us on the slope had a better vantage point to cover the overall cemetery. When we reached the last berm, Bill repeated his plan, telling us where we should place our fire. After a deep breath and exhale, Phifer crawled out alone into the cemetery, went to the grave mound, and lobbed a grenade on top of it. We were aghast when after he started to slide back down the mound, the grenade was thrown back out. We screamed at Bill to watch out, and fortunately, it exploded on the side opposite from the three of us. Unflustered and looking somewhat disappointed, he crawled back up but this time with the pistol in one hand and a grenade in the other. When he was almost within an arm's length of the hole, he stopped momentarily to get both hands forward and slightly raised himself on his elbows to peek inside. He immediately dropped down and pulled the pin on the grenade with his trigger finger. With one continuous movement, he dropped the grenade in and blindly fired all the rounds in his pistol into the hole. The concussion of the exploding grenade lifted him off the ground, but he was okay and wasted no time sliding back down. Jason and I kept our M-16s aimed at the top of the mound just in case.

When Bill crawled back and slipped over the muddy berm, he was huffing and puffing but very calm. Between deep inhales he said he saw four guys in the hole when he peeked over the edge. Jason was trying to get more out of him, but he was still searching for more breath. No, he wasn't sure if he hit any of them with the .45; he just wanted to keep them busy. He thought they were really big for NVAs. Then wondered if they might be officers because their uniforms were so clean. As we kicked the possibilities around, we wondered if they might be Chinese soldiers. Jason suddenly got very animated and said, "souvenirs!" In spite of Phifer's cautions, he immediately crawled up the mound on his hands and knees. It was bad decision.

When we crawled back to our squad, Bill explained that there were tunnels leading from the burial mound in all directions, probably linking the other grave sites. It explained why we had been receiving fire from so many different locations without being able to clear any of them the previous day. It also explained why our helicopters kept getting hit when they tried to hover with both door gunners shooting straight down. The information was relayed back to the CO, and I guess not wanting to lose any more guys, we were ordered to pull back. Phifer saved a lot of guys because of his selfless deeds that morning. Looking back on it now, I find it ironic that Custer's 7th Cavalry and we had the same problem and solution. If he'd had a hot-air balloon to see over the rolling the hills and we'd had a drone the day before…

When we finally reached the safety of the hamlet we'd stayed in the night before, Jim asked Phifer why he had exposed himself to enemy fire like that. Twice. William Phifer simply shrugged and said rather matter-of-factly, "I was getting pretty hungry." Now what was *he* thinking of?! Later that day rumor quickly circulated that he was being put in for the Distinguished Service Cross[38] for his actions, our nation's second-highest medal for valor. When asked about it, Bill frowned, shrugged at the suggestion, and continued shuffling toward the cases of C rations that had finally been dropped off along with our packs.

It would take another day for the battalion to complete its mission objective—the bridge over the moat at the northwest corner of the Citadel in Hue. On a serious note, the 5/7 Cavalry suffered twenty-seven KIA and 203 WIA over the twenty-two days afield in February.

---

38   Specialist Fourth Class William Phifer was presented with the Distinguished Service Cross for exceptionally valorous actions on February 23, 1968.

Photo by John Taylor
From left to right: Capt. Ralph Miles (CO, B Co.), sitting: Lt. Col. James B. Vaught (CO, 5th Battalion, 7th Cavalry), Capt. John W. Taylor Jr. (CO, A Co.), driver (unknown), Capt. Mike Davison (CO, C Co.), Capt. Frank Lambert (CO, D Co.)

Fleas. Please

There were some guys who knew exactly what they were doing, yet everyone around them thought they were nuts. Some did things for glory and medals or just to goof around. Some because they were scared to death and would do anything to get out of the field. Think back to the old M*A*S*H television series and Corporal Klinger, the guy who was always trying to get out of the military by wearing dresses. His character was not really that far-fetched.

On two different occasions, the company had to call for a tracker team, which was composed of one trooper and one dog. It was always fascinating to watch how GIs changed their behavior when they came in contact with things or people other than GIs. Put a dog with a grunt and the guy will jump in front of a tank to save its life. The same held true for a civilian, especially a kid. I suspect many guys would do the same thing if the other grunt were a female. That's the only reason I don't believe females should be assigned to combat units. Don't misunderstand me. It's not because I don't think they could do the job but because we would probably have squashed male grunts lying over all the roads with tank tracks across their chests. But maybe times have changed since fifty years ago and now guys don't put women on a pedestal.

Anyway, we had called for a dog team while trying to find a bunch of the little fellows who had somehow escaped our sweep of an area. We knew Charlie was there because he welcomed us with his usual greeting of letting loose with a burst from his AK, just enough to make us jump into the mud and get our fatigues wet. While we waited for the team to be brought out by chopper, we took a short break alongside a trail and munched on cookies and crackers. It was rather relaxing because the operation we were on was not bad at all. The beautiful May weather had cooperated for the six days we were out and contact with the enemy was nowhere near as bad as it had been back in February, March, and April. The current operation consisted mainly of sweeping areas and looking for trouble, and that was the first day we had found any.

We sat along a low rise and tried to figure out where Charlie had disappeared to in the wide-open expanse of sparsely vegetated fields, a terrain that was fairly common to that particular part of the country. We were working the areas located closer to the east coast than the mountainous chain that ran north to south through the western side of the I Corps region along Laos. The relatively flat terrain was a nice change for us, a reprieve from humping the mountains for weeks at a time. After a relaxing thirty-minute wait, we heard the distinct sound of a Huey in the distance and assumed it was the tracker team headed our way. The unmistakable sound of the big blades slapping the air meant it would be down soon and we would again be off to continue the search.

While everyone started to prepare themselves to saddle up, the chopper landed some distance to our rear. We watched in excited anticipation as the lightly equipped trooper jumped off the left side of chopper, followed by his big-boned German shepherd. The Huey pilot stared intently straight ahead, knowing that there was enemy activity in the immediate area, and was ready to take off in an instant if necessary. He kept the roaring engine powered up, the rotor wash flattening the grass and blowing the loose dirt in all directions, waiting until his crew chief gave him the okay to lift off. As soon as man and beast cleared the blades, the Huey gone, and the silence of the landscape returned.

Our CO walked back a short distance to greet them and spent the next ten minutes briefing the trooper. By his arm and hand actions, the CO must have been filling him in on what had transpired, where the enemy had last been seen, the direction they were traveling, how many there were, how well equipped they were, and what he wanted done. While stroking the dog's head, the tracker stared at the immediate terrain. With complete indifference, he occasionally responded to the captain's monologue by nodding and shrugging as if totally bored. When it appeared the CO had finally finished talking, the handler dropped to one knee and started talking to the dog as if translating the English into a language only they could understand. Once satisfied and ready, he started to walk in the direction the CO had pointed, holding the dog on a short leash.

They walked point for about fifteen minutes with our own point man just a few steps behind them and the rest of the company in tow. The shepherd, soon off his leash, got more animated when he picked up a scent while his master continued to direct his efforts. They started to lead our long, spread-out column of grunts toward a small river that cut through the flat "bottom lands." The scent trail eventually ended at the river's eroded mud bank, which dropped about ten feet straight down to the water's edge. Our immediate impression was that Charlie had jumped into the slow-moving brown water and swum fifty feet to the other side for one of his vanishing acts. The dog, however, sensed differently. When the handler asked Bob where Charlie was, the dog walked to the edge of the riverbank, put his nose down, and started digging. That finished their job for the day, and they moved out of the way so the grunts could do theirs.

Our point man crawled on his stomach to the edge of the drop-off and looked down. What had at first looked like a sheer mud riverbank, undercut by occasional fast- moving waters, turned out to be a one-man opening dug into the side of the embankment. We knew it was a rare occasion when Charlie allowed himself to be cornered. The hard part would be trying to figure out how to convince him to come out. Heads were put together, and the first plan of action had our Chu Hoi interpreter yelling in Vietnamese that anyone in the cave had better surrender before they got hurt. The Chu Hoi fellowship was comprised of former North Vietnamese soldiers who had surrendered and were assigned to US companies as translators, guides, trackers, and very often saviors. They were paid by grunts taking up collections every payday, and as far as we were concerned, the Chu Hoi were worth more to us than US savings bonds.

We named our Chu Hoi, or Kit Carson, as they were also known, Chewy. He was standing above the cave entrance, screaming and shooting his M-16 on full automatic straight down into the river, right in front of the cave's opening. Chewy's not-so-subtle dialogue didn't work. A common tactic of many scouts was to threaten Charlie with increasing amounts firepower, using full automatic bursts from a 16 to emphasize each pause. Like using a period after a sentence. When his suggestions were not agreed to, he would shout that the Americans had "run out of patience" and were "calling in jets to blow them into tiny bits so that their families would never find a piece of them." During the rare, quiet interludes between Chewy's intimidating offers, we could faintly hear voices coming from beneath our feet. It seemed to validate what we thought the little fellow really was. Make that little fellows. They were most likely debating among themselves the pros and cons of each alternative offered. After about fifteen or twenty minutes of shouting and threats, a grenade flew out of the cave and landed in the river, soaking everyone standing within range of the waterspout. We had Charlie's answer.

We had a real dilemma, because there was no way to approach the cave opening other than from the river, and that would have been suicide. Butch Barrett, the gung-ho guy who was now a member of my fire team, still wanted medals, and he said he could get them out if someone held him by the ankles and lowered him down next to the mouth of the cave. He would then throw a concussion grenade in and get their attention—let them know we were serious. Well, Butch was in my team and therefore my responsibility, so I called him aside and gave him my thoughts on his idea.

"What the hell are you thinking of?" I demanded. He told me to lighten up, challenged my backbone, and assured me it would be fun. Fun? Our new platoon leader, a lieutenant fresh from the states who had not seen any action yet, thought it would work too, so their plan was hatched. We old-timers could only lift our eyebrows, shake our heads, and walk away.

Because no one would volunteer to hold Butch's ankles, the lieutenant had the honor. The rest of us nonchalantly drifted away from the bank and the surrounding area. No one knew what Charlie was hiding in the cave and didn't want to be too close when a grenade went off. We just didn't know what the big spark could touch off. Meanwhile, the tracker and Bob the dog had also walked away and were playing with the leash now reattached to the dog's collar. The insanity of the entire scene would have made a great Kodak moment.

With everyone in position, or out of position as it were, Butch was "hung by his stockings with care" and threw the grenade through the opening. Not surprising to many of us, the grenade flew right back out, landed in the river, and exploded. That naturally scared the hell out of the lieutenant, who was running out of strength anyway. Butch of course was released head-first and slid straight down the muddy embankment and into the river like an otter, where he frantically swam to get out of the way of the cave opening. I think demonstrations of stupidity are even funnier when two people have to be asked, "What the hell were you thinking of?" Usually there's alcohol involved when a guy says, "Hey, watch this!" but not always. Bob, the dog, also looked like he was smiling as he sat with his ears straight up, tongue hanging, and shaking his head at the two morons who had just embarrassed our entire company. The CO must have reasoned he had better come up with a better solution fast before those two guys killed themselves. Or worse yet, before the rest of us got bored and decided to go swimming. Sanity prevailed and an alternate plan was made and executed, so to speak.

It was decided to retain the tracker for the remainder of the operation, being that it was already very late in the afternoon. That evening, after the packs had been flown out, we went through our nightly ritual. While some found straight saplings for erecting hooches, others began setting up the defensive perimeter. First, any potential cover the enemy could hide behind was cleared away from the areas to the front of each dug-in position. Then we would place the overlapping trip flares around the entire perimeter, position the Claymores, and dig our foxholes.

By the time all was completed and we started preparing our C-ration meals, it began to rain. The tracker had come out with very little equipment, except his weapon and canteens for himself and Bob, so we knew he was ill prepared for rain. We offered him a couple of ponchos to build a hooch, but he gratefully declined, saying he and Bob enjoyed the rain. That did not make much sense to us, because when the rain stopped, and we knew it would at that time of year, the mosquitoes would come out and attack anything warm.

No matter how much we insisted, he said, "Thanks, but no thanks." Well, the sun had set, the rain continued, and as we retired to our dry hooches and mosquito netting, we could see the tracker and his dog huddled together under one poncho while the rain pelted them. We figured the guy was crazier than Butch, and that was okay, but why hurt the dog? The following morning over some hot coffee, we learned the insane reason for his behavior. Ken, the tracker, was from Southern California and told us he slept in the rain with Bob as often as he could. "If you noticed," he said with a sly grin, "Bob was covered and protected from the rain, and only my neck and head were partially exposed." We still missed the point he was trying to make. With a growing grin, he looked around to make sure no officers were listening and, moving his eyebrows up and down like Groucho Marx, said, "The mosquitoes come to Bob's coat like a magnet. He can't get malaria, but I can!" Ken's insanity was so logical—it was the right wrong decision. He had probably stopped taking, or kept forgetting to take, his daily or weekly malaria pills, hoping to contract the lifelong disease just to get out of the field alive. Contracting malaria would, in all probability, insure him a longer if not healthier life. To Ken it was worth it, and no one could fault him for his reasoning. And no one ever asked, "What was he thinking of?"

Because of his ongoing actions, I requested Butch be transferred out of my fire team when we had our next reshuffling of squads. I didn't want the lunatic endangering any of my guys with his ridiculous acts of bravado, or constantly challenging orders so he could get decorations. My request was granted a few weeks later. Butch and the new lieutenant's contracts with the military were terminated at the end of June, when they both received medals posthumously.

If a Tree Falls in a Forest . . .

We were assigned a new platoon leader who had already served a tour in Vietnam. Whereas most platoon leaders were 2nd lieutenants fresh from the states, Tim Pasquarelli was a 1st lieutenant who had transferred from the combat engineers for an infantry assignment. Because of his training, skills, and past experiences, he would eventually change our entire platoon into fledgling pyromaniacs just like himself. By doing so, he altered the contents and weight we normally carried—from over a dozen hand grenades to pounds of plastique explosives, detonation cord, and blasting caps. LT just loved to make *big* explosions!

Most operations with the new LT were back in the mountains. He was used to climbing out of a Huey with his platoon of engineers, walking over to where some grunt company wanted something destroyed or an LZ cleared, and then have his men blow it up. Then a short walk back to a chopper for a quick extraction. Walking all day looking for trouble in river valleys, mountainsides, and high ridgelines was new to him as an infantry officer. To his credit, unlike most new 2nd lieutenants, "butter bars" that had passed through our ranks at an alarming rate, LT knew it was dangerous in the bush. He wasn't looking for medals. He wanted to do his job, protect his men when possible, and eventually become an infantry company commander. Many unfortunate new officers, it seemed, did not realize that rank only had its privileges in the rear. Charlie did not care whom he hit. For LT to do a good job and survive, he understood he could and should place a lot of faith in his sergeants and seasoned enlisted men.

One of the biggest difficulties we had in mountain operations was knowing where we were at any given point in time. Another was trying to get supplies down through the heavy jungle canopy. Because of those two problems, we would often have to stop the patrol and fix our position with the battalion commander flying five thousand feet above us in his command chopper. One thing that always bothered us, as I am sure it did every grunt that ever experienced it, was that from the chopper's altitude, the vegetation always looked like grass. Looking down from his aerie, the BC would direct the companies below him as if they were out for a leisurely walk in a park. In reality we would be sweating our brains out, slashing through dense jungle, slogging through leech-infested undergrowth and water, while trying to be as quiet as possible. And it was not uncommon for him to yell at the COs because they were not moving fast enough for him. Or better yet, they could not be where they said they were because he couldn't see anyone from where he was!

At times like those, we would have to stop and figure out a way to signal him so he could locate our position. As simple as that may sound, we occasionally had real difficulties doing it. If we were lucky, we could find an opening between tree branches. That allowed us to fire a star cluster[39] above the treetops. Other times, some-one would climb a tree and force the marker through the canopy. That method would occasionally backfire, literally, when the cluster ricocheted off an unseen limb and flew right back down at us. Typically though, star clusters would not work, nor would smoke grenades. With some jungle canopies being so dense, smoke would rarely escape, or the trees were just too tall, and smoke would dissipate before it could rise above the profusion of branches and leaves. When we were in situations like those, which were not that uncommon, we improvised. Someone would have to construct a "signaling" pole made by using one or more lengths of long bamboo or saplings, tied together to make a longer pole if necessary, with a smoke grenade lashed to its tip. Sometimes the canopy was so high and thick that using a single pole wasn't feasible. Misplaced as we were, we would have to continue traveling until finding an area where we could clearly signal our position.

Trying to signal a chopper with a hastily construct-ed pole was usually pretty funny and at times very frus-trating. Imagine tying two dozen licorice sticks together end to end, fastening a can of soda to the end of the last piece, and trying to push it up through tree branch-es so you could pass it to a friend. It was usually that ridiculous. First, we had to locate bamboo or suitable materials that could be tied together that were only slightly flexible and not weigh a ton. There had to be the correct number of lengths that when tied togeth-er could reach near the top of the canopy on the first try, without snapping. Once construction of the multi-

---

39   Star cluster –signaling device consisting of a metal tube and firing cap to launch free-falling pyrotechnic stars or illumination parachute. Military version of a roman candle

length pole was completed and we had enough guys ready, we'd find a suitable spot to try and thread the probe up through the branches and leaves. Anyway, that's where the game would begin and hopefully end.

As fast as the "smoke team" could, someone pulled the pin on the grenade, and each guy involved would then begin to lift the smoking end of the pole and each segment up—and by the way, the pole could be thirty feet long. Each guy/segment quickly moved forward and helped maneuver the probe up and through the tree branches, vines, and leaves while trying to keep the multiple segments in one piece. The entire task had to be done before the smoke grenade stopped burning. If it did, the pole had to be snaked back down through the foliage by the same legion of guys who had pushed it up. They'd re-formed in reverse order to grab the pole as it came down, thus preventing any hastily tied joints from separating. It was a tricky maneuver because they also had to be careful not to hit anyone in the head with the falling smoke grenade or burned branches that might also come down. The pole bearers then held the massive contraption while someone retrieved and lashed a replacement grenade to the end and the whole process attempted again. Anyone not involved on the "team" sat down, relaxed, and enjoyed the show.

Sometimes these events could be pretty funny, similar to the old *Beat the Clock* TV game show back in the fifties. An inane show where people had to do crazy things and beat a timer to win a prize. Our timer was the battalion commander yelling at Capt. Taylor, our commanding officer, to "pop smoke!" No matter how the CO tried to explain that we were trying to signal, the BC would keep barking impatiently. Occasionally, we would have to move to a "thinner" area because the canopy was just too impenetrable, while at other times it would actually work, and a small puff of colored smoke would escape to the BC's satisfaction.

What seemed to never fail was that when we humped to a more suitable area to signal our position, the BC would radio down telling us to move. "County Line Six, this is Cold Steel Six. I've got your marker. Head November Whiskey, one-five for Jack Benny[40] minus thirty-eight from your position. Looks like we should be able to get some log into you tonight. Cold Steel Six, out!" In English it meant, "Go fifteen degrees northwest for one kilometer from where you are." Naturally, he had just ordered us to return to an area a kilometer away that we had been in an hour earlier. He didn't want us stop then because it wasn't late enough in the day. Every grunt was absolutely certain the army, especially that BC was doing that to us just to break our balls.

Once we were able to get into a position where we could be supplied, we would sometimes have to make sure the clearing was wide enough to fit the forty-eight-foot-diameter helicopter rotor blades. The CO usually ordered LT to make sure it was safe to bring a chopper down into the clearing. Making it look official, LT would then walk around for a cursory survey, checking for rotor clearance, stumps that could puncture the ship's hull, and large rocks that might hang up one of the skids. Of course, the clearings were never large enough, which meant we would have to take down a tree or two. LT was always very serious when talking to the CO, describing how he could take down such and such a tree with a minimum of effort and noise. If

---

40   Jack Benny was a vaudeville comedian who always claimed to be 39 years old. We assumed Charlie never watched any of his shows.

the CO agreed with the need, their conversation would end, and LT would call us over for our orders.

The scenario rarely changed. With a grin on his face and a sparkle in his eyes, he would tell us what to do: where the tree should be notched so it would fall a certain way; how much explosives he wanted packed into the notches; how we would detonate the charges. It always sounded very professional, maybe for the CO's sake. LT, though, had one basic flaw—he loved to make really, really big noises! Hey, let's face it: As kids, we would all have rather thrown a cherry bomb instead of a tiny little firecracker. On one particular occasion, he "misjudged" the required quantity of explosives and almost put the first teak tree into orbit. The same launch almost showed the battalion commander and his helicopter crew what the surface of Vietnam really looked like from ground level.

We had been in the mountains for over two weeks and were going to have a hot meal brought out to us. The CO told LT to open a clearing to be used for a Log Bird[41] that night, as well the choppers that would extract us the next day. He nodded his usual affirmation to the CO, did his usual survey of the area, and we began the preparations. Because we would be leaving the next morning, LT figured there was no sense in bringing back any of the "stale" plastique explosives we had been carrying for two weeks, so he wanted to go out with a really big bang. We cut notches with machetes into the rock-hard tree with great difficulty. A half-pound of the C-4 explosive was packed into each of the many notches made about eighteen to twenty-four inches above the ground. The tree's enormous

---

41   Log Bird –a helicopter, typically a Huey, carrying supplies or cargo, logistics

circumference and the explosives were wrapped with det cord, an explosive detonating fuse that looks like your typical, every day, white plastic clothesline. After the blasting caps were inserted and the ignition system prepared, LT was ready for his really big noise. Warning the rest of the company that the tree was ready to blow, LT yelled, "Fire in the hole!" that was repeated a number of times by other guys. Then he looked around to make sure everyone had taken cover and gave the order to light the fuse.

The ensuing explosion was so loud, Charlie must have thought we had started using nuclear weapons. We at ground zero thought we were being honored with bags of confetti thrown out of tall buildings at a parade, when in fact we were being showered with a gazillion wood chips, leaves, chunks of vines, and branches as the tree was launched almost straight up but with just enough angle that it would fall where LT said it would. From the air, the battalion commander was shaken by the shock waves of the blast and probably also sprayed with wood-chip debris from the launch site. As everyone on the ground ran around holding their ears and looking for a safe place to dive for protection from the fallout, the immense tree crashed down to earth, dragging miles of vines and raining tons of leaves over everything. And just like that, we had our landing site. The BC, of course, went ballistic too. He demanded to know who did it and proceeded to chew out LT, finishing with, "What the hell were you thinking ?!" We just loved Tim[42] because he was one of us.

---

42   Tim Pasquarelli did in fact become an infantry company commander. Afterward, he returned to the states, became a helicopter pilot, and returned to Vietnam for two more tours.

Photo Tim Pasquarelli
Tim Pasquarelli showing holes in his Huey

Chapter IV
The Wild Kingdom

Over the years people often asked about the types of animals we experienced in Vietnam. "Did you ever see any lions, or tigers and bears?" Now how can you answer that with a straight face? Anyway, some guys claimed to have heard the guttural roars of big cats prowling at night in the A Shau Valley. I've read about two tigers killed farther south where flatter jungle terrain was more prevalent. No one could doubt them, of course, because most of the areas we patrolled were so remote and wild that the dense jungle could easily have sustained extended families of extinct beasts with no overlapping territories.

Most of the critters we encountered were harmless by comparison—small deer, mongoose, snakes. And let me not forget to mention insects and crawly things of truly monstrous proportions. Without exaggeration, many of them could have been used in the post-atomic-bomb-era horror movie genre of the 1950s. As an example, a few wigglers instantly come to mind. Late one evening somewhere in the boonies along a streambank, we were digging in for the night, and I unearthed some worms. Now, if I were to have been going fishing at the time, and had an empty one-pound coffee can to put worms in, like we used to do as kids, I could have filled the whole thing with just three or four of the mutants: a foot long and thicker than my thumb. At least I think they were worms because they didn't have eyes. And on another occasion, after waking one foggy morning, I was shocked to see an enormous beetle trying to copulate with my helmet. Maybe it was the noise or the vibrations from M-16 rounds bouncing off his armor plating and my steel pot, but he eventually got the hint and crawled off. He was frustrated, I'm sure, and slightly dented in a couple of spots, but at least I got my helmet back. God were there big bugs over there.

So, even though we knew most of nature's inhabitants in the western mountains of Vietnam weren't life threatening, doesn't mean they didn't bother us at times. On the contrary, it usually scared the hell out of someone not expecting one of their surprise visits. Knowing that these monsters lurked in the bush was almost as bad as knowing Charlie did. One crystal-clear memory comes to mind is when we were on one of our mountain hiking expeditions. Our entire company was almost paralyzed for half a day after Big Joe stared into the dark, piercing eyes of the unimaginable. It happened one eerie morning in July of 1968.

Name That Tine

We were again going to look for trouble in the mountains far to the west of Camp Evans. Two guys sat in each door opening of the lead Huey, and from time to time each of us glancing over at one of the two gunships that flanked our formation. I don't know if it was interest, curiosity, or just to fill the little boy in all of us with excitement, but it passed the time. Both modified Hueys were there to prep the LZ with miniguns and rockets, and hopefully to be around quickly later if needed. A little farther back and flying slightly to the side of us was another slick with the rest of our squad. Behind them were two more slicks. You couldn't help but shake your head in wonderment looking back at the other guys just looking around in every direction as if they didn't have a care in the world, even though in a short time they'd be soldiers again going into the unknown. Completely relaxed and swinging their feet back and forth as though sitting on a split-rail fence back home and watching the sun rise.

There was room for three guys to sit in the open doorway: directly behind the copilot, holding onto the doorframe; in the middle, sitting back, feet inside the bird and holding onto anything within reach just in case; and next to the door gunner, where there was no need to hold on because the wind kept your shoulder pinned against the open bulkhead. I guess guys had their preferences. The cool air rushing past at about ninety knots against dangling legs made the baggy cargo pockets on our trousers flap in the wind. For whomever chose to sit behind the copilot's seat, the buffeting air movements would slowly slide them on the worn-down steel floor away from the doorframe. If or when that happened, they had to readjust their seating arrangement from time to time, scooching their butt over while pulling themselves toward the front of the chopper until their shoulder was once again tight to the doorframe, just to make sure they remained in the chopper with the other guys. I preferred sitting against the doorframe next to the door gunner. The downside of that position was having your hearing assaulted when the door gunner started prepping the LZ just before the bird landed. From our vantage point on the floor, we could watch a gunship rise and fall at the same rate as our Huey. Any significant changes in the air temperature or density made the choppers look and feel as if they were a boat trolling on gentle one-to-three-foot ocean waves. At other times they bounced like they were hitting a city pothole.

To pass the time, we'd typically search the ground for potential trouble and/or admire the lush scenery below as it streaked past. As the miles floated by, I was always grateful for the increasing warmth provided by the rising sun's rays. Just that little bit of direct sunlight washing across my face and chest was enough to slowly take away the chill from flying at three thousand feet in an open doorway. This particular mission happened to be my first since returning from a one-week R and R spent with my wife, and the fresh memories were making it a little difficult to maintain any prolonged concentration. I closed my eyes, feeling the warmth of the sun, and imagined myself back on the beautiful white sandy beach of the Royal Hawaiian Hotel in Honolulu, smelling the air that had just been filtered across thousands of miles of open ocean. Long, yellowish green palm fronds swayed above me while I leaned against its trunk, watching the unmistakable triangles of a far-off sailboat. Rolling my head slightly, I could see the silhouette of my wife approaching with a tall drink in her right hand, an orange slice draped from its rim. She appeared to be pointing up with her left hand and saying something. I squinted into the bright sunlight, straining to hear her over the sounds of the breaking waves, but by the time I understood, it was too late. "Bano!" *What the...?*

Jackie, sitting on the bench seat that overlooked my position on the floor, shook me from my daydream by banging the M-60 gun barrel on my helmet to get my attention. Who could hear anything over the roar of the Huey's noisy engine and rotor blades spanking the air? Apparently, I had dozed off and was leaning back against his legs, which guys typically don't do to each other. He was banging on my head because of either his ingrained Texas homophobia or more likely because I was keeping him awake.

As the first wave of four Hueys flew on, the strengthening sun continued to stay in our eyes. It meant that this particular operation was going to be farther to the north, an area we had never patrolled. The terrain, though mountainous and severe, was somehow different from all other areas we had searched in the past. Going into unknown territory was not our idea of a good start to the day. Besides, it was always a little unsettling to be in the first wave of helicopters to reach a two-ship landing zone. The inserted lead elements of the company would instantly head for the cover of tall grass or trees away from the LZ and set up a small defensive perimeter. It was a nervous time because we could only wait, undermanned, while the second pair of Hueys with the rest of our platoon could be inserted, all the while hoping Charlie wasn't too nearby. When we felt our slick slowing down and dropping lower, we knew we were probably about two kilometers or so away from our LZ. At that point everyone typically changed from admiring the scenery to studying it. This unknown area would be our home for the next two weeks.

Fortunately, after the gunships sprayed the area with miniguns and rockets, they circled the LZ, and everything appeared quiet that morning. Much to everyone's relief, our final destination was not "hot." The air assault seemed to be going as smoothly as could be expected, though we were somewhat surprised to find the landing zone large enough to bring in two helicopters at a time. Not only was that different from what we had become accustomed to, but we would be landing on a flat plain of tall grass at the foot of a mountain rather than our typical landing at the top of a ridge. One is never comfortable with change of the status quo, but it's even worse when people want to shoot at you.

As the helicopter prepared to land, those of us in the doorways cautiously slid out from our seated positions on the floor. With weapons at the ready in one hand, and holding onto a doorjamb or a metal seat leg with the other, we dropped down to a standing position on the helicopter's skids. Moments after the big bird flared its nose up to land and we sensed its forward motion almost stop, we were off the skids and running for cover before the Huey had even touched down. In a matter of seconds, the remaining guys occupying the canvas seats were up and out as well, allowing the helicopter pilot to quickly tilt the tail section up and gain speed as it angled away from the LZ. Very fast. Very efficient, the way the pilots liked it. A helicopter sitting on the ground was a juicy target for Charlie.

Everyone knew where to go to form the perimeter because all landings were choreographed beforehand: Guys on the first Huey covered the twelve o'clock-to-three-o'clock firing positions, second bird covered three to six, and so forth. Looking around through the swaying grass for any signs of danger, I noticed the trees on the mountain's sides appeared neither as tall nor as close together as in other parts of the mountain range we had previously traversed. And oddly, the undergrowth appeared less dense, which, gratefully, offered us unimpeded sight lines for fifty yards or so to our flanks. Those two natural terrain and vegetation features gave me hope that while patrolling this new area of operations for the next two weeks, we might actually be able to see the sky every now and then instead of the perpetual low light of a triple-canopy jungle.

The surroundings, though tranquil, emanated an all-too-familiar eerie feeling that many old-timers sensed when something wasn't right. The terrain was just too nice not to be inhabited or traveled. We studied every bush and tree for any signs of movement while waiting for the rest of the company, hoping we were just jumpy because we had been lazing around for the past three days. But that wasn't the case, and right from the beginning of the operation, many of us had the feeling of not being alone but of being watched. After the choppers returned with the other platoons, we started to form the column of march for the day. Our platoon would have the point, and we reluctantly left our defensive position, walking past old friends in other platoons who were assembling before we could start to head up the mountainside. Quite a few guys, more

BULLETS IN MY BOTTOM DRAWER

than the usual suspects, mentioned having a strange feeling about the place.

"Go extra slow today, man," one guy said as his eyes darted left and right.

"I don't want to hit the shit today, Ski, so keep a good eye out" came a solemn request from a platoon sergeant to our point man.

"Somethin' jus' ain't right here" offered a perplexed veteran who had survived many bad days, adding, "I'm too short for this, man."

Our squad had the lead for the company that day, with Bob Jablonski walking point. Bob, "Ski" for short, had been drafted out of a college in New Jersey and had a real easy manner to him, always smiling or laughing. Following Ski was Ed White, who hailed from Oklahoma. Eddie was a nice, friendly type built about like me, had short blond hair, and spoke in very slow, deliberate sentences. "Okie," as we naturally called him, left no doubt in anyone's mind that he was there to do his patriotic duty to the best of his ability, then get home in one piece to his wife and family. Although Ski wasn't a gung-ho type, he would often volunteer for tough assignments so married guys like Okie and me would not have to face unneeded dangers. Totally selfless. That often led to some very interesting discussions, because Okie and I argued that we were there to pull our own weight and didn't want anyone getting messed up because of us. Following them was Big Joe, who at that time was the acting squad leader, followed by me as the squad's RTO carrying the PRC-25 communication radio. The rest of the squad and company were spread out single file down the mountain behind us.

Joe and I had moved up in the formation and were walking very close to the front because of what we felt

rather than saw, a sense recognized only through experience and one that was most always correct. Oddly
though, the feeling many of us had was somehow different from the other "normal" times when the hair on
our necks stood on end. It's complicated to explain a
feeling, but what we all sensed was a strange *atmosphere*.
Not necessarily one of impending danger but just eerie,
like the supernatural, goose-bump-type stuff. Like how
you might feel being alone at the edge of an old cemetery on a dark foggy night, walking under huge old
trees with long human-shaped strands of Spanish moss
hanging from their bent and twisted limbs. You swear
you can hear or feel footsteps behind you, and low guttural sounds of moaning coming from a different direction...that kind of eerie.

The author with his CAR-15

It appeared as if we were walking up a very old, well-worn, narrow trail having a lot of exposed tree roots, some high enough for a foot to slide under. Big Joe and I reasoned with Ski and Okie that based on the amount of exposed stone, it might just be a depression cut into the hard rock and soil after years of heavy seasonal rains. Or it could be a well-used trail, but we weren't certain. There were no tire tread marks from Ho Chi Minh sandals. There were other such depressions on both sides within eye sight. There were no signs that it had been used recently, but we intended to stay alert. I wasn't sure if Ski bought our theory, because we couldn't even convince ourselves. The higher we climbed, the more the trail narrowed, allowing shrubs and tall grasses to lean in closer. Between that and the tree canopy getting denser, our surroundings grew darker. It all added up to everyone feeling more uncomfortable. After a nerve-racking hour climb, the CO ordered a halt. He wanted everyone to check for ground leeches. There were some reported.

We hated those disgusting things and wanted to make sure we weren't wearing any either. Now, for leech examinations, we would go through a routine that was meant to insure we were clean. Step number one was to first check our own arms and legs, then help other guys near us to make sure they didn't have any on them that they couldn't see. If just one leech was found, it urgently called for immediate steps two through five.

Ground leeches are really weird creatures. Unlike their slimy-looking, dark-skinned, arrowhead-shaped cousins who live in water, ground leeches look more like skinny, gray-brown, hairless caterpillars. Think one-inch broken twig. That is, they look that way until filled with blood, at which point they begin to resemble their aquatic cousins. They start out looking like half a Q-tip but end up about the size of a man's middle finger. We'd rarely see the little bastards because their camouflaged bodies blended so well with the dirt. That and the fact that most of our visual concentration was directed at any signs of movement in the foliage surrounding us. While we walked and searched for Charlie, leeches searched for us by picking up vibrations from our footsteps. Once their targets were located, they would crawl like hell, inching forward in their odd head-to-toe movement seemingly as fast as we were walking. Their attack looked like a herd of dismembered human pinkies flexing open and closed as they dashed from their cover of rotted leaves to the barren trail.

Once they caught up and hitched a ride on a mobile GI restaurant, they'd immediately crawl to an unprotected area. Once a leech reached bare skin, it could either attach itself immediately or crawl to a spot more to its liking. Then, having found an area with the appropriate ambiance, it would dine in uninterrupted comfort until completely bloated with blood. The worst part of a leech attack, as far as we were concerned, was that the anatomical areas leeches preferred most were the armpits or crotch. So sharp was their "bite" that we wouldn't know if we had any on us unless a complete physical exam was performed right then and there. That fact certainly explains the urgency of steps two through five. When someone in the company announced having a leech in a sensitive area, everyone would immediately jump into action, telling new kids what to do if necessary.

Step one, again, was the quick visual inspection of our own exposed skin, followed immediately by step two, which was to light a cigarette. Step three had everyone swearing and stripping as fast as they could to prevent the filthy things from penetrating any "delicate" areas. As our urgency grew, step four called for very accurate poking of the little bastards with the business end of a burning cigarette. That usually got them off our bodies or anyone who was nearby and needed help. Step five was to check our clothes and quickly get dressed—rolling pants down to boots and tying them off, rolling sleeves down to the wrists, buttoning them and our shirts up to the neck. We then pulled up our collars and were acutely attuned to any odd feelings, anywhere on our bodies, for the rest of the day.

Being attacked by leeches was not funny, but it was always good for a few laughs, nonetheless. Imagine what would be running through someone's mind if they had been camping alongside the trail and saw a column of heavily armed men slinking silently through the jungle. They all suddenly stop, strip off their clothes, and start spinning around naked, sticking each other with lit cigarettes. Who ever said war wasn't romantic?

Operations in unfamiliar territories always had us a little neurotic, and we felt from the start that this one was surely going to be a strange journey, and thus far it was. We must have climbed higher than the leeches' territory, because intermittent body searches found no more hitchhikers. Yet as unnecessary as the examinations were, everyone was sure they still had at least one in hiding. Every drop of sweat that trickled down an overheated body caused by climbing with buttoned-up and tied-down clothes and flak vests felt like something crawling. Every once in a while, when I looked down the trail behind us checking spacing intervals, I'd notice someone drop out of formation, drop his pants, and bend over. I couldn't hear what was being said, but I had a pretty good idea, having been there myself. He was probably pleading over his shoulder to the guy behind him in hushed whispers, "I know dare's one of dem bastids on me! Can ya see it? Whadda ya mean no? I can feel it, dammit! Look closer!" To which his companion would reply, "What the hell do I look like, a fucking proctologist? Pull your pants up and keep moving!" Lord, what we wouldn't do back then to help a brother grunt!

After another forty-five minutes or so on the trail, Ski and Eddie started finding old signs of human activity and called Big Joe forward to check them out. Where the trail ascended rather steeply and made an abrupt left turn, Ski had found an old "Himalayan gate" that had probably sprung years earlier due to its age. The primitive antipersonnel device was made by lashing a sapling ten feet long or so between two closely growing trees and positioning it horizontal to and a few feet above the ground. The sapling was then bent back like a bow until parallel with the trail and held in that position by a triggering device. When sprung, it would snap back into its original straight position. Usually the booby trap was rigged to be sprung by an unsuspecting soldier who stepped on or released a trip wire. The sapling would then snap back across the trail about waist high and impale its victim on sharply pointed sticks tied along its length. Very crude but effective. A booby trap of that type was completely unheard of in the areas where we operated simply because Charlie used the trails more often than we did. In fact, booby traps of any kind were very rare for the troops who operated in NVA territory, thank God. The guys working in other areas of Vietnam were not so fortunate.

Joe had me radio our platoon leader and alert the rest of the company to what we had found, and that everyone should keep their eyes peeled. Once notified of the findings, Lieutenant Pasquarelli ordered us to clearly mark any traps found in order to alert the rest of the company on their way up. We continued looking in the immediate area while LT and the CO made their way up to our position for a firsthand look. After arriving and examining our findings, they discussed the situation at hand and notified the battalion commander flying above the operation. The CO also explained that because of the increased danger posed by the booby traps, we would proceed at a slower pace, using extreme caution.

Besides the sprung gate, its deadly release frozen in a half-bent position, the sides of the trail were pocked with small punji[43] pits just large enough for a single foot. Much of the grass and leaves, originally placed atop twigs crisscrossed over the holes for camouflage, had dried and blown away. The debris that remained sagged into the traps, revealing a slight depression that easily exposed their locations. Closer examination of the pits revealed some that contained a very old rifle cartridge positioned upright above the point of a nail. The makeshift firing pin had been driven through a piece of wood and carefully placed in the bottom of the hole. Had someone stepped on the trap, he would have caused the bullet to fire through his boot sole. The crippling devices had probably been put there decades earlier, still waiting for some unsuspecting Frenchman.

---

43   Punji stick or stake—Used for booby traps, punji's are wood or bamboo sticks that are sharpened, heated, and most typically placed upright in a camouflaged hole.

We continued to find other threatening devices in the immediate area, fortunately with no casualties. The placement of the traps and the surrounding terrain at the bend in the trail suggested the location had once been a planned ambush site. It's human nature that when the first rounds were fired, the natural tendency is to jump off the exposed trail into the safety and cover provided by tree trunks and vegetation. Had that happened, many guys would have met almost certain injury. As well planned and executed as the ambush site had been years earlier, it now appeared completely out of place and somewhat surreal. We knew what it was intended for, and the horrifying results the booby traps could cause. Yet, as strange as it may seem, the area looked more like one of our training exercises back in the states. The traps were too obvious and exposed.

The overall effect of our surroundings, coupled with uncommon leeches and unexpected ancient booby traps, validated what we sensed hours earlier and the eerie atmosphere around everyone. When we started to climb again, everyone was much more alert then when we had first started the patrol. No one said a word, coughed, smoked, or stepped on a branch. I remember thinking, *Gee, we only have thirteen more days of this!*

We continued slowly up the winding trail, scanning for any signs of movement, as well as trip wires or booby traps. Oddly, as the elevation increased, so did the plant growth. Each step forward exposed us to even denser vegetation, reducing our visibility to less than twenty yards to either side. As the jungle closed in on us, so too did the trail. It had started out at the bottom of the mountain sufficiently wide where five people could comfortably walk together side by side if they so choose. We had reached a point where it now approached the size of a single-file path. Sometimes just a space to squeeze through.

The birds must have sensed something in the air too, because they stopped chirping and calling out to each other. Rather than hop and flit about, as was so often the case, they held their positions on the high branches that had started to block out the sky over-head. Each complication encountered continued to increase our anxiety. There was no doubt in my mind that the new territory had us all spooked, but we pushed on. Occasionally, Joe turned around to check the interval between us, and I could see his eyebrows furrowed as if he were confused or in deep thought. On one such occasion, he looked at me with the same concern and quickly cocked his head off to his right. I realized then that he might have heard something and was trying to listen to the silence around us. I wasn't sure if we were just letting our imaginations get the better of us or if it was just a coincidence, but I started to *feel* a presence too, as if being watched.

Trusting instincts and working methodically to insure the trail was clear, Ski had slowed the company's pace even more by being extremely cautious and deliberate. Sharp turns in the trail, and the spacing we tried to maintain between us, caused me to lose sight of the three guys from time to time, making me feel even more vulnerable. I could no longer see Ski at the front. From time to time, I would hear our company platoon leaders alerting their squads over the radio to be careful with their spacing. It was obvious the whole column was having the same problem with visual contact. We continued at the same pace, nonetheless, being careful not to make any sounds or bend any foliage at the sides of the trail.

As we continued through the shrinking surroundings, we automatically started to lower our bodies into
a crouching stance. At a turn in the trail where I could
no longer see Ski, I saw Eddie and Joe stop and slowly
drop to a knee, signaling me to do the same. The signal
instantly started my heart pounding as I too immediately passed the message back, dropping down and using my own hand to signal those directly behind me. I
watched Joe slowly turning his head from side to side,
cocking it slightly as if he were listening to something
and trying to pinpoint the location of the sound. From
what I could see, he was obviously in contact with both
guys, who were probably signaling something back to
him. With a "stop" motion of his hand, telling me to
stay where I was, Joe dropped down and crawled out of
sight up the trail and around a bend.

I had waited along with the entire column for almost five minutes when the CO radioed down the
chain of command to find out what was holding us up.
I informed LT of our status, telling him our point man
had stopped because of some noise up ahead, and that
Two-Three, our squad leader, had gone to investigate.
I followed that by saying I'd contact him when I had
more information. Waiting for another few nerve-racking minutes without any sign of either one of them had
the same effect on me as it did on Lieutenant Pasquarelli, who again radioed and asked what was happening.
As he was ordering me forward to get them moving,
Joe came back into view while crawling downhill toward me. I too dropped onto the moist soil and began
to move forward to cut the time and distance in half.
Once together, I told him the CO and LT were getting
antsy and wanted us to start moving. I then asked
what he wanted me to tell them, and Joe whispered,

"Ski heard something off to our right, but by the time I got to him, the noise stopped. Then I heard it, but it stopped again. Something or somebody is shadowing us just off the trail." Joe frowned, rolled his eyes, and took the handset from my sweaty palm.

"County Line Two-Six, this is Two-Three, over," Joe whispered, almost leaning on my shoulder.

"This is Two-Six. What's the holdup, over?" came LT's instant response.

"Two-Six, my number one and I heard movement from our Romeo. Do we have any friendlies in the area, over?"

"Wait one, Two-Three." We could hear Lieutenant Pasquarelli radio the company commander, "County Line Six, this is Two-Six, did you copy that, over?"

"Ah, roger that, Two-Six, we're checking for friendlies now, over." The CO must have already begun the calls on another radio tuned to a different frequency. Though he had been briefed otherwise before the operation began, he would still ask if there were supposed to be any other "friendly" troops or civilians near us. Friendly fire was just as deadly as enemy fire. The last thing another unit or we'd want to do would be to call in an artillery fire mission on the wrong soldiers. While Joe and I waited for the response, Ski and Ed crawled back into sight to where Joe had originally been. By their looks, it was obvious they didn't want to be out of our sight for too long. Captain Taylor got back to us after a few minutes and gave us an answer we didn't feel too comfortable with.

"Line Two-Six, Line Six. Cold Steel informs me we have ARVNs in the area, but they shouldn't be anywhere near us. Get your number one to proceed with caution. Six, out."

"Wilco, Six. Two-Three, this is Two-Six. Did you copy that, over?" LT asked Joe.

I was holding the handset again and responded using my call sign. "Two-Six, Two-Three India. Copy that. We are moving ahead with caution, out."

Joe stared at me while I relayed the message, after which I filled him in on the "friendlies" situation. We both had the same look of confused surprise on our faces, mouths twisted, shoulders shrugged, and eyebrows up. We agreed with each other that if there were friendlies in the form of ARVNs,[44] and they fired first, we owed them a good return volley. During February we had had to put ourselves in real danger to clear one of their villages because their own militiamen would not go in to do it themselves. Of course, we hoped we wouldn't hear *any* firing that day.

Ski and Ed had been looking around, listening, a little spooked, but showed no signs of alarm. When Joe asked them if he heard anything by holding both his palms up and shrugging, Ski replied by shaking his head no. Joe then got up slowly and walked up to Ski to relay the CO's message and Lieutenant Pasquarelli's order. Just like that, we were on the move again, jumpier than we were before, but moving. I watched Joe, Ed and Ski appear and disappear from view. As the trail continued up, the twists and turns became more frequent and even more abrupt. Every five minutes or so, Joe would again drop to his knee and signal a halt. Time and again the column stopped, each time heightening everyone's anxiety. Two-Six always asked what was going on, and I always whispered the same response: "We have movement ahead. Checking it. Out."

---

44   ARVN—Army of the Republic of Vietnam; the South Vietnamese Army.

After twenty minutes of mounting stress from the stop-and-go, I was stopped once again on a bend where I could see none of them in front of me. Naturally I was surprised and anxious when Ski crawled into view and back to me with no sign of Joe. He was definitely spooked at something up ahead and said, almost apologetically, "Bano, Joe wants you up there with him and Eddie. He thinks he just saw some movement and wants the radio closer—you know, in case he has to call in an air strike or something." We always seemed to crack a joke at times like those just to ease the tension, sort of take the messenger off the hook for bringing bad news.

I informed LT of what was happening and said that I would contact him as soon as I reached Two-Three's position. Before low-crawling up and around the bend to find Joe, I told Ski to make sure my antenna was tucked down into the rucksack frame. That was something we always did because there was no sense in advertising or waving a target when it wasn't necessary. Assured by Ski that it was okay, I slithered as quietly as I could, hoping the pounding of my heart would not give my position away to Charlie or any leeches that might be in the area. I rounded a bend in the trail in little time and could see Joe from his shins down. He had positioned himself behind bushes at the side of the trail with his 16 pointed at something. He either heard my heart or was getting nervous out there, because he started to slide backward instead of waiting for me to reach him.

"What the hell's going on?" I asked. "Ski looks like he just saw Ho Chi Minh." Joe looked more curious than scared, which was not at all surprising to me. I mean, this is a guy who came back to the field two weeks after being shot through the left shoulder and pulled a bunch of wounded guys to safety near Hue. When we asked him why he came back to the field so soon, he just shrugged, rotated his left arm a couple of times in a big circle, and said, "It's a little stiff, but there's a lot of other guys who needed a hospital bed more than me."

Joe said he thought he saw something moving about fifty yards ahead of us, and Eddie heard something. Apparently, the trail opened up ahead where the area had been bombed in the past. He added that it was completely cleared of trees and vegetation from an air strike, so he had a clear view. I asked him what he saw and if it could have been friendlies, but he said all he got was a glimpse of movement from inside the rim of a bomb crater. I knew why Ski was spooked. It is the unknown that terrorizes the mind. He would have been less alarmed if he had actually seen NVA soldiers. At least then he would have felt in control of the situation and had some say about his own future.

I stayed behind the brush and radioed LT with a status report. "Line Two-Six, this is Two-Three India, over," I said, my voice barely audible. When his response came back, I almost jumped out of my skin because it was incredibly loud in my ear.

"Two-Three India, this is Two-Six. What have you got, over?"

The first thing I wanted to tell him was to keep his voice down but realized it was loud because I was mashing the handset into my ear, afraid that some of the sounds would leak out. "Two-Six, Two-Three India. Two-Three and number one have definite sound and movement ahead. I say again, definite movement. I am near his position now in case we need support. He's gone ahead for a better view. Please advise, over."

Knowing that Joe and I were seasoned veterans, he knew it had to be serious for us to even consider an air strike or artillery. I listened to LT and the CO talking back and forth, discussing the situation, when after a very long minute, LT responded, "Two-Three India, this is Two-Six." I noticed his voice was a little softer and hushed this time. "Six wants clear identification and count. Can you comply, over?"

"Wait one, Two-Six." I knew we had their attention now.

I crawled up and told Joe what was wanted. He nodded and crawled a few more feet forward again. I waited a few minutes, staring at the bottoms of his well-worn boots, until finally he slid back. By the amount of time he spent staring straight ahead, I figured he was having trouble counting that high, that we had indeed run into real trouble, not friendlies like the best-case scenario hoped for. After what seemed like an eternity, he turned back to face me, and his expression had not changed at all. He wore a curious, confused look, as if he were trying to understand the theory of relativity. I was about to go nuts waiting for him to say something, anything, because I was struggling with my own mind creating possible scenarios—vacillating between having a horrible firefight such as in Hue or being attacked by a berserk tiger. I finally punched Joe in the arm and asked him what he saw. Still whispering, without any change of expression, he said, "I think it's a moose."

It was like I'd gotten hit with a cattle prod. Oh no, no. I couldn't believe what I had just heard, so I asked him again, "What did you see, Joe?"

"I think it's a moose," he answered again in a flat tone as if sure.

"Joe, there aren't any moose in Vietnam. In fact, I don't think there are any moose in Asia!" I couldn't believe I was lying in a cold sweat one moment and then discussing the probable existence of moose in a tropical jungle! "Joe, maybe you saw a deer or some branches moving."

With a straight though insulted look, he assured me, "I saw moose in Alaska, and that was a moose!"

Now, I had never been to Alaska, but I had been reading *Outdoor Life*, *Field and Stream*, *Sports Afield*, *American Rifleman*, and every other hunting magazine my father would buy for as long as I could remember. With LT whispering on the radio for a response and not hearing any, he notified the CO that he had lost all contact with his lead element. I knew I had to stop the nature debate immediately and calm down the brass before all hell broke loose.

"Two-Six, this is Two-Three India," I said, trying to sound like we were in control of the situation. "Two-Three has confirmed movement but is unsure of number and identity. He has gone for closer look. Wait one, over." I immediately jumped back into the debate. "Joe, are you sure you saw a moose? Did it have palmated antlers like this?" I asked, holding my free hand on my helmet with my fingers spread out. He looked at the display carefully, and after studying it for about twenty seconds, his eyes got large like he had just remembered something important and said, "Yeah, just like that. It was a moose all right!"

Tim Pasquarelli, John Taylor, the author

I couldn't believe it and didn't really feel we were in a position to discuss it much longer. I got straight to the point and asked him, "Joe, is that what you want me to tell LT?"

"Well, I think it was a moose," he answered, not so positive anymore, adding, "Come on up there with me and check it out for yourself."

"Okay, as long as you're positive it isn't any bad guys. By the way, did it have a big rack?" As soon as I asked, I knew it was a stupid question, Alaska service or not. I mean, I loved the big guy, but he was an inner-city kid from Philadelphia. How could he know what a rack was if he couldn't even identify a moose?

"Uh, yeah. It had a big rack," he assured me.

I decided to radio LT and tell him what was going on as I crawled just behind Joe for a personal view. Because of a few nights in the past when LT, Okie, and I had sat around swapping hunting stories, bragging about how hard it was to hunt in our home states, I at least knew LT was somewhat aware of animal populations and habitats. I also knew Pasquarelli was going to go ballistic from the call, especially after being uptight about his platoon holding up the company and causing unneeded tension. I thought I had better hold the handset a couple of inches away from my ear, just in case, before I told him what Joe had seen.

"Line Two-Six, this is Two-Three India. Be advised, Two-Three has positive ID on noise and movement. It is a single moose." I just had to pause. "I say again, one moose. Going up to verify myself, over."

I stayed next to Joe, positioning the handset and myself so he could hear the reply himself. There was a long pause on the other end, then a simple, nonmilitary, yelling whisper from LT, "A what? There are no goddamn moose in Vietnam! What the hell is going on up there?"

"I knew it. I told you, Joe. It can't be a moose," I chided him, grinning from ear to ear because we were still whispering as if an enemy battalion were waiting for us around the corner. "Come on, show me where it was."

As we started forward, Joe sheepishly said, "Well, it looked like a moose to me."

We continued discussing the anatomical differences between various members of the deer family until reaching the area where Joe had seen the moose, when a thought crossed my mind. Still grinning, I called LT and asked, "Line Two-Six, Two-Three India. If it's a moose, can I have the antlers?"

You would think I was asking him for a date with his sister the way he started screaming. "You can carry that goddamn rack all over stinkin' Vietnam for all I care! Now get this column moving, *now!*"

I had heard all I needed to and calmly replied with a slow, deliberate drawl, doing my best impersonation of a southern pilot, "Ah, roger that, Line Two-Six. This is County Line Two-Three India, out!"

Joe, Eddie and I got to the spot where he had seen the moose, but there was nothing in sight. We visually scanned the clearing and as far into the underbrush as we could. All the while, Joe was swearing that there had been a moose there before. Fortunately for Joe and Ed, they could at least verify they had heard and seen movement that might save them a little embarrassment later. We didn't want to wait too much longer looking for the phantom moose, because LT had sounded as if he were ready to run up the mountain and bayonet the two of us. I looked where Joe thought he had seen movement last for a little closer examination.

Cautiously, I made my way from the cover of the trail to the open area that was indeed pretty chewed up from a previous air strike. After a brief search, lo and behold, I found tiny little hoof prints in the mud next to where water had collected in the bomb crater. We went down into the crater, where I got down on one knee to examine the tracks. I thought it was a good time to explain to Joe the difference in the size and depth of a moose track compared with this track, so I moved a foot away and stomped my boot heel into the mud four or five times and shaped the depression with the toe of my boot. That way, he was able to compare it to the track I was pointing at. LT suddenly appeared above us on the crater's rim, all sweaty and flushed from running up the mountain. He didn't look like a happy trooper when he stormed over the top. He said, both relieved and pissed off, but still in a cautiously low voice, "It's a good thing you found fresh tracks, or Joe was going back to Alaska for more jungle training!" Then, as two jets roared past just over treetop level, he added a little more vocally, grinning at the way we had handled the stress we had already gone through that day, "I'm moving another squad up to the point so we can make better time the rest of the day. You guys are so spooked you might start seeing Martians with ray guns!"

LT shuffled the squads and once again we were headed merrily on our way. That was really a shame, because we might have had a wonderful hot meal if we had only waited a bit longer.

Can I keep him, Dad, pleeease?

During an operation in late May, I was to find out Big Joe had come across a live but very helpless little mongoose. The last of our choppers had just dropped us off on a smoldering mountaintop, where we scrambled into the bush for cover. The noise of the four Hueys had faded into the distance, and, while kneeling behind a shattered tree stump, he said he had heard whining coming from under some debris next to his foot. Curious about the strange sound, he described pushing some shredded leaves aside with the muzzle of his 16 and discovered the little fellow. Thinking he would decide what to do with it later in the day, he scooped it up and put it in one of the billowing lower pockets of his fatigue shirt without telling anyone.

A few hours later, we stopped to take a "break for beans," as lunch was called. Usually when the order passed through the ranks, everyone simply looked where they stood for a soft, dry spot to sit on. Once a suitable location was found, we dropped down and took a can of C rations out of a pocket. Joe, on that particular occasion, took out what appeared to be a moldy piece of bread. It was at that point that he explained his discovery to a few of us around him.

The squirming ball of fur appeared to be only a few weeks old, very much alone and frightened by all of the unexpected commotion around him. The bombing and strafing runs of two US Air Force jets prepping the LZ before the assault had probably orphaned him. Like the other guys standing next to me, and forming a circle around Joe, we had a hard time believing anything could have survived the bombardment, especially something so small and fragile. It seemed to me an ironic coincidence that the mongoose was very much like all of the human males looking down at him. The war had separated him from his family and would forever change his world.

Joe, being the selfless, kindhearted person he was, decided to adopt the mongoose as his own and raise it back to health. I think from the beginning we all knew it was a bad idea, because it was hard enough to keep ourselves alive. Yet no one would argue with Joe's reasoning, both because of his logic and his bulging biceps. Besides, he had already saved more than one of us in the past. The mongoose deserved the same opportunity. We had seen so many casualties over the previous three months, so much suffering and destruction, that the mongoose sort of represented hope, maybe even a sign of a new beginning.

The possibility of the war ending seemed real to us at the time. Peace talks between all of the warring governments had been announced a month earlier while we were at Khe Sahn, and rumors naturally circulated suggesting we might get home by Christmas. Everyone could only pray that sometime during the year, we would see the end of war, and could resume our own growing up in safety. How hopeful and naive we had been. I mean, what do eighteen- and nineteen-year-olds know about politics? More than a month had already passed, and the negotiators couldn't even agree on the shape of the conference table, let alone who should be there.

After we saw the mongoose and guessed what it was, we put our heads together to figure out what should be done to take care of it. That posed a little dilemma, because most us were just learning how to take care of ourselves. It was finally agreed that first and foremost was to get the thing to eat, and what else would you give to a baby but milk? Right, run right down to the corner grocery store and get some. If the military had taught us anything, it was to improvise, adapt, and overcome any obstacle. We had gone without food, slept wearing only lightweight nylon shirts and pants in fifty-degree pouring rain completely exposed to the elements, and had suffered severe thirst. And so improvise we did. The C rations brought to us almost daily had a packet of powdered milk in every unit, so we had a start. We further reasoned that if we soaked small bits of meat in the milk, it just might make a nutritious brew. After all, mongoose ate snakes and stuff, so it must eat meat. If the plan worked, we would finally have a use for the B-1A unit's "green" eggs and ham. So, after only a few tries of dipping his finger into the milk and putting his dripping pinkie to the animal's mouth, surrogate Mother Joe and baby were doing fine. That meant one canteen would have to be sacrificed for the "formula."

As soon as we finished eating, we saddled up and headed out for the remainder of the day. That fact presented Joe with his next problem: transportation. He decided to make a nest that would provide the little guy with warmth, fresh air, and protection from the heavy afternoon rains we usually experienced. Starting with an empty pouch from a LRRP ration, he lined its mylar insides with toilet paper and formed a flap that could be opened or closed, depending on the weather. He then put the "house" in his left breast pocket and supported both sides so the little guy wouldn't get crushed from the pocket collapsing inward. It was a perfect nest under the circumstances. If Big Joe found any more animals, our mission might turn into a safari.

We continued the operation after lunch, always looking for Charlie or signs that he'd been in the area. The battalion commander high above us would provide the direction to the next bombed area. Once the area was reached, we would sift through the torn-up trees and plants, report our findings, and continue on to the next destination that he wanted investigated. Some areas looked like a waste of taxpayer dollars, while others had the unmistakable smell of decaying bodies. In either case, as long as we did not receive enemy fire, the day was good.

The latter situation was horrible in a number of ways. First, the smell was awful, an odor never forgotten. Second, it brought us face to face with our enemy. Going through Charlie's personal belongings for documents he might be carrying often revealed him as a human being rather than the sneaky little coward he appeared to be every time we walked into an ambush. Invariably we'd find photographs of his wife, girlfriend, mother, sister, family, children, friends, whomever. The backgrounds would show gardens, lakes, and dinner tables with smiling people. It made him human, not un-like us at all. The more we saw him in this state, and we did very often, the more human he became. Just a pawn for his political superiors to sacrifice. The more we wit-nessed death on either side, the more we lost pieces of our own selves, our ability to mourn or have pity, the very emotions that make us human beings and not low-er animals on the food chain. That little mongoose re-minded us that there was indeed hope for the future.

Big Joe cared for the critter whenever we stopped for a break, making sure it was okay, feeding it as often as possible, changing its bedding. As the days went by, the little fellow appeared to be gaining strength, growing and taking on the appearance of a real animal rather than a drowned rat. The mongoose eventually got a name and changed from a stray and orphaned animal to something very close to all of us. It was just natural to call it "Little Joe Two," and consequently, he became one of us.

Big Joe was very protective of the animal, not want-ing to see it harmed or teased in any way. When we left the field and went on our stand-down, guys from other squads would come over to hold and play with the little guy. Joe would occasionally allow it, but always under his watchful eyes, and only then for a couple of min-utes. That was okay, because after all, who could argue with a man that had sixteen-inch biceps? The bond-ing continued between Little Joe and a number of guys during our four days of rest. Others wanted no part of it.

Big Joe Kochman having fun at LZ Jack

We all started out in-country wanting to make friends with our teammates, but after a couple of fierce firefights, those "friends" could be lost forever. Try as we might, the longer we survived, the less likely we were to get too close with anyone. We could only lose so many pieces of our heart before we lost ourselves. It's been over fifty years now, and many still have trouble getting close to people, even their own children. That fear of loss can change a lot of things in a person.

By the end of our stand-down, almost three weeks had passed, and I think Joe started getting second thoughts about trying to raise a pet. As it grew, it naturally wanted to eat more, get out more to play, and explore his new world. Those things would become increasingly hard while we traveled. Joe figured we'd be on our next operation for only two weeks, and by that time Little Joe might be ready for release. If not yet ready, he would be given to the artillery guys at LZ Jack for more rearing. In any case, while waiting to saddle up and board the slicks the guys joked around with him, trying to manufacture a little rucksack and helmet for the rodent. Little Joe, the youngest member of the 1st Cavalry Division (Airmobile), was going on his first combat assault.

Everything went smoothly during the assault, and we began the operation like so many others; walking, listening, searching. At the end of the day, we climbed until reaching a new perimeter another squad had started. We were sitting around that night, like many others, groaning about all of the things "army." Food, orders, brass flying five thousand feet above us pushing hard. Your basic military bitch session. Carl, the CO's RTO, who was sitting with us, asked Joe if he could keep the mongoose during the night because he had radio watch. He reasoned that he could then leave Little Joe with the forward observer's RTO, who was to stay behind with the packs the following day. He pleaded, saying he would have the night to play with him, feed him, and even show him to the CO. Like a father about to let his son take the car keys for the first time, Joe was not too sure but reluctantly agreed. We tried to pacify him when Carl walked away with Little Joe held securely in his "mobile home." One of the guys explained that the kid came off a farm and knew how to take care of animals. Joe eventually lightened up but was still not sure he did the right thing. It was the first time in over two weeks Big Joe would be sleeping alone.

We got up just before daylight and prepared ourselves as lead squad to head down the mountain. At the last moment, a very nervous Carl went over to Joe and said, "Ah, Joe, I'm sorry, but Little Joe died during the night. After I fell asleep, I must have rolled over on him. I'm sorry, Joe. I didn't mean to do it. It just happened." The radio operator was scared to death because of his admission and probably didn't think he'd survive the morning. Joe just listened to him, and for the first and only time since I had met him five months earlier, I saw him lose his composure. He stared at the frail RTO, who kept repeating, "I'm sorry, Joe, I'm sorry. I didn't mean it. Punch me in the mouth, get it over with. Say something, at least." In the dim light of the fading moon, we could see the pain and fury on Joe's face. No one knew what to expect next as he stood gritting his teeth, hands clenched at his sides and his huge chest heaving through his open shirt. Almost spitting out the words, he finally said in disgust, "Aw, what the hell did I expect. Everything else in this damn place dies. It doesn't matter who you are. You'd think He would let some things live." Joe turned and walked towards the perimeter, away from all of us. He needed to be alone.

We could see his broad outline silhouetted against the dawning sky, head lowered and shoulders shaking. Everyone felt terrible, not only for Little Joe but for the big guy as well. Many of us felt responsible because we told him it would be okay to leave the mongoose with someone else. Carl left us and returned with the limp little body, still in its "house." There was nothing any of us could say as we watched silently when Joe buried it. We all lost a couple of more pieces of our hearts that morning.

Three Grunts and a Water Buffalo

Occasionally, the animals we met while on patrol during the month of March were not of the wild variety, but rather the domesticated type. Yet, to the young and uninitiated among us who had never traveled beyond our own "world," such as me, all animals in that mysterious land were still considered exotic creatures with unknown and potentially threatening behavior patterns. The old adage goes, "If it walks like a duck, swims like a duck, and quacks like a duck, it's probably a duck." Through many experiences during our tours of duty, we found that the adage also holds true for chickens, pigs, dogs, and cats, even though many looked different from those we had back home. We were to learn, however, that an Asian water buffalo is not a cow as we know them.

The operation had brought us to small hamlets during the aftermath of Tet. Our mission was to sweep through the area looking for the remainder of any enemy concentrations that might still be there from the offensive. We sensed that the area was somewhat secure after a few days because of the civilian population's daily activities. There was calmness in the air as they went about putting their land and possessions back in order. Overall, the mission thus far had been nice and quiet, in dramatic contrast to our earlier experiences in the same villages. Making our days even better was the broad, flat terrain drying up due to a few extended periods of pleasant weather. This time around we weren't being physically and mentally taxed by constant cold rains, wet clothes, and oozing mud. Oh, and flying bullets.

Many of the Vietnamese people we encountered were not exactly pleased to see us, because we were soldiers. It was very obvious to even naive, nonpolitically minded nineteen- and twenty-year-olds that these simple farmers just wanted to get on with rebuilding their worlds. This was especially true after the horrible devastation done during January and February by both enemy and friendly troops alike. It felt as if with every sight I absorbed, and with each step I took, I lost a little more of my innocence. I knew deep down I would never be the same person I was before I left home only few months earlier. I was becoming so much richer in experience but poorer when it came to emotions.

As we slowly walked through small clusters of thatched "houses," I reflected on the events of the past few months and realized I was now experiencing the saddest part, the actual result of any war. The civilian wants to continue his life, preferring not to get involved in political issues, but always winds up paying the biggest price—in terms of property, life, and limb. The simple peasants before me were living examples. They wanted only to be left alone to raise their crops and families in peace, without any unwanted interruptions. Yet for the older ones, over the course of their entire lives, they had already witnessed many different-looking men, wearing many different uniforms, walk into their homes and villages. They had good reason to fear anyone in a military uniform because they usually brought trouble. We were about as welcome as a frigate flying the Jolly Roger coming to the aid of a merchant ship with a broken rudder.

We continued the mission, searching each hut, hay pile, and shelter for caches of weapons or anything of military value. Doc usually checked the civilians as we passed, looking for cuts or wounds that might need to be cleaned and dressed with sterile bandages. The ever-present kids just stood there with their hands out, begging for some GI food, candy, or a surprise. Watching Doc do his thing and seeing the kids made me realize how so many not in the fight were affected. It occurred to me that during a firefight, when everything happened so fast and there was so much confusion, a grunt's own physical exposure to the pain and suffering of war was limited to just those horrible moments during enemy contact; get the wounded to a medevac, then jump back into the fray. It was the field medics, the doctors and nurses at the MASH units, who really saw the horrible results of war. So did the civilians, old and young, male and female, weak and strong, rich and poor; all of them embodied in the eyes of the kids in front of us who had never known peace. How could it not have an effect on us? Ernie Pyle, a WWII combat correspondent, wondered how anyone who survived war could "ever be cruel to anything, ever again."[45]

The hamlets in the general area looked very much the same. A few small bamboo and grass huts with dirt floors, each having one or two rooms. Occasionally

---

45   Ernie Pyle, Here is Your War, January 1944, Black Dog & Leventhal Publications

the huts were positioned opposite each other, forming a "town square." When many such hamlets were near each other, they formed a village. Many of the typical shelters had a covered "porch" created by an overhanging grass roof, supported by bamboo columns. Most had a small courtyard in front where pigs, chickens, and ducks roamed freely. Many yards were surrounded by their version of the "little white picket fence"—a two-foot-high structure, usually leaning because of the bent "fence posts," built of saplings lashed together with vines or dried reeds.

When standing in the open doorway of a hut, we would often see how dense the air was, as dirt, dust, and soot danced in the narrow shafts of sunlight passing around our bodies. The furnishings both in and out were always very simple. A few large earthen containers, like huge flowerpots, were placed in and about and used for holding water, rice, or even peanuts. Crudely hewn and assembled benches and tables were located strategically. One would support a small oil lamp to augment the light afforded by the two small windows at night. The largest table, roughly three by four feet, positioned in the center of the hut, was used for dining.

Each kitchen, located against the back wall directly opposite the usual door less entryway, sported a few blackened and battered pots and pans. Some hung from wooden pegs for convenience, while others sat on ancient wood-burning stoves. Wood bowls stacked on crude shelves served as dinnerware. Interior corners and sides of the hut were saved for the one-to-two-foot-high sleeping platforms covered with grass mats. A small burning candle beneath a crucifix was not an uncommon sight. Walls were usually barren, though an occasional calendar could be found, used primarily for its bright picture rather than scheduling or reminders. As crude as their interiors were, they were usually neat and tidy, with everything in its place.

In the small outdoor courtyard, most families tended a small vegetable garden of carrots, beans, radishes, celery, and the like. A low fence to keep out intruding pets surrounded the straight rows of carefully tilled soil. In another area of the yard was often found a stone or concrete lantern-like structure, looking like a small pagoda that served as an altar of sorts. Most showed the harsh results of the monsoon weather, with flaking white paint exposing their inner construction materials. Upon them were placed simply framed photographs of deceased relatives, sometimes encircled with the rising smoke from burning incense in honor of and respect to their memory.

I guess the richer folks in the villages also owned a domesticated Asian water buffalo to help with the heavier chores. Although the buffaloes ran on grass and had different horns, they were identical in purpose to our own John Deere and Ford tractors, and just as valuable to their owner. Much to our chagrin, the peasants kept the huge, menacing-looking beasts next to their huts in crudely made corrals of sticks and saplings. I think I know why, but it seemed all water buffaloes in Vietnam hated green, as in olive-green jungle fatigues worn by American grunts. I stood transfixed that day, watching one staring in our direction, and a very clear memory filled my thoughts.

That well-known "fact" always created tension when we were patrolling through a hamlet and came upon a water buffalo. If the monster wasn't in a corral, it was usually being led by a small Vietnamese kid of about eight or nine years old. Slightly different than a

kid the same age here walking his chihuahua with a
collar and leash. A forty-eight pound Vietnamese lad
"controlled" his two-thousand-pound pet by smacking
its rump with a small switch or twig and using a short
section of old rope tied through the beast's nose ring.

There was always tension in the air when anywhere
near the huge horns that curled out from each side of
its massive head like the handlebars on an old bicycle.
Even if the buffalo appeared to be completely passive,
it seemed the moment it saw green, or maybe it was
round eyes, it would start lowering its head and pawing
the ground as if getting ready to charge, just like their
cousins in a Spanish bullring. So just to be safe, whenever forced to move near them, we were always very
conscious of not making any sudden moves that might
provoke an attack. That is, unless the day was boring
and the guy behind you needed some "cheering up."

Before we continued our patrol that day, I thought
back to when I was a new kid during my first week in
the field. We were walking past a corral that held what
I thought was the biggest water buffalo in the world.
The damn thing looked like a garbage truck with its
doors open. For some reason I can't remember, we had
to get around its corral by turning sideways and squeez-
ing between it and a large tree. We couldn't go around
the tree because of a hut that was strategically placed
there. I'd been around cows back home, so I wasn't too
intimidated. Maybe just anxious. Wanting to be one of
the guys, I started laughing at my squad's old-timers in
front of me, breaking their chops about being tough
combat veterans afraid to wake up a sleeping cow.

Rat, the little guy from Philly, was walking in front
of me and kept telling me to shut up, explaining that
water buffaloes hated green and GIs and all that stuff.

I just laughed at him and said something about city kids being afraid of anything with four legs. As we approached the narrow passageway along the corral's side, I decided maybe discretion was the better part of valor and I should stop the taunting, just in case Rat was actually telling the truth. His turn finally came, and as he got ready to slide through the opening, never taking his eyes off the buffalo, he said in a very low voice, "New kid, if you make one noise while I go through, if I survive, I will shoot you." I think at that point I started to believe him because few guys in the squad who already passed the corral with great caution, stopped walking, and waited to help us in case of trouble.

Rat took a deep breath and started to slide between the tree and corral as quietly as possible, but the strap holding up the large bag he was carrying, bulging with shells for the grenade launcher, hung up on one of the fence rails, and shook it. While the buffalo stirred and looked around at what had caused him to wake up, Rat frantically worked the bag free and gently continued through the tight opening while holding his breath. As soon as he cleared the tree and sprinted away with the ammo bag flying straight out behind him, I started my passage, laughing at his unfounded fear because the buffalo was still in the same position.

I casually turned sideways to face the animal and began to sidestep through the opening. Though quiet, I noticed the buffalo had lowered his head and was shaking it from side to side. I assumed it was just shaking flies off its ears until it scraped the ground with a front hoof the size garbage pail lid looking as if he was actually going to charge. I figured if I just kept quiet like everyone else, I'd be okay. I probably would have, too, if Rat hadn't started yelling and beating on the fence rails with his weapon. I was immediately transformed from a cocky FNG to a rodeo clown as the buffalo snorted, bellowed, and launched itself in my direction. I almost trampled Rat and the other guys as I barreled past the end of the corral. Well, they thought it was just great, especially when I stopped and spun around with my 16 in case the "truck" was still behind me. I didn't think it too funny for them to take advantage of a new kid like that, get him killed by a rampaging locomotive. I could imagine the letter home: "Dear Mr. and Mrs. Montalbano. We are sorry to inform you that your son John has been mortally injured in the Republic of Vietnam while playing with a cow." I was glad I made the other guys laugh, maybe lifted their spirits a little that day. Yet, over the years, I often wondered if they thought I was really scared.

I came out of my daydream realizing it was now months later and I was about to pass a corral with a new guy following me. I smiled to myself, remembering that day so many months, so many bad days, so many replacements ago. Maybe I was not quite the tormentor Rat was, or maybe just not in the mood. It could have been that I just wanted to keep that experience to myself, so I passed the corral without spooking the buffalo. I did, however, explain to the new kid why he should never make any sudden noises. I looked past his shoulder at Jackie walking directly behind him and who was grinning from ear to ear, probably remembering the early days too.

Strangers in the Night

There were times when on guard duty it would be so dark, we honestly couldn't see our hand in front of our face. If you don't believe it's possible, go into a closet, at night with no lights on, and close the door behind you. That's how some people go through life. It was on just such a night that a new kid named Chris Harding almost died of fright. In fact, the entire company almost died of fright. I have to confess now that it was partially my fault.

Within sight of every village and hamlet in our area of operations were small, densely vegetated parcels of land. These dry platforms rose above the rice paddies that stretched for miles in all directions. The effect made the area look very much like our own farmland where, in the middle of hundreds of acres of plowed and cultivated land, could be seen a few acres of trees. I knew we weren't home because I was seeing dark-green swaying rice marsh grass instead of amber waves of grain.

After completing almost a full day of inspecting every hamlet or village in the immediate vicinity, and our interpreter interrogating the civilians, we headed off in the direction of another "island." We never knew if we'd find just another hamlet, action, or nothing at all. Approaching the wood line from the open paddies gave us old-timers chills, remembering our past experiences, and the guys we had known. Once we completely entered the treed area, our search continued at a much more deliberate, nerve-racking pace until we were sure the area was secure.

Fortunately our new destination revealed nothing but a couple of old concrete buildings built during Vietnam's colonial past. The day was getting late, so the CO had the lead squad keep their eyes open for a good place where the company could set up for the night. After walking all day, it was always good to hear the old cavalry order to "Circle up!" meaning our "workday" was over. We collapsed as soon as we reached our designated position, and once recharged a little, we started the daily routine of clearing the area outside our perimeter with machetes. Anything that might hide Charlie during the night was knocked down if possible—weeds, bushes, banana trees, bamboo plants. Everything out to one hundred feet.

When our packs were flown in, we started building the night perimeter in earnest. While guys were salvaging hooch poles from the cleared firing zone, others started digging a roughly three-by-six-by-four-feet-deep foxhole. We kept switching our efforts—one would dig while the other erected the shelter. Once completed, we ate dinner, then waited until almost dark so Charlie couldn't see what and where we were doing things, like the all-important final job of setting out and camouflaging the trip flares and Claymore mines, fastening trip wires between the overlapping flares, running the Claymore ignition wires to the foxholes, and carefully placing all of the Claymore trigger mechanisms, grenades, weapons, ammo, and munitions within easy reach of the foxhole. Most every position was laid out in similar fashion in case we needed to be at someone else's defensive position in the dark for whatever reason.

It was almost completely dark by the time the squad leaders walked to each of the positions under their command. Every link of our "circled wagons" was checked nightly to insure the perimeter provided the best security for the good of the company. Everyone was told the password for the night, where the overlapping firing zones were for each position to cover, the schedule and amount of guard duty each of us would have for the night, and the reminder not to shoot at anything with an M-16 unless it could be identified. If not sure, use the M-79 grenade launcher. Don't give our position away. After that was completed, the only thing left for us to do would be to blow up our air mattresses and pass out.

We took sanctuary for the night, feeling a false sense of security within the island's still confines. The atmosphere created by its dark closeness gave us comfort in knowing that our movements were cloaked by the protection of its dense cover of trees, shrubs, and vines that enveloped us. In some ways, operations in the populated areas were much better than those in the mountains far to the west. The anxiety and exhaustion were similar, but here we didn't have to force our aching muscles to carry us to the top of a mountain, dig into rock-hard dirt, and set up our perimeter.

On this particular night, we were lucky, because we could dig four-man holes instead of two-man. The work was spread out a little better, the guard duty wouldn't be as long for each of us, but the hole had to be dug larger. It also meant we had a pretty tight perimeter, probably because some of the huge trees and buildings dictated a smaller area than we would have liked. It could've meant good news or bad, though we'd never know which until the bad news was delivered, accompanied by a lot of noise. We didn't expect any trouble there because the entire countryside in that particular area seemed very quiet, and the villagers were not at all nervous—the best sign. Even though, we set up the same way every night, everywhere, regardless.

Our hole was just to the left of a massive, towering tree, its limbs spreading well over our position. The other trees in the area, though not as tall, had long reaching branches almost as wide, creating the familiar leafy canopy we had come to expect in the mountains. The only problem with canopies, besides sometimes keeping us from getting hot chow, was that they blocked out and absorbed all visible light at night. No matter how we tried to adjust our eyes, we were completely blind unless one of the very new night-vision Starlight[46] scopes was used. Silhouettes of the nearest branches and limbs could not be seen, making the area potentially very dangerous. I'm talking *really* dark.

When confronted with visual sensory deprivation, we learned to memorize positions of things and to trust our other senses, such as smell, hearing, and touch. I still make sure I know where all my stuff is at night. I can find whatever I'm looking for in pitch blackness if I have to—my shirt is on the floor next to the bed, pants next to the doorway, one sock is in the bathroom, one in the hallway, my sweater is on the kitchen chair, and so forth. Hey, you never know when you might have to run out of a house with the lights out. We learned that

---

46   Starlight scope—early generation of today's night-vision goggles used by the military.

if anything happened at night, you had better know exactly where everything is, or you could be in deep doo-doo. Seriously, it made an impression on me, because I still live by a lot of those lessons today, as I'm certain others do as well. I just can't remember where I put stuff now.

When the total darkness fell on our positions, we retired to our hooches for much-needed sleep. After what felt like only minutes had passed, I was in a deep sleep until awoken for my guard shift at two-thirty in the morning. I was awake but still in total darkness as if I had not even opened my eyes. Okie whispered he had tapped on my foot, then twisted it, then had to drag me for a few inches. I sat up on the end of my mattress, shaking the cobwebs from my head and constantly blinking to make sure my eyes were indeed opened. My ears seemed to pick up the slack left by my eyes, making the slightest mosquito sound seem like an amplified dentist drill. Experience with these conditions had taught us that to communicate with each other, we had to whisper into each other's ear, a target that neither of us could see. As if telepathic, we groped for each other simultaneously and put a hand on the other's shoulder. At least we'd located each other and, by proximity, where a head was supposed to be. Talking to each other was still not easy because we would occasionally bump heads or inadvertently "kiss" an ear. For all I knew, I was talking to the back of Okie's head, but as long as a reply came back correctly, we knew we got the point across. Assured I was alert, Okie warned me to watch out for a monkey in the big tree next to our hole.

"A monkey?!" I asked, having never seen one there.

"That's what I was told. Well, it's either a monkey or something else trying to get on the ground."

For whatever reason—curiosity, hunger, or just plain mischief—the small rodent kept climbing down the tree as if it wanted to jump off. Each guy who had been on guard before me, had been forewarned and instructed to slightly rattle a small bush at the base of the tree to scare it back up. We never liked animals roaming around our perimeter at night because they might set off a trip flare and leave a void in our defenses. I told Okie I understood his instructions, wished him a good night, and listened to him crawl off to his hooch. I could not see a thing, but I didn't hear him fall into a hole either, so I assumed he made it okay.

I groped my way to the foxhole located just four feet in front of my hooch. Once the freshly dug dirt of its inner edge could be felt, I slowly worked my way to the right end. Once in a sitting position, I hung my legs down into the hole. From where I sat, I could visualize the position in my mind as if it were daylight by recalling where the trees and bushes were when putting out the trip flares and Claymores, in relation to our hole. To insure nothing had been moved, I reached across the hole and found hand grenades lined up on the right, ready to be grabbed, armed, and thrown. A couple of feet to the left of them were the three trigger mechanisms for our Claymores. I touched each handle to make sure the safeties were up. To the left of the triggers was the grenade launcher. My 16 lay by my side. The squad radio was within easy reach and monitored throughout the night. Everything was as it should be.

Ah yes, one more thing. I leaned over a little to the right and located the branches of the small bush at the base of the tree. I checked the time on the radium dial of the watch Eddie had handed me and reviewed my mental notes on the shift's duration, whom I had to wake up and pass the warning to next. It wasn't long before I started thinking about how amazing it was and what could be "seen" when sightless. I guessed being unable to see creates a state of relaxed concentration, a greater awareness with our other senses. I could smell the environment better, the freshly turned-over dirt and surrounding vegetation that had been cutdown, could hear air movements by the slight fluttering of leaves, could differentiate the sounds of insects, someone turning over on an air mattress, something coming down the tree to my right! I snapped out of my trance and cocked my head slightly with my right ear pointing upward. As the sound got closer, I shook the first branch I could reach and heard the noise of something scrambling upward, followed by a few small pieces of debris falling onto the bush in my hand and a nearby hooch. Moments later, the rustling in the branches far above me stopped, and complete silence returned. When all was quiet again, I'd try to hear if there were any new sounds coming from our perimeter.

I stared at the radium dial of the watch that was handed off to each successive guard and placed it to my ear every thirty seconds just to make sure it was still ticking. No one ever wanted to lose more sleep than necessary. Assured it was, I again focused on the surroundings for unnatural sounds. Perimeters like this were tough because we couldn't even count stars. So, most times, thoughts of home and life would fill the lapses in concentration, and rhetorical questions came in droves. Would I survive the next one? Why did I make it through the last one? Was I a father yet? Were Donny, Mello, and the rest of the guys I went through training with okay? Would we eventually invade North Vietnam? On and on, having conversations with myself to stay awake. I'd think about what was in the last letter I read or the person who wrote it and wondered what they were doing at that very instant, almost halfway around the planet and in broad daylight. Now and then my focus was broken by the sound of small pieces of debris landing next to me. Our little game of cat and mouse, or rather grunt and monkey or more likely a mongoose searching for eggs or some other delicacy, happened a couple more times during my shift, which broke the monotonous boredom. Either I had unknowingly let the interloper get farther down the tree each time or it was getting braver before I could reach over to shake the bush.

When at last my shift was up, I had to find and wake up Chris, the FNG, for his shift. I crawled over to where his hooch was but could not remember if he was sleeping on the right or the left side, so I just reached in until I felt a foot and tapped it. Little Joe mumbled something about already pulling guard duty and nudged the new guy. I could hear someone slowly rising and sliding off their air mattress until at last I could feel a presence. With the same routine Okie and I had used, I whispered to him while he pulled his boots on. When his replies sounded relatively lucid, I told him to follow me, holding my boot heel if he had to. Because he was new to the field, I had to make sure he knew what to do in an emergency and remind him of where everything was located at the hole. It was necessary for us to do that until new guys got the routine down pat.

He followed me to the hole, where I "showed" him where everything was, asked him for the password, told him where the radio was located, and went through the call signs with him, telling him to "keep it quiet, but you can call County Line Six India, the CO's RTO, and he would answer. When he answers, you tell him, 'This is County Line Two-Three India, need a commo check. Over.' He'll tell you if he heard you. You can ask him for the time. He'll tell you. Those few seconds will help keep you awake. If you can't stay awake or have a problem, wake up the nearest guy." He kept saying okay or got it, and I reminded him of what he should do in case a trip flare went off. "Be ready! Don't panic. It just might be an animal, or maybe something fell on the trip wire. If you see someone and think it's a real attack—fire a Claymore." When he assured me he knew what was going on, where everything was, when his shift was over, who he was supposed to wake up, and where he was sleeping, I handed him the watch and said I'd see him in the morning before adding, "Stay awake and stay alert." I leaned back and turned to where my hooch was supposed to be and groped around until I felt the edges of the ponchos. Angling to the left, I crawled onto my air mattress, pulled my poncho liner over me, and prepared to sleep for the remainder of the night. My last waking thoughts were of the monkey, and did I tell the new kid about it? During my internal interrogation, I passed out.

At some time during the new kid's shift, and after nervously hearing something to his right for almost five minutes, he had prepared himself for the worst. Apparently, the monkey or mongoose or whatever decided he wanted off the tree, but instead of quietly climbing down and hopping off on the opposite side, he decided to jump onto the thing below him that had been playing with the branches all night. Imagine the little fellow's surprise when he landed on a human's shoulder and about a pound of plastique explosive detonated, fracturing the silent night with a tremendous earth-shattering roar. He was instantly deafened, and his night vision was destroyed by the intense white light. Both of them, man and beast.

The terrified new kid fell screaming into the foxhole. Horrified grunts on the whole perimeter jumped from their hooches, grabbed their helmets, and landed in foxholes, ready to start pulling a trigger. The new kid, having hit the bottom of the foxhole and having the presence of mind to get back up to see how many were attacking, was then completely blinded from looking at the white phosphorus trip flares that had been set off by the seven hundred steel ball bearings launched when the Claymore was triggered. In a split second's time, the seasoned grunts on either side of the glowing flares were pouring M-16, machine-gun, and M-79 rounds at the glowing perimeter that they assumed had been breached. All radios came to life, trying to find out what had happened and where, how many were there, did we need Artillery support, anyone down?

After less than two minutes of incredible outgoing fire, a ceasefire was ordered. Along with the instant silence came big flashing red and white spots in front of our eyes, because when the firing stopped and the trip flares burned out, we were again cast in total darkness. Everyone was half awake, half in shock, and completely sightless. In the ear-ringing silence, we could hear the new kid babbling on and on about hand-to-hand combat with a VC sapper. Coming from somewhere in the night, in the accent of a giant rooster, was someone saying in a hushed whisper, "What, Ah say what da hell wuz zat?"

What happened next was almost as bad as what had happened to cause it. The order was given to move out because of the security breach to the defensive perimeter. The entire company was to move a few hundred yards in total darkness with only our weapons and munitions, no sleeping gear. If Charlie didn't know where were, he knew now. Of course, he wouldn't know where we had gone, because he couldn't see either. As one might expect, even though you were walking behind someone with your hand on their shoulder, and someone else was behind you with their hand on your shoulder, it was very difficult in the absolute darkness. We walked, or shuffled is a better word, into or tripped over everything in our way, including trees, hooches, foxholes, buildings, and guys bent over tying their boots. Even our own trip flares that hadn't gone off on the rest of the perimeter were now being compromised as the company walked through them, again destroying any hope for some vision as we were blinded again by the fifty thousand candlepower burning for over a minute. The move was a complete disaster because we were blind and stumbling around, trying to find safety where we couldn't see. After about thirty minutes or so, everyone was ready to shoot the CO, but of course no one could see where he was. I guess he was just as frustrated and confused, because he finally called a halt. Everyone just dropped in place and continued guard duty to protect our new position.

When dawn broke, we carefully headed back to our old positions to retrieve our gear, disarm, and collect the good trip flares and Claymores, and at least have a cup of hot coffee before saddling up. The funny thing about that night was that everyone yelled at the new kid for not knowing the difference between a human and a monkey, and we had all learned a few lessons: 1) Always let the new kids have the first guard, because someone else will usually be awake to help him, 2) Disaster can happen even in a "safe" place, and 3) Don't play at night with monkeys or mongoose.

Chapter V
Dining Out

All combatants since the beginning of time would probably rank food as their third most important concern during a war. Staying alive is obviously number one, except for martyrs and kamikaze pilots, with sleep ranking a very close second. I had to leave the field in April of '68 and weighed myself for the first time since I had left the states. The farther left I slid the hanging chrome weights along the scale's notched bars, the higher my eyebrows went. The line on the tottering pointer finally leveled off at 112 pounds. Drawing from my memory of advanced mathematics, I was stunned to realize I had already lost thirty-three pounds in a little more than three months. Always trying to look at the positive side of things, I rationalized that the meat remaining on my bones was at least solid muscle. Another quick mental calculation, using a loss rate of eleven pounds per month, suggested there was a good possibility I might weigh thirteen pounds by the end of my tour. I think Sam Morris did as well.

There are a number of contributing factors to losing weight other than serious health issues, exercise that burns off calories and a balanced diet among others. I'm sure the rear-echelon support guys in supply did their best to sustain us troops in the field. Try as they might, though, sometimes it just wasn't possible, or maybe things just went wrong (the army way). In my case, I was probably just melting away from water loss. Hey, who knows, maybe it was the sixteen-to-eighteen-hour days. Could have been stress or prolonged periods of acute concentration or loneliness or... Then again, it could have been an unappetizing diet. What can I say, I've been a picky eater all my young life, despite having an Italian mother who cooked great meals. But I took it to a whole new level when it came to C-ration meals that contained slimy, greenish yellow foods like Eggs and Ham, Chopped, or Ham with Lima Beans. Speaking of water loss, I remember a water delivery we received while working high in the mountains with a triple-canopy cover, away from any natural water supply.

Ho Chi Minh's Revenge

The month was late July, when the intense summer sun really beat down on the countryside. Doc continually reminded everyone to take their salt pills and drink at least a quart of water each day. Those health suggestions were fine when water was readily available, but that wasn't always the case.

Operations in Vietnam's western mountain ranges rarely posed a water shortage problem for us. Millions of years of lashing wind and rain had shaped their jagged peaks and steep rocky faces. Each deluge had created erosive cascades that clawed their way downhill, uniting in abrasive torrents that sliced through stone and rich soil with impunity. And although the forces of nature had carved an ominous terrain for us to walk through, the surroundings were beautiful, nonetheless. The heavy rain might have defaced the mountains, but it rewarded the lush valleys below with plenty of good clear, moving water. Fortunately (or unfortunately, depending on your point of view), our battalions spent most of their time in those mountains. It was known as Rocket Ridge because Camp Evans was often showered by rockets coming from there. It had become an

area for concentrations of NVA troops since the Tet
Offensive. An ideal area for Charlie's hospitals, mess
halls, R and R and resupply centers. Also, a good place
to go if you like being shot at or wanted to collect some
souvenirs from Asia.

Photo Vince Laurich
Left to right: John Taylor, Boyd Osler, Vince Laurich, Tim
Pasquarelli

On a typical CA, we landed on or near a mountain
peak and worked our way down into a darkened valley,
hoping to find Charlie before he found us. Whenever
we located one of the pristine streams during an operation, we filled our canteens at will. And as a rule,
finding one usually wasn't a problem. Once we reached
a valley floor, we just had to look down around our ankles. A few procedures had to first take place before we

consumed river water. To purify water and assure it was safe to drink, we were instructed during army training to add an iodine tablet to each quart of water we carried. Without any of us being chemists, we guessed the iodine couldn't really neutralize the sprayed defoliants and other chemicals that occasionally fell from the sky. And we didn't think it could remove caustic elements like arsenic and lead leaching from the stagnant pools that collected in artillery and bombshell craters. No, in the name of higher morale, it was supposed to make us *think* the water was okay. That was all well and good to please the army, but anyone who humped a ruck for a living knew that to really make water *drinkable*, a packet of Jolly-Ollie Orange, Lefty Lemon, or Goofy Grape Kool-Aid had to be added to kill the taste of the iodine and whatever else was lurking in a canteen.

One mission had us traversing high along a mountain ridgeline. After three days, fresh water had become scarce. We were informed early the fourth morning that a log bird would be bringing supplies and water later that night, so for that day, it was business as usual. Unfortunately, on that same day, some sort of problem with the water purification system back at Camp Evans had occurred and was beginning to cause a universal supply shortage. When later we heard the news, everyone knew that we were about to get screwed. If a decision had to be made as to whether to fill a REMF's[47] electric water cooler or a grunt's one-quart canteen, we knew who would lose that one.

So, in typical army fashion, it was decided that instead of extracting us too early from wandering around aimlessly looking for trouble, as if that particular mission was so critical, the new battalion commander de-

---

47   REMF—Rear echelon mother f—r.

cided that we should push on ahead. The hot water remaining in our canteens would have to be shared, if necessary, until we could be supplied the following morning. Due to our worsening condition, most of us hoped we wouldn't surprise our little adversary before then. Nothing could cause dry mouth faster than the unwelcome crack of an AK-47 round breaking the sound barrier just above one's head.

The going was tough in that area, requiring us to hack our way through dense underbrush. One point man at a time flailed and chopped in thick, humid air, with temperatures in the nineties and the sun breaking through each opening he'd just created, while the rest of the company sat back, relaxed, and waited for the formation to move another ten feet forward. The tool of choice was a machete. Easy to carry, not too heavy, and used every night to gather hooch poles for our temporary sleeping quarters. It was also used every night when hacking a clear field of fire around the perimeter. Kind of like having a very deep backyard behind your house with nothing but mowed lawn. Deer are nervous about being so exposed in the open, so they'd go to your neighbors' overgrown backyard to get at his garden instead. In our case, the deer were unwanted NVA soldiers.

That evening after our packs were dropped, we went about our normal daily routine for setting up the company's defensive perimeter, starting by removing the necessary articles and tools from the rucks. Every guy in each squad, responsible for their own area, would take turns digging defensive holes, while the others were cutting down vegetation outside the perimeter being sure to keep the six-foot-long saplings needed for erecting each hooch. Once everything that someone could hide behind was gone, and just before darkness fell, it was time to put out overlapping trip flares and Claymore mines to encircle the entire perimeter. After completing that critical chore, blow up one's air mattress and lay out the weapons, ammo, grenades, and Claymore triggers atop the dirt mounded in front of the defensive hole, making sure each item and weapon was in same position every night. The same routine every night in a different location. *Then* we could prepare our own dinner. The same routine over and over and over until your tour was over. Afterward, we would hang our socks out to dry, down a scrumptious meal, put our slippers on, and watch some TV for a while. Squad leaders walked through their teams' positions, checking equipment, coordinating fields of fire, giving out that evening's password, and asking if there were any requests for needed supplies. Most importantly on this mission, they checked the water situation with each guy, making sure everyone had some for the next day.

Hard decisions had to be made by everyone as to how to address their own water situation. Things previously taken for granted were now nearly impossible. Drinking only a mouthful or so of water for dinner would prevent one from eating any of the breads, crackers, cookies, or fruitcake that came with the Cs.[48] No coffee or hot chocolate could be brewed to help us wake up or take the edge off the morning's chill. Washing and other hygiene needs weren't even considered. That evening we brushed our teeth with only the toothpaste, preferring to save what drops we could for the certainty of the following day's sweltering patrol.

---

48   Cs—C rations, canned foodstuff.

In addition to our packs, the log bird had also brought cases of beer and soda to substitute for the missing water. Receiving alcohol in the field was un-heard of to us for obvious reasons. Nonetheless, we were provided the option of taking any two-can com-bination we chose. This brought to light a minor ob-session a few people had adopted recently. Rather than drink a beer allocation immediately, they hoarded the cans until they had a six-pack or more. In that way, they could really tie one on during a stand-down with little chance of danger. Oddly enough, others did the same thing with soda. Why anyone would stockpile noisy twelve-ounce cans weighing almost half a pound apiece confused many of us. It was common knowledge that there was always the possibility we might have to carry our packs on any given day. So why drag around the extra weight? In any case, with the packs arriving, many had access to their existing stash plus two addi-tional cans. Now, on the other side of the equation, some guys always carried two two-quart canteens of water, while others carried just a single one-quart can-teen. Naturally, that meant some had plenty of water left, and others had almost none. Therefore, with wa-ter being at a premium, and supply and demand being what it was, crazy negotiations took place well into the night.

Some guys considered small amounts of cash for a full canteen of water, though not seriously. So, what's a quart of water worth? Well, to some it was worth a six-pack of warm beer or soda. To others, five dollars (which in my case would have been half a month's sal-ary). To guys like Big Joe, who walked around looking like Gunga Din at times, it was free, something to be shared. Funny thing about those trades, though—it was hard to figure out who got the better deal.

After an early breakfast the following morning, we broke camp, undoing, collecting, refilling, destroying, and repacking everything, piled our rucks in the sling still lying in the same place, saddled up light, and headed out. In no time at all, everyone was soaked with sweat. By nine o'clock the terrain had begun to change from the tall jungle canopy to areas only sparsely populated with trees and dense shrubs. Intermittently, an unimpeded morning sun beat down on us each time we lost the overhead protection. Captain John Taylor, our CO radioed the battalion commander riding in a chopper high above us that our water situation was very serious, and he didn't want to push us too hard or too far in the heat. "Cold Steel Six" said he understood and assured "County Line Six" that he would have emergency water rations brought to us as soon as he could. Until then, keep moving. Word of the command decisions trickled back to us in the ranks, and it certainly didn't make the new battalion commander any more popular. If not for the helicopter crewmen, there were more than a couple of guys who wanted to shoot the poor excuse for a battalion commander out of the sky. And that was just our squad. Probably a couple of officers who'd like too as well.

So, we staggered forward, one step in front of the other, praying we didn't make contact, walking through the thickest vegetation imaginable. Every step was precious because no one knew when their tank would empty. Unfortunately, we had to make a slight detour because the point man hacked the trail straight to an undetonated 250-pound bomb lying in the weeds. *Column right!* Other than the chopping noise of the machete, there were no other sounds effectively announcing our presence so Charlie could set up an ambush, while the new battalion commander enjoyed the scenery and air temperature from five thousand feet above us. To those of us who had been in-country for a while, it didn't sit well at all. We knew things would be vastly different if Lt. Col. James Vaught[49] were still with us. As much as we hated the war, being drafted, and making contact, we would have walked through fire for that guy. When he commanded, it wasn't uncommon to see him walking right along with the grunts, through the worst rain and slogging through the deepest mud. He endured every hardship and discomfort that we did. Including being shot at. He'd climb into the C&C,[50] look down to assess the situation, then land and join the fray. The current battalion commander couldn't even spell *Leadership*.

We pushed on as the sun got higher and we got hotter, both physically and emotionally. The precious little water remaining in our bodies was literally trickling out, trying to cool us off. The perspiration-soaked fatigues, rifle slings, and Claymore bags became heavier, making us use even more energy and naturally increasing our sweating. Worse still, our brains began to bake in our overheated steel helmets. When exposed to direct sun for long periods, a metal helmet becomes somewhat like an inverted portable Hibachi worn on the head.

Doc was showing his anger and frustration with the situation more so than we. He was getting pissed at the CO because the effects of heat exhaustion were beginning to show on a few guys. Like all combat medics, he watched over the well-being of the entire company as if

---

49   James B. Vaught retired a three-star general.

50   C&C—Command and control helicopter.

we were his children, even though he was younger than many of us. Medics take their job responsibilities very seriously. God bless them all. Captain Taylor listened to Doc's pleas and warnings, but we had to continue moving forward. He did, however, radio the information to the battalion commander, who again responded that a delivery was coming "soon." By midafternoon, when many guys had already started getting headaches and cramps, and others were becoming extremely agitated, Doc insisted we stop for the day, and the CO agreed.

The request was radioed back to the C&C bird. The new battalion CO again replied he understood our situation but said, "Push on a little farther, troop. I can see a clearing along a ridge not far from your current position." He and the pilot felt a chopper would be able to land and offload the water for us. Of course, from their vantage point thousands of feet up, riding in a chopper while drinking all the water they wanted and surrounded by nice cool air, the clearing wasn't far off. We again had no choice but to continue our walk in the sun.

The point platoon for the company that day, specifically the guys in the lead squad, had it especially hard. Typically, it was their job to get the company to its destination as quickly, safely, and quietly as possible. On that day, every man in the lead squad took a turn walking point, and swinging a two-foot-long machete through thick brush and bamboo. Each guy hacked out a trail until exhausted and was then replaced by another. That had already happened a number of times by midafternoon, except that one guy was replaced not so much from exhaustion as nerves. He was the one who had inadvertently chopped his way right into the bomb sticking out of the dirt. *Talk about dry mouth.*

Collectively, we moved like a giant caterpillar, very slowly, one segment at a time in jerky, twenty-foot increments. When not moving, we knelt or stood for ten or fifteen minutes at a time, gasping in the humid air and, as always, wondering about what was holding us up. Guys in the back of the column never knew if enemy was spotted or we were just lost. As the day progressed, the winding trail became a dense, chlorophyll-scented, gaseous envelope of hacked vegetation. Like the rapidly wilting branches, grass, and leaves that were trampled underfoot and lining the trail, we too roasted under the sun, grumbling about our plight. With each step there was an ever-increasing popular train of thought throughout the ranks as many spoke about their desire to prove their marksmanship. "I'd shoot that sum bitch right outta the fuckin' sky if it weren't for the chopper crew. Make the bastid walk back to Evans if he survived the crash"—that pretty much summed up most statements. We had all heard or said those same words on other operations recently, but on that occasion, he was coming closer and closer to having it become a reality.

The situation deteriorated further, and we started taking turns carrying others' equipment due to their depleted condition. Some guys were in such bad shape that they asked to be left behind, saying that they would catch up to us later. It wasn't even taken seriously or considered, no matter how desperate the plea. After a brutal two-and-a-half-hour climb that had begun "not far from our current position," we all collapsed from dehydration and exhaustion when we reached a wide-open rocky area on a mountainside. The clearing itself was mainly exposed bedrock about seventy-five yards long, strewn with large boulders that had broken from a ledge one hundred yards above. The dull sandy-colored topography framing the bedrock stood in stark contrast to the cloudless deep blue sky that framed its uppermost reaches. A few scraggly, browning plants and dying weeds grew from fissures that traversed the area like veins. The relentless sun beating down on the barren surroundings made them hot to the touch, as if the bedrock were a result of recent volcanic activity. And to make matters worse, there wasn't the slightest hint of a breeze stirring the thinnest blade of dead grass.

Being completely exposed ourselves, we too could not escape the sun's intensity. And there was no sense backtracking, because the last section we had passed through was tall grasses where the air was so heavy, it was difficult to even inhale. Some guys were able to locate a boulder or ledge that afforded a small shadow, but with few places to find shade and without our ponchos to create shelters, we had little choice but to endure the debilitating heat, just as we had endured sleeping in the open during the cold rains of February. Shirts, flak vests, ammunition belts, and helmets encircled each guy as he sat slumped over, arms hanging at their sides, looking as if they were melting.

About the only thing anyone could do until the chopper arrived was minimize any nonessential movements and save energy as best they could. The only movement was our eyes searching for a threat of danger, and occasionally a canteen was seen being passed about. Most of us drafted enlisted men released steam by venting about Vietnam and the army. Poor pay, long hours, and people we didn't know trying to kill us; people we did know not appreciating our sacrifices; ambivalent countries both here and back home. Lousy food, forced marches, clothing that didn't fit, living in the bush like an animal for weeks at a time, and to top it off, they couldn't give us water.

When at last we heard the familiar sounds of an incoming slick, a smoke grenade was popped, and we watched through a purple haze as two choppers with cargo slings dangling below their frames approached from a distance. When near our position, one circled while the other dropped lower, flaring about one hundred feet above the clearing and slowly descending toward the ground. Instantly we were enveloped in a maelstrom of swirling smoke and pelted with stinging granules of sand that instantly coated our sweat-covered skin. Between the hot exhaust from the whining turbine engine forced downward by the huge rotor blades and the hot bedrock we were perched upon, it felt like an open-air blast furnace. Despite the additional heat and blinding squall, the air movement was welcomed. Like using a big window fan on a hot day back home, it was better than nothing.

The grunt who had gotten up to mark our location with smoke now directed the chopper into position. Holding his rifle overhead with both hands, he slowly lowered it parallel to the ground in sync with bottom of the twisting sling's descent. During the entire maneuver, the pilot watched both the signals and ground surface approach through the Plexiglas nose bubble below his feet. We could see him talking, his mouth partially covered by the microphone jutting from his helmet as he moved his head from left to right and back again. Most likely conversing with his navigator, crew chief, and door gunner. Aware of the mountain's severe slope and the large boulders that loomed beneath them, he was using extra caution with the approach, assuring the chopper's main and rear stabilizer rotors remained clear of any obstacles. As soon as the grunt signaled that the large cargo net containing our packs was positioned sufficiently near the ground, the sling was released, and dropped into a tangled brown-and-green heap. Almost instantly upon the release, the pilot pulled away from the LZ, clearing it for the second chopper.

Hanging beneath the second bird was a large, cylindrical, black rubber bladder that contained our precious liquid. With its four-foot diameter and five-foot length wrapped in canvas netting, it looked like a giant burnt pretzel nugget wrapped in cheesecloth. The sequence of the first drop was repeated. When the bladders, or blivets as we called them, had been safely released, the Huey lifted, banked slightly, and quickly accelerated down toward the valley below. Once the speed increased sufficiently, it climbed to join the other slick still circling the area for protection. As quickly as they had come and dropped their payloads, the Hueys were gone. In less than a minute, the silent stillness, and unbearable heat of our surroundings returned.

Squads from each platoon alternated going through the jumbled pile of rucksacks to retrieve their "homes." If you think trying to identify your luggage on an airline carousel is hard, you should try finding an olive- green backpack in a jumbled pile of identical government-issued olive-green backpacks, all wrapped up in a tangle of an olive-green canvas webbing. While one squad was getting their packs, another was getting water. There is nothing that tastes better or is more refreshing than a big drink of cold water when you're parched. Unfortunately, the bladder that was delivered had been lying in the hot sun at Camp Evans for who knows how long before being deposited on us. Just about everyone spit out their first mouthful in disgust.

It was hard for us to believe that that was the best they could do for us. We took it as just another insult to the guys who were doing the actual fighting and sacrificing the most. We just knew there were REMFs back at Evans drinking cold water from a water cooler at that very same moment—certainly the ones with brass insignias on their collars. To compound the insult, besides the water's temperature being hot, it tasted like rubber. No matter how many Kool-Aid packs were added to a canteen, it still tasted like liquid rubber. It had a slight hint of iodine, and its aroma did not exactly have a fine bouquet. The concoction was horrible, but we forced it down because we needed it to survive. Our overall condition was so poor from stomach cramps, headaches, and exhaustion that our CO decided we would stay at that location until late the following day before continuing the operation. Though that was good news, other things continued to go badly for us.

We tried as best we could to put up our hooches, but the ground was solid bedrock, with only small patches of dirt trapped between the cracks and fissures. Instead of tent pegs to hold down the corners, we had to find, carry, and use large rocks. To compound matters, the only reason we were putting up tents for the night was because mosquitoes were descending on us to satisfy their own thirst. We would have just slept under the stars, but we needed the hooch framing to hang our mosquito netting from if we were to survive the night with our sanity.

Once the hooches were up, we tried to address the next problem of digging foxholes. Our entrenching tools were useless, so instead we built small walled structures out of the loose rocks and boulders that were lying around, just in case we'd need some protection from unwelcome visitors during the night. The routine was the same as any other night—dig in, set up the perimeter, put up the hooch, and heat some Cs. The only difference on that night, besides not having to cut fields of fire in the barren outcropping, was that we had to force vile-tasting water down our stomachs if we wanted to recover some of our health. And believe me, that was no small feat.

It was difficult to sleep that night due to the unrelenting heat. Adding to our discomfort, the solar energy stored in the bedrock transferred the heat into our air mattresses, making us sweat even more. It was unbearable, especially due to the mosquito netting's density being so tight, the heat trapped within couldn't escape, nor could any air movement enter. But without it and an air mattress, we'd be sleeping directly on the hot, hard stone and being sucked dry by mosquitoes the size of hummingbirds. Sleeping without either was not an option. As if our conditions weren't bad enough, worsening stomach cramps persisted throughout the night, and so did the horrible aftertaste of the water. During guard duty that night, I found it increasingly difficult to remain still, because severe cramps were doubling me over. It looked like guys purposelessly walking around in the dark behind me were in the same state of discomfort. By Three-thirty I was clutching my stomach and rocking back and forth, I prayed for the pain to subside and an end to my shift. I felt that if I could crawl back into my hooch and assume a fetal position, it would relieve the muscle spasms.

On some nights, guard shifts seemed unbearably long, and that was one such night. I tried to remove my mind from the stomach pains, headache, and throbbing muscles by looking up at the clear, star-studded night sky, awed by the billions of flickering lights. When at last it was time to wake up my replacement, I made my way over to his position and tapped his toe a few times until quietly waking him. We sat and whispered about the headaches, cramps, and lousy water just long enough to insure he was awake. I handed him the watch, reminded him of the time duration and password, then said good night and crawled over to my hooch. Jack was sound asleep after having already pulled the shift before me, so I didn't want to disturb him.

I crawled into the hooch as quickly and quietly as possible to leave the bugs outside the netting. Jack stirred a little but continued to sleep. I immediately collapsed on my air mattress, lying on my side with my knees drawn up to my chest, but it did nothing to relieve the pain. After tossing and turning for a while, I somehow dozed off, trying to ignore the pains, heat, stinging mosquitoes, and their annoying buzzing around my ears.

I don't know how much time passed, but I was awakened by a more urgent stabbing pain in my stomach, leaving me with no doubt that my cramps would soon be gone if I didn't do something. In other words, if I didn't get out of the hooch fast enough, my pain would be relieved right there in my pants. My eyes popped wide open as I bolted upright and dove for the hooch opening in one quick motion. I pushed and spread the small opening in the netting to escape, but the only thing that happened was Jackie's legs and feet rose up into the air as though levitating. I tried pulling the opening again but with the same results: feet and legs rising and falling. Panic hit me in the darkness of the hooch's interior when I realized his feet were wrapped in the mosquito netting, thus sealing the opening and blocking my escape. After three or four desperate attempts to free his feet, I frantically tried to ease him awake by tapping him and whispering his name as loud as I could without scaring him, but it was too little, too late.

After a panicked span of only ten to fifteen seconds since awakening, the cramps were gone. Now I really needed to get out of the hooch. I elbowed Jackie and he stirred a little, mumbling that he had already pulled guard duty. Another shot to his ribs, and he finally awoke, leaned on his right elbow to face me, and asked what was wrong. Despite my terrible discomfort and the diminishing air quality within the confines of our little sauna, I told him as calmly as I could that I had just shit my pants because his goddamn feet had me trapped in the stinking hooch! Half-awake and not at all shocked by my embarrassing admission, but definitely beginning to share my discomfort, he untangled the netting for the next few minutes until the opening reappeared and I gingerly crawled out on all fours like a crab.

Okay, now what? I thought. Step number one was to slither out of my pants. Step number two was to get myself cleaned up, and step number three was to clean my fatigue pants. I figured the best thing to do was go over to the water bladder in the cover of darkness and do the best I could. After successfully completing step one, I kept a low profile and made my way bowlegged over to the water bladder. I wore only unlaced boots and my fatigue shirt to protect my upper half from mosquitoes, all the while dragging my pants behind me. I approached the bladder and could see two other guys standing there in the buff, obviously doing their laundry. By the amount of water running off the mountain, it appeared there had already been a steady procession of GIs who had visited the "Laundromat."

The following day found everyone limply draped over rocks or lying down spread eagle as if completely drained of every ounce of energy. Heads were propped up on packed rucksacks. We waited for choppers to extract us, because our CO had finally convinced the battalion commander that we were in no condition to continue the operation. For the first time in the seven months I'd been in-country, we were going to leave the boonies five days earlier than planned. Good thing. It was going to take some time recharge our batteries back at LZ Jack.

Recharging the batteries on a stand-down

Buon Appetito

Because of the terrible health problems experienced by our company on the earlier mountain operation, supplies became an even more important issue to us. Our next forays afield usually had us eating a hot meal almost every night, and good fresh water was plentiful. That is, of course, if the jungle canopy allowed for a helicopter delivery. The initial operation, after the bad water episode, had us using several methods for resupply. Sometimes we walked all day and headed for the top of a mountain that was sufficiently clear for a helicopter landing. That was usually our standard operating procedure. Other occasions found us in a terrain where it wasn't suitable for a chopper to deliver supplies on the ground, so improvisation was in order.

The first operation after the tainted-water incident had started like most others. We ended a four-day stand-down at an area along Highway 1 where we had "guarded" a bridge spanning a wide river. Frolicking in the water and just lying around getting some rays was exactly what the doctor ordered to recharge our batteries. By the time the choppers staged for our next mission, we were rejuvenated, in good spirits, and wearing nice clean clothes that fit. And just in case, most guys had traded in their one-quart canteen for the two-quart model. Our previous couple of operations had been rather noneventful for our company, so stress and anxiety levels were as low as one could expect for a grunt. But as most old-timers knew, nothing could ever be taken for granted in the bush. There was always a reason why we were flying to a specific area.

We boarded idling Hueys lined up for us, glancing at the two gunships circling the LZ waiting to escort us to our destination. Once we were all settled in, I felt the increased vibrations from the accelerating rotor blades and watched as the warrant officer pushed the cyclic forward, pulled up on the collective, and twisted the throttle. Almost instantly the tail of chopper wagged left and right, and the Huey tilted slightly forward as if poised on the front of the skids. It looked as if the fuselage was being pulled forward in the same position until the heavily laden slick lifted slowly into the air as it gained speed. Below and behind each slick was a yellowish orange cloud of sandy dust blowing up from the ground. It was like watching an old Western movie with a line of wagons heading west.

We continued a steady climb over the river valley and rice paddies, constantly accelerating and gaining altitude. While flying west at about fifteen hundred feet, we absentmindedly stared at the familiar landscape below. At that altitude objects appeared to slowly glide past us even though we were traveling at over one hundred knots. When we flew at treetop level at up to 120 knots, the landscape was a blur, and it seemed we would reach an LZ faster than we might have wanted to. At five thousand feet, though, helicopters appeared to be just hovering, with very little forward motion.

Flights at high altitudes seemed excruciatingly long as the chopper's noise and vibrations numbed our senses and cold air gave us goosebumps on our exposed arms.

We had no idea where we were going, only the direction: toward the mountains. Glancing around the cabin, I could see everyone lost in his own thoughts. The three grunts on the webbed seat and three others on the floor fiddled with their equipment to get a little more comfortable, occasionally glancing out the open doors to take in the scenery. The crew chief, door gunner, pilot, and copilot scanned the all-too-familiar terrain below with a somewhat bored detachment. The distant mountain range that had become our semipermanent home for the past three months grew larger as we approached, and I knew it would be our home again for next fourteen days or so.

On to the next mountain mission

The mountains were still a few miles away when the four slicks slowed to maneuver for the hilltop assault. The two slower gunships escorting us at about eighty knots pulled away from the formation and, when within a mile of the planned landing zone, started to prep the area by blindly raking the hillsides with their incredible firepower. With the slicks still slowing to about seventy knots, we watched the ground below for any signs of activity while the gunships continued to dive well ahead of the lead slick firing their ARA[51] and miniguns. Our excitement built as we watched, felt, smelled, and heard the events of the CA unfolding before us. When the gunships completed their strafing runs, they abruptly angled up and away to either side, leaving in their wakes clear blue skies streaked with long, black, tapering smoke trails that pointed toward the ground, the dissipating reminders of their discharged rockets. Lazily floating down far behind the gunships were sparkling cascades from hundreds of ejected brass bullet casings, shimmering in the sun like a suspended golden chain.

As soon as the gunships stopped firing, the slicks started their approaches, with both door gunners in each helicopter spraying their machine-gun fire into the vegetation immediately surrounding the LZ while we prepared to climb out onto the skids. An adrenaline rush always hit me as I watched and participated in the choreographed ballet of six or so drab, olive-green Hueys with brightly painted crossed yellow sabers of the 1st Cavalry Division emblazoned on their fronts. The entire ensemble cast of choppers darted up and down, in and out, the weapons, engines, and massive blades making an earth-shattering roar. Compounding

---

51   ARA—Aerial rocket artillery.

the excitement and noise were cautions and orders being yelled by fire team leaders on where to go once on the ground. Not easy to do or hear, competing against the stereo jackhammer reverberations of machine guns blazing only a few feet from each side of our heads.

By then totally pumped up for the insertion, the guys climbed out of the moving chopper at thirty feet or so above the ground, carefully lowering themselves onto the skids on both sides of the slick. As if suspended in air with no means of support, we watched far below for any signs of a hot LZ. The lead Huey dove toward the LZ, then flared its nose upward sharply and almost instantly slowed from fifty knots to zero. From our angle far above, it looked like its forward momentum would surely drive the big eight-foot tail rotor into the ground. But it became obvious that the Huey was flown by an excellent and experienced pilot, because his ship suddenly leveled off only feet from the ground. His flawless execution was what we had come to expect from all of the Cav pilots, and they rarely let us down.

Even before the Huey came to a complete stop to land, the squad jumped off the skids into the maelstrom of flying dirt and debris. Once the crew chief announced the cabin was clear, the slick rose slightly, tail tilted upward like a scorpion, and flew down the side of the mountain at treetop level to help it rapidly accelerate to begin its climb. With the lead bird out of the way, our ship began to angle down in a slow dive. We stood on the skids and clung to the door openings and seat framing while watching the guys already on the ground running in different directions to start forming the defensive perimeter around the LZ. In a matter of seconds, we too were on the ground, running to enlarge the circle, diving into protective cover, and looking for enemy movement. When the first wave of four slicks had completed the insertion, they quickly departed and ended the show's first act. We remained at that location in silence, hidden amid the vegetation, waiting for the same group of choppers to return with the second and third waves of the assault.

Once everyone was on the ground, the squads reformed and headed down the mountain single file to begin another nature walk. Over the past month, we had picked up a few new guys who fit in with the rest of us very well. They were intelligent, fit, and familiar with the outdoors to varying degrees. Overall, I'd say we had a solid squad of very capable troopers, made up of various races, religions, and backgrounds from numerous states. You just couldn't help but get close to some guys once you were together for a while, or maybe through just one firefight. And still, after fifty-plus years, I still smile when thinking about the other guys and wonder how they're doing today. I think the CO of Bravo Company said it best: "With the exception of the bond between a mother and her child, the brotherhood of those who fought together in battle may be the deepest bond that human beings ever form."[52] *Amen.*

We descended the mountain and reached the valley floor with no interruptions. The operation, we were informed, would have us again walking along a small stream meandering between rugged mountainsides. Hopefully, the entire operation would be just a quiet hiking trip. After a few hours, we stopped and spread out along stream banks to eat and relax before heading out for the afternoon portion of the patrol. Except for

52   Howard T. Prince II, Brigadier General, USA Retired, Commanding Officer Bravo Company, 5/7 Cavalry (January to February 1968); severely wounded in combat during the Hue Tet Offensive.

the heat and humidity, it was easy going. By two p.m., our nice clean fatigues were soaked with sweat, and our butts and elbows were muddied from sitting on the damp riverbanks. But as many of us had learned earlier, it didn't matter if we were naked, as long as no one was shooting at us. We just never knew when it would happen. Even during a lunch break. We walked quietly for hours, looking for any signs of human activity—footprints, a dropped piece of paper or equipment, a broken stem on low vegetation, or the matted grass of a possible trail. Though concentrating on the surroundings, we also had the opportunity to study the exotic plants and occasional animals that happened by, or the beautifully colored birds calling to us in yet another unfamiliar language.

The country of Vietnam is quite beautiful. Along most of its five-hundred-plus-mile eastern coastline are long strands of sparkling sandy beaches where white-crested waves crash in stark contrast to the incredibly dark-blue South China Sea. In other areas of the coast, where mountain peaks descend precipitously into the sea, small, isolated beaches accessible only by boat or helicopter lie safely hidden between jagged stone walls. They look very much like they belong on a travel poster for other countries like Italy and Greece. Small, ominous-looking islands with fractured pinnacles, hidden caves and battered rock formations dot the coast beyond the breakers. The diversity of the terrain is best seen during the harvest season, when much of the country's interior is covered in an emerald-green plaid quilt of mature rice plants. The low, narrow dikes and footpaths of dark-brown mud encompassing each paddy, crisscross the undulating landscape like that of a quilted blanket. Far to the south, a complex network of muddy water and lowlands forming the massive Mekong Delta dominates the topography. And at the other extreme, running along the spine of the country from the central highlands north, is the Annamese Cordillera Mountain chain separating it from Laos far to the west, flaunting rugged peaks over eighty-five hundred feet high and deep foreboding valleys shrouded in a vaporous mist. This was the place we had come to know as home. Without politicians both there and in the states, I think our generation would have liked that place. Now it's called ecotourism because no one is trying to shoot you.

I was always fascinated by the plants and trees. Most of us grew up surrounded by hardwoods like tall oaks, sycamores and maples that have defined trunks and broad, spreading limbs that form huge spherical profiles. The smaller vegetation at home looked pretty much the same as the trees—a trunk supported by thin roots disappearing into the earth, topped by branches covered with leaves. The foliage in the mountains of Vietnam is tall and densely spaced, often blocking out the sun. Almost everything alive is some shade of green, or yellow, or brown. Even on the ground. Root systems of some trees ended on the trunk five, ten, fifteen feet high, rather than at ground level on the bottom of the trunk. If you were to cut a section out of the tree, its profile would look like a star. Branches forty, fifty, sixty feet above our heads struggled with each other to capture enough sunlight to sustain their very existence. For those trees that failed to reach the light of day, they were doomed to support the vegetation that found its nourishment from the fallen and decaying wood lying on the dark, moist moss on the ground.

There were ferns, mushrooms, and palm trees of unbelievable shapes and sizes, and leaves on some so large we used them as umbrellas during the spur-of-the-moment torrential downpours. Towering bamboo was so hard that it defied a chop from a machete if struck the wrong way, yet yielded the cool water locked within its hollow trunk if hit at just the correct angle. Where sufficient light reached the ground, banana trees twelve inches in diameter could be found, their trunks so soft that a single blow from a machete could cut them in half. In the morning the same decapitated tree would have already grown eight inches tall at its center. Each day it would grow ever wider and taller in concentric rings like an onion, its new trunk looking like the terraced crown of a New York City skyscraper.

Lurking everywhere were insects and other creepy-crawlies of unbelievable proportions, the type that Achilles would have encountered in Homer's *Odyssey*. We would often see centipedes a foot long and as thick as a cigar, beetles the size of a man's fist, worms so large they would choke a largemouth bass. I assumed they were worms because they didn't have eyes. We northern boys were not used to that kind of stuff, but the boys from Florida, Louisiana and the deep south in our ranks said they saw larger things back home. *So much for retiring to Florida. Maybe North Carolina instead.*

As usual, the end of each day would have us climbing a mountain and digging in for the night. On that particular day, the climb through thick vegetation required everyone in our squad to take a turn at point, slashing at the undergrowth and tall grasses with our machetes, clearing a trail for those who would follow. Although the work was exhausting for the lead squad, the advantage of getting to the top of a mountain first was being able to pick the best spot to set up. That usually meant flat ground, good clear fields of fire in front of the position, no brush or trees that would have to be cut down, and no rocks, so the foxhole would be easy to dig. Those squads farther back in the column would remain on the trail for some time because of the nature of a company-sized patrol. Unless a loud, steady cadence was being used, and that wasn't a very good idea in the bush, an "accordion" effect occurred. Let me try to explain this jungle traffic-pattern phenomenon. When we left a campsite each morning, everyone would spread out along a trail in relatively equal intervals. As a day progressed, any change in the lead squad's speed influenced the column's spacing intervals. Each time there was a bend in the trail or obstacle requiring extra caution, it slowed or stopped the point squad. The compounding result was the entire line constricting and potentially coming to a complete halt. When a stop at the point did occur, the trailing squads eventually remained stationary, advancing again only when the people in front of them moved. Although the end of column might be waiting to move, the point squad might have already restarted minutes before and reached a normal pace. The resulting effect was a stretching of spacing intervals throughout the entire column.

Every twist in the trail, suspicious bush, potential ambush site, movements, or strange sounds allegedly seen or heard by the point man compounded the differences in the company's tempo. When the time difference between the lead and last squads became too great by the end of a day, the last squad had to run full bore just to reach the main part of the company. For many of us, it was our first real exposure to stop-and-go traffic, and it was not enjoyable. On many occasions, the last squad would still be at the bottom of a mountain waiting to begin its climb while the lead squad was finishing their nightly defensive positions. Even after they reached the top, they might have to continue their walk around the site to complete the company's circular perimeter. It wasn't uncommon to see the last squad begin to set up in the dark. It also wasn't uncommon to see guys from the lead squads digging their foxholes for them. I think it's called brotherhood. We all took a turn in the same barrel eventually.

And this day was no different, because by the time the last guys reached the top and passed us, we were almost completing our foxholes. Furthermore, hooch poles had already been cut down, and our fields of fire had been cleared. Boots and socks were hanging inverted on sticks shoved into the ground, taking advantage of the sun's last rays to dry them. All we needed was our packs, maybe a hot meal, and we would be set for the night.

As the company filed past us, we heard the usual groans and complaints that were always directed at the day's lead squad. "What'd you guys do, run up here?" they'd moan. "When our squad cuts a trail, you could drive a truck through it. You guys just trimmed some bushes." "Thanks for taking the best spot, guys. Did you at least leave us some straight hooch poles?" It was always in good humor, I hope, because we would all have a chance to be first and last. When the CO and his entourage walked by, "Mac," Top's exhausted and flushed radio operator, said almost apologetically, "Hey, Bano, we're getting some hots tonight, so don't get too comfortable!" I wasn't sure what he meant because he didn't look or sound so happy, and that made us all a little curious.

While we lounged about wearing only our pants, taking full advantage of the setting sun's last rays to dry everything, Little Joe, our RTO, who always had the radiotelephone nearby, announced a slick was inbound with hots and mail. That good piece of intel immediately made us wonder where the chopper might land. With mouths already beginning to salivate, we made a quick scan of the hilltop, but it revealed no obvious area large enough for a chopper to set down. There could always be an area just out of our line of sight where we could quickly walk, taking turns leaving the perimeter. When we saw and heard the log bird circle, we were surprised when it suddenly veered from our position and disappeared from sight below us. No one had heard any incoming fire, and the Huey had sounded okay when it went over. There must have been a very good reason for such a tight maneuver so close to us. Suddenly we heard the staccato sounds from two M-60 machine guns. The door gunners had opened fire in earnest very near us. Muscles tensed and minds raced as reflexes instantly threw everyone toward their own equipment.

Little Joe yanked the radio handset up and listened intently for orders or an explanation. He wasn't monitoring the chopper's radio frequency to hear what was going on and heard no alerts coming from our own CO as the two M-60s continued to pound the landscape. Hearts beat louder as we could only speculate as to what the problem might be. None of us had noticed any flat areas on the way up the mountain, so we didn't think the chopper was prepping a landing sight. Wet boots were yanked on, helmets donned, weapons lifted, and ammunition bags quickly slung over shoulders in preparation for a worst-case scenario.

We had waited an unusually long time since the chopper had first opened fire, yet we hadn't heard any explanations since the firing stopped. Bodies began to relax slightly as speculation changed from the potential for a firefight to complaints about the army.

"I'll bet the pilot thought he saw something, so he pulled out," someone said.

"Nah," someone else countered. "I heard we were getting real steaks tonight, but they were probably still too hot. So, he decided to fly around for a while and test-fire the guns."

"Yeah, typical. First, they pump us up, then they scare the hell out of us."

Everyone's frustrations built as we fueled each other's thoughts to a frenzied level. "I heard some goddamn REMFs are going to get our chow tonight, I just know it. Fuckin' army."

"Why is it that grunts are always getting the shaft? Can't they just leave us alone once in a while?"

"Ah shouldah, Ah say, Ah shouldah joined the navy!" That voice always took the edge off a little.

Mac, the obvious nickname given to Bertram MacAllister, was a real good guy from Maine. He wore thick glasses, had a big bushy red mustache, and spoke with a pronounced New England accent. He casually sauntered up to us and had a funny look when he said, "Hey, Bano, you might as well stay dressed and saddle up light, because the chopper just landed on the other side of the river! Said it was 'a nice flat sandy beach that the grunts would appreciate.' Looked like a picnic ground to him, so they mowed the lawn for us." He couldn't stop grinning, knowing that our squad's clothes, especially our socks and boots, had probably already dried.

Of course we weren't alone in the bitching. "Stinkin' pilot did that on purpose just to piss us off. Always screwing with our minds."

"If they knew they were going to use that LZ," Joe asked, "why didn't we just stay down there before climbing up? Now we gotta get dressed, saddle up, climb down the damn mountain, wade cross the river, and get our socks, boots, and pants wet again."

I took it to the next step and added, "Yeah, and that means they'll be wet when we saddle up again tomorrow morning."

"Well, I ain't goin', 'cause by the time we get there, the food will probably be cold anyway."

Bill Ebel was the thinnest of us and the last one who should ever refuse a meal. "Hey, don't forget, boys and girls," he said, frowning, "after we go down there for the chow, we'll be climbin' back up humpin' our rucks because they're over there too." Damn, we forgot about that!

There wasn't much we could do except saddle up and head down the mountain. Surely there could have been a better way to bring us hot chow. Hell, we would rather eat Cs and have dry socks than have hots and wet socks! Our nightmare wasn't over, because after we stumbled back down the mountain, sloshed across the river, and got online for chow, we discovered the meal wasn't steaks, but liver and onions! It isn't smart to piss off heavily armed, twenty-year-old guys who are very hungry, tired, angry and hate liver!

Most of us stood stunned with our mouths hanging open. Some guys, me included, went from salivating to dry heaving when the odor from the open marmite[53] cans of liver wafted into the surroundings. The pilots standing next to their chopper and the door gunners serving the chow kept apologizing with concerned looks, saying, "Hey, guys, it wasn't our idea, so don't shoot the messengers, please." Of course, some guys just loved liver and would have eaten it every day if they had a choice. Those few had plates with the vile-tasting organs stacked high like pancakes and were grinning from ear to ear, saying, "Hey, this liver is great, why don't you try some?" I, on the other hand, had a scrumptious meal consisting of 2-slices of white bread, a half pint of milk, and by the time I reached the mountaintop again, a small cup of chocolate milk that started out as ice cream.

That was probably one of the lowest days of my tour in Vietnam and just added to the proof that Hollywood had duped us by romanticizing war. That day exemplified what a grunt's life was really about. I'm not sure if Mac was joking or not the following morning when he told us the CO had slept with one eye open. It probably had something to do with him sending Mac down the mountain to bring his pack and dinner up for him.

---

53   Marmite container—Insulated steel container about the size of a medium cooler for transporting hot food, ice cream, et cetera.

Attack of the Killer Tomatoes

The operation continued uneventfully, as did most of our recent forays. We walked for days, guided by the command chopper above us always circling, always giving orders to speed it up. At times, we'd hear that one of our brother companies was in a firefight somewhere nearby. Little Joe would monitor the radio transmissions and keep us informed as to what was happening. The worst thing we would hear or see was medevacs heading in the direction of the other company. If the fight was big enough, we'd be forced to get to an area as fast as we could for a helicopter extraction and subsequent insertion into the fray. That was the whole purpose for the development of the 1st Cavalry Division (Airmobile). It sure seemed to work well.

Those were nervous times because there was no guessing as to what our mission would be; we were going into a firefight. It was at least comforting to know that if it happened to us, another unit from our battalion would come to our immediate aid too. That was a very strange part of the war as well. One company could be walking in peaceful silence while another, not too far away, could be engaged in a fight for their very

lives. Every company probably felt like they were doing most of the fighting in Southeast Asia at one time
or another. I know we did at times. We always knew
Charlie was in the same area we were, because that
was why we were inserted in that particular location
in the first place. Knowing that, and struggling through
terrain that could easily hide and support enemy forces, always kept us on our toes. Of course, being young
and burning up millions of calories also kept us alert.
Someone was always speculating about when and
where we would stop for the night or if we would get
a hot meal and fresh water. The severity of the terrain
dictated whether a slick could land, so we never knew
for certain if the day would end with hot chow. The
landscape often changed during the day, especially if
we were working along ridgelines or on the sides of a
mountain. One minute we could be hacking our way
with machetes through dense jungle and then suddenly
we'd be walking into a clearing created by a B-52 strike,
with craters the size of house foundations, enormous
trees shredded down to small stumps, and not a leaf or
fern for hundreds of yards.

Chopping our way through

We could never see the open areas in advance because of the dense vegetation, but with the command chopper five thousand feet overhead providing us "guidance," we could be blindly steered right into a detour sign. And with our new battalion commander at the controls, that was not unusual. In fact, it was typical. We couldn't see the sky. So how the hell could he see us from five thousand feet? Must be an FNG. If it was late in the day when we reached the LZ, we usually stayed for the night. Typically, a log bird would deliver our supplies and rucksacks. When we located an open area too early in the day, we'd patrol around it looking for enemy signs, then continue walking for the remainder of the day. When that happened, it usually meant that by the end of the day, we would be back in dense jungle, sometimes unable to get supplied. That naturally drew complaints about how "they" were always screwing the grunts. "Why couldn't they just let us stay at that opening we were at this afternoon?" a new guy would ask.

"Ain't the army way." came the reply from a veteran.

"This really sucks. I'm sick of eating Cs" would come from a short timer.

"Ah shoulda joined da navy" usually echoed during any discussion.

Well, on this one particular mission, it turned out to be a good news/bad news day for us. We were told a log bird was coming that night with hots and water. The bad news was that we'd been marched into one of those areas where the canopy was so thick, there was no way a chopper would be able to land. To overcome a situation like that, we had gotten what was called a "kick-out" on a few occasions, but never to deliver a hot meal.

The basics of a "kick-out" are fairly simple. A helicopter would hover at whatever altitude was necessary to clear the obstruction below, and then a door gunner would literally "kick out" whatever supplies were to be delivered. If it was munitions, they were usually in metal cans that could withstand the drop from treetop level. Drinking water was put into "elephant rubbers,"[54] as we called them, capable of surviving a kick-out. We had received that stuff before, but never through a triple canopy, and certainly not a hot meal.

It was obvious from the very beginning that there were going to be a number of problems with this kick-out. First, the canopy was so thick and high that the helicopter pilots couldn't locate the colored smoke we'd popped at our position. Therefore, we had to build an incredibly long "smoke pole" to push through the canopy. The second problem was that once the log bird's pilot had located us, gotten into position, and hovered above the treetops for the drop, we still could not be sure of each other's exact location. When the contents started raining down through the leaves, limbs, and branches, it was anybody's guess as to where they would land. And our last problem was that we were not on a flat part of the mountain. The severe angle of the hillside would probably cause the cans and boxes to roll downhill before they could be retrieved.

When all was ready, we veterans of past kick-outs were uneasy because we couldn't see the chopper. May-

---

54   Elephant rubber—A four-foot-long, five-inch-diameter, clear, pliable rubber tube. When filled with drinking water and placed in a corrugated cardboard box, it was used for "kick-outs" when a helicopter had no place to land for resupply.

be this was an experiment, a trial thought up by some genius sitting at a desk in the Pentagon. We could see leaves high above us being blown around, but with rotor blades almost fifty feet long creating a huge downdraft, we couldn't be exactly sure where the chopper was. Instead, most of us got strategically positioned where we thought stuff would land and stood tight against tree trunks, hugging the side that had the biggest branches above our heads. This time we also hung on because the slope of the mountain threatened to pull us, and for that matter anything else that was not growing, downhill. Kick-outs could be a lot of fun.

When it finally began, we watched in amusement as four-foot cardboard boxes of water broke through the canopy like spears, only to hit huge tree limbs that stretched out far above the ground. The sudden stop at one end of a box's motion caused the other end to start cartwheeling, making them look like propellers that had disengaged from an old biplane. Like a pinball machine on a grand scale, they broke through the canopy, only to careen off other limbs. Some landed safely, then began sliding downhill. They ricocheted off tree trunks in every direction while guys chased after them. Other boxes made it through the upper leaves in a freefall for twenty or thirty feet. When their speed had increased significantly, they often hit protruding limbs squarely in their midsection. The abrupt stop made them instantly fold in half and explode, spraying water in every direction. Others that survived intact all the way to the ground but couldn't withstand the impact also erupted like miniature geysers, spraying their precious liquid across the landscape.

Interspersed with the water boxes were shiny one-gallon metal cans of stewed tomatoes. Now, they really looked like pinballs bouncing off limbs and branches. Unfortunately, or fortunately if you didn't like stewed tomatoes, most of them exploded on impact, flinging sticky red globs all over the trees, ground, and grunts diving for cover, making the area look as if a herd of cattle had just been slaughtered. While everyone ducked, dove, ran, and laughed, the food, drink, leaves, branches, limbs, boxes, cans, and vines rained down from the heavens. But the best was yet to come. Our "hots" hadn't been delivered yet. As soon as the storm of stewed tomatoes stopped, we saw the olive-green metal marmite containers, that could hold hot or cold food, follow the same paths as the water and stewed tomatoes. They too bounced, deflected, and spun in flight, causing many lids to open in midair. At that point, we knew what we were having for dinner— pork chops and one-pint containers of cold milk to go with our tomatoes. It would have been better if they had just dropped menus.

Pork chops and milk containers showered down from the heavens and erupted from the ground upward when the marmite cans couldn't take the impact. The one-pint milk boxes were cartwheeling all over the place looking like giant hailstones, bouncing off limbs, branches, tree trunks, and legs, then continued their unpredictable path by rolling downhill. The pork chops, on the other hand, pretty much stayed where they landed due to their flat profile, except for those whose marmite container landed at an angle facing downhill. Those puppies were launched into never-never land when the lid popped open. Otherwise, they stayed right where they landed, unless one happened to land too close to someone in hiding. An arm could be seen darting out from behind a tree, like a frog's tongue zapping some unsuspecting dragonfly. When a grab was on target, the tasty morsel was quickly retrieved, blown "clean" of dirt and debris, and consumed in earnest.

As soon as the chopper's rotor pitch changed, signaling its departure, all hell broke loose. Everyone started diving and running for the pork chops as if it were an Easter egg hunt. Meat and sloppy tomatoes were being picked up from the ground, scraped off tree trunks, and caught in flight while dripping from overhead branches. Guys drenched with water, tomato "sauce," and milk were in a feeding frenzy, stuffing their shirts with chops, some filling their helmets, still others instantly eating things as they were picked up before looking for more.

We laughed and continued our searches while the officers ran around, slipping and falling on the layers of fallen leaves, trying to get some semblance of order. When at last everyone was finally calmed down, we were ordered to drop all of the food in a pile at the CO's feet. It was hysterical watching guys with sheepish grins slowly opening up their shirts and dirt-covered pork chops slid off their grease covered chests, and crushed milk containers fell onto the disgusting-looking heap. It was also obvious that some guys had quickly dispatched a few chops before dumping their loads, because they were coyly spitting out dirt and leaves while trying to stifle smiles. Even the CO had trouble staying serious.

Once everyone and thing was accounted for, the chops were divided evenly. Each guy could take two greasy brown things off one pile and some red stuff from another, or not, depending on his appetite. Fortunately, enough water had survived the fall to both fill everyone's canteens and wash off the pork chops. Although the meal wasn't exactly hot and had a slightly gritty texture, it sure tasted better than Cs or liver.

Can du Jour

No description of a grunt's Vietnam experience would ever be complete without special mention of the food we ate daily, the infamous C- ration. When we were FNGs, we didn't know any better and tried to act as if Cs were all right. We wanted to impress the old-timers that we could eat anything. We were tough enough to be out in the boonies with them. After a while, though, we realized we had only been fooling ourselves. The only things that made C- ration units edible were seasonings and preparation learned through many weeks of trial and error. Some guys actually became gourmet chefs in their own minds. When they added sufficient amounts of Tabasco sauce, Cheese Whiz, crackers, and the contents of a few selected items from other boxes of Cs, they created masterpieces.

Unfortunately, time, place, and ingredients were not always readily available. Especially time. We did, however, have one such occasion on a mountain overlooking the marine combat base at Khe Sahn. Besides carrying our normal "light" but heavy loads of sixty to seventy pounds, Operation Pegasus also had each man carrying a full twenty-five-pound case of Cs. That was like adding insult to injury for me, because most of the stuff in the cases I couldn't or wouldn't eat. Just because a can read, "Ham, chopped" didn't mean it wasn't Alpo. However, having everything available to each person allowed us all to experiment, pick and choose, mix and match, and learn how to make some interesting and tasty combination platters, like pizza, stew, strawberry shortcake, and Parmesan dishes. I don't think I would order any of those dishes in a restaurant today, but back then it really wasn't all that bad at times.

Perhaps the best way to explain those tasty morsels, sealed in olive-green steel cans, is to describe them in detail. There were twelve separate meals in a case. Each meal was individually packaged in a light-brown cardboard box about the size of two James Michener novels. Stamped on each flimsy lid was a cryptic military description of the "meal" and one of three different designations indicating the type of meal. After we were in-country for a short time and were left to consume only those meals the old-timers didn't select, we quickly learned to translate the cryptic designations on each box to assure getting a digestible meal when it became our turn to pick first. It probably took me longer than most guys, which is why I lost so much weight in my first few months there.

Some meals were downright nasty and were to be avoided at all costs, like Ham and Eggs, Chopped, or Ham with Lima Beans. Then again, I'm sure some readers are saying those were their favorites. Other entrees, all in olive-green cans the size of a dog-food can, were tasty when they came straight from the can, such as Soup, Chicken with Noodles, and Meatballs with

Beans. The remaining meals, like Loaf, Turkey; Slices, Pork; and Beef, Gravy with Potatoes, required careful blending, preparation, and seasoning.

Each meal fell into a different category and was designated as B1A, B2, or B3. Those designations indicated what was inside the box along with the main course. The four B1A units contained fruit, which was greatly sought after by all. Included in each of the units was a can of applesauce, crushed pineapples, fruit cocktail, or peaches, each fruit matched to a specific meal. The remaining eight units contained tuna fish-sized cans of pound cake, white bread, crackers, cookies, fruitcake, or date-nut bread. Completing each meal unit were small cans about two inches in diameter and a half inch thick that contained cheese, peanut butter, or jelly. A packet of hot cocoa mix was a special treat if prepared with the correct proportions of water, Cremora, and sugar. The different combinations of breads and spreads were matched to specific meals, just as the fruit was. Every ration box included a brown aluminum foil accessory pack. These provided all the necessary condiments for both the meal and for afterward—plastic fork, knife, and spoon; two Chiclets; small packets of salt, pepper, sugar, Cremora, and coffee; matches; a small four-pack of name-brand cigarettes; and, thankfully, a few pieces of toilet paper. Included with each case of Cs were four or so P-38 can openers, a small metal device about the size of a single thumb joint that could be worn on a necklace or carried in a pocket. The same can opener was used in WWII, so it had certainly proved itself after having passed the test of time. I'm sure there are a lot of guys who still carry one, just in case.

The way the rations were distributed was to give one case to each squad and have each fire team take a turn picking from the open case first. In that way, everyone was assured a favorite once in a while. When a squad was below eleven men, which was common, or a new guy had just joined the ranks, the odds of getting a preferred meal two times in a row was pretty good. All you had to do was tell a new kid to grab something you didn't like, because until they knew what each box contained, they were just taking a shot in the dark anyway. You could only screw over a new kid a few times, though, because he was a brother grunt. To make things fair, we would flip the case of Cs upside down, open the bottom, and select from the unmarked box. In that way, all the boxes were the same for everyone. Veterans still had the advantage because they knew the exact location of every meal in the case based on where it originated, like Texas. We didn't feel bad about a new kid selecting poorly. After all, we gave the new kid the first pick of the open case. Everyone experienced a trial-and-error period for a short time until savvy.

The location of the different manufacturers forewarned us of the differences in the food itself. For example, if the Slices, Pork came from Texas, they were good. If the Cs came from another state, it meant they had too much fat. Cases were also stamped with a date that meant something entirely different. The earlier variety didn't have many of the good meals or fruits. And you thought ordering from a French menu was hard.

Eating and meal preparation became almost a science to most. There were many variables to consider when choosing a lunch and dinner meal before moving out each morning. In addition to the selection process itself, we had to make a number of assumptions about the entire day—if our rucks containing seasonings would be there at night, if the proper cheese could be gotten, if crackers were available, and so on. On some very lucky occasions, we received LRRP rations—individually packaged dehydrated meals in a clear plastic bag. They're now called MREs, Meals Ready to Eat." LRRP rations didn't have all of the accouterments found with the Cs, like fruit or cake, but the meal itself was far superior. To prepare them, we just had to open a plastic bag of what looked like sawdust, add boiling water, and presto, Chicken and Rice, Chile Con Carne, or some other "scrumptious" meal. Then again, we had to have water and be able to boil it to prepare them. Which brings up another point: how we heated our food or boiled water for soup, coffee, hot cocoa, tea, or LRRPs.

Heating a meal or boiling water required a "stove" to place the can, canteen cup, or pot upon. To make the stove, one would remove the top of one of the "tuna" cans with a P-38, empty its contents, and lay them aside. The small can would then be turned over, and a few triangular air holes were put into the sides of the can using a regular church-key-type can opener. Turned back upright and placed on the ground, it became a perfect little stove waiting for a source of fuel. We were provided with small "heat tabs," a chemical substance that looked like a used two-inch bar of soap about a quarter-inch thick and made of dried Sterno. Each tablet was packaged in aluminum foil to protect the chemicals from evaporating. Laying the heat tab in the can and lighting it would provide a few minutes of a low flame. Feeding a new one into the can when the other was almost gone provided sufficient energy to boil water or heat a soup-sized can of Franks and Beans.

Most of our guys used an alternative energy source that was far more efficient: plastique explosives, of which we had plenty. The stuff looked and felt very much like the white modeling clay we played with in grammar school. First, we'd break off a small piece from what looked like an oversized bar of white butter, roll a small amount between our fingers into pea-sized balls. One ball would be placed in the stove and lit with a match, and other pieces added as needed. The heat was so intense we could boil water or heat food in a third of the time. Faster than a microwave! I don't know what type of chemical vapor they put out, but considering the other stuff we inhaled or was sprayed on us, a faster cooked meal was more important. Somewhat like our mosquito repellant and gun cleaning oil. We used them for the opposite purpose- gun oil on our skin for mosquitos and repellant to clean our weapons.

As mentioned, some guys got really good at preparing a meal. First, they created the proper blends of the beef and pork meals and seasoned them with the appropriate amounts of Tabasco sauce, orange marmalade, or a dab of cheddar cheese spread. Then they'd toast bread or pound cake over a little stove and cover it with fruit for their dessert from yet another meal. Boil water in a canteen cup blackened from months of use and they had a perfect cup of instant coffee or hot cocoa. It was pretty darn good stuff after about six months of a steady diet, and the whole meal could cook in under a minute using plastique! Depending on how hard it was raining, of course.

At the end of every meal, all cans and wastes were crushed and buried in a foxhole so they couldn't be used against us as some type of IED[55]. If we didn't get a hot meal brought to us, the entire process (except selection, which was done only in the morning) was re-

---

55   IED- Improvised explosive device

peated two or three times a day, every day, month after month. We had to be very creative and adaptable to survive even our meals. How else could you open a can of Alpo and decide how best to prepare it?

Chapter VI
Letters from Home

Whether in the field, on a stand-down, staging in the mountains, or after a long day of action, sometimes a small canvas sack containing mail was included with supplies brought out by helicopter. As for our outgoing mail, it was either placed in the outgoing sack, or if express mail was wanted, handed to a door gunner while his idling chopper was being unloaded. Fortunately, we didn't need stamps to mail letters. In either case, the mail would begin its processing when the chopper returned to Camp Evans. We could never be certain if a letter would make it back to the world or even if all of the mail sent from back home actually reached us. A lone Huey flying over enemy-occupied jungle is inherently more at risk than a US Postal Service vehicle driving through a residential neighborhood. Unless, of course, you live in...

The military did the best it could under the circumstances. One of the interesting things about our mail delivery was that even though it was purported that the enemy suffered greatly when it came to resupply, his mail delivery was faster. His was hand-carried from

North Vietnam using the Ho Chi Minh trail, through the jungle terrain of Laos, over towering, rugged mountains into South Vietnam. The entire trip to our area of operations was less than one hundred miles as the crow flies. On the other hand, the mail we received had to be flown across the continental US and the Pacific Ocean, then routed in-country via military transport planes and trucks and ultimately delivered by helicopter out to the field. The letters were probably hand-sorted at every transfer point along their incredible journey almost halfway around the planet. Our incoming mail could take upward of two and a half weeks to reach us in the field; Charlie's took one to two weeks.

The military's version of the pony express could present problems for us. For example, trying to follow the box scores listed in a hometown newspaper was a problem. Ordinarily, the long wait between sending a letter and receiving the long-awaited response didn't bother us, though there were always exceptions—like when one could not remember the questions originally asked weeks earlier in the letter they had sent. Realistically, unless we needed a timely response to something, such as when I needed an answer from my wife two weeks before I was to meet her on my R and R in Hawaii— "Where are we staying?" or "Am I a father yet?"—the delays were tolerable.

Some letters from the world were funny, not necessarily because they were intended to be but rather because of the circumstances under which they were read. Some communications kept us up to date on "current" events or town gossip. Others put life's trials and tribulations in a clearer perspective, teaching us at our tender young age that many things should never be taken for granted, like food, clothing, and shelter. Sometimes the contents of a letter provoked anger, frustration, and pain, making it difficult to stay focused on the immediate job at hand: staying alive. Occasionally a letter would be handed off, asking how the other guy interpreted the writing. "Do you think this is supposed to be serious, funny, or is she just busting my cubes?" Correspondence from home contained both good news and bad, but it was always welcomed. A letter meant someone thought enough about you to actually take the time to write. Things are a bit quicker these days, but you still don't know the tone of voice or frame of mind the sender was in when the email was written. Now you can just hit "Reply." For us in Vietnam, it might take a month.

"Care packages" from home were an entirely different story. As great as it was to receive them, it always seemed they came at the wrong time. *Damn army always screwing with our minds.* Understand that anything we received had to fit into a rucksack and potentially be carried. Couple those concerns with the knowledge that some items, if stored in a rucksack, could be damaged. And there were many ways things could be damaged there, like being one of thirty rucks piled onto a sling and crushed during a helicopter drop. Plus, there were the elements—ruined by rain, destroyed by mold from high humidity, or melted by the sun's intense heat. We always had to take into consideration that at any time, an item could potentially meet some destructive force that nature or man could deliver. Therefore, all items of questionable longevity had to be completely scrutinized at once and a determination made as to whether it should be traded, sold, read, eaten, drunk, worn, saved, or sent back to the rear immediately. When anyone received a package the night before an operation started, funny swap meets, and outrageous feasts resulted.

I can't say I remember the contents of every letter I received, but a few are forever tattooed on my brain. In late February 1968, after some intense action one kilometer outside the city of Hue, I received a letter that was so good that I had to share it. I read it aloud, interjecting "the severity of the situation" to the other guys around me. I wanted to put our plight at the moment into perspective: Things could always be worse. We could always use some humor during our days there. Especially after three straight weeks of rain and heavy action.

Wet Is a Relative Term

It was late on a cold, dark afternoon when we got word that hot chow and mail were on its way out to us. Helicopter flights, whether for resupply or gunship support, were not very common during the Tet Offensive due to low cloud cover and horrendous weather conditions that month. In fact, we would be exposed to rain, dense fog, constant drizzle, and heavy mist almost nonstop for twenty-eight of the twenty-nine days of February. Yep, it was a leap year, one more day to stay in Nam. The dismal conditions we had already endured made the delivery especially terrific news. To top it off, the CO said we'd also be getting some dry socks. We were about as happy as someone who just won the Publisher's Clearing House sweepstakes. Just think of it— hot food to warm our bodies, dry socks to warm our feet, and mail to warm our hearts, and all at the same time! Yeehaw! Happy days are here again! Like I said, it's amazing what's taken for granted in a comfortable world. And people wonder why Vietnam veterans— hell, any combat veterans—think a little differently.

We had set up a perimeter near the small hamlet just outside of Hue where Bill Phifer had performed his incredible act of bravery, just because he was hungry. So it was appropriate that food would be delivered to us at that location. This particular day followed the same script and was characteristic of our luck of the previous eighteen days. The food, mail, and rucksacks were about to be delivered just as the weather started to worsen. We waited with very little to do except keep our eyes peeled for Charlie and look for a suitable place to dine while sitting on our inverted helmets. When at last the chopper landed, some guys ran out to quickly unload food, munitions, and a mail sack. After an anxious minute on the ground, we turned our heads to protect our eyes from the swirling debris as it took off. The Huey banked right across a rice paddy, bringing its path directly over the stripped skeleton of the less fortunate Go-Go Bird helicopter shot down only days before. Gaining speed and altitude, the pilot pointed its nose north toward darkening clouds, heading back to Camp Evans to retrieve the sling containing our rucksacks.

During the chopper's absence, the marmite cans of hot food were set up next to each other on the ground. Positioned behind each can was a "volunteer" grunt wielding a ladle like a machete. Squads were immediately called up individually to form a chow line because once the containers were opened, it didn't take long for the hot food to become cold food, or the little ice cream cups to melt. It was all orderly and very similar to occupants at a party getting up from each table and heading for the buffet. The only difference being there were no tables, chairs, and clean, dry clothes. Come to think of it, we didn't have the buffet either, but we usually savored the "hot" meal just the same. But not always.

The initial squads started the procession standing in a light drizzle, being careful not to stand too close to each other, more so for safety than the smell of those around them. By the time our squad was finally told to get our chow, the weather had worsened to a light rain. About all we could do was stand in the deepening mud and take it. Our packs had our rain ponchos, and they hopefully would be flown out to us before the weather deteriorated any more. If not, another night trying to sleep in the rain. We watched in nervous anticipation as an increasing volume of water dripped down from the edges of our helmets. Guys from the other squads hurried past us with mounded plates, trying to inhale their food as fast as possible while it was at least still warm. We craned our necks, guessing aloud as to what they were eating, similar to sitting on an airplane when flight attendants walk down the aisle handing out...whatever it is they hand out on planes. It's easier to guess these days because it's usually a small bag of pretzels.

Where the line queued at the first station, paper plates and plastic utensils were handed out, and because of the steadily increasing rain, we naturally blamed the army for planning it that way. Try as we might to protect them, the plates began to resemble wet napkins, so we hurried through the line with arms extended. Cupping the plates into the shape of a bowl out of necessity, we received separate ladles full of different foods that all drifted to the center. While we progressed past each food station, the rain seemed to be picking up and began to form little puddles on top of our food piles. Left exposed to Mother Nature's warped sense of humor, the meal eventually looked more like a school science project of an extinct volcano with a crater lake in its jagged caldera.

Once the last serving position was passed, we each ran to what little shelter we could find, and the instant we got settled down to eat, it was, of course, time to get back up for mail call. The conditions had created yet another problem for us to overcome because the rapidly dissolving paper plates had to be carefully placed on the ground before we stood up. Just like holding one of those little plastic games where you try to get wildly rolling tiny steel balls into marked holes, we had to observe extreme caution to prevent the Jell-O that was sliding around in the collecting rainwater from slipping off the dish.

Usually, as soon as mail was retrieved, we couldn't wait to tear it open and read its contents. I say usually because on rainy days like we were experiencing, some mail was saved. A letter from a wife, girlfriend, or parents was put inside our dry helmets and stored for later reading when dry privacy with enough light could be found. All other authors, however, were typically read immediately. There was only so much room inside a helmet, and some of the room was reserved for photographs.

The problem that day, however, was twofold. We had to race the increasing rain before it washed our "hot" meal away and to read our mail before the ink came off the paper. But try as we might, many were fighting a losing battle against the green Jell-O blobs slithering off their plates. Fortunately, they matched the color of our boots. So, while sitting our butts on our helmets, trying to balance the slop on our laps, we shoveled food into our mouths with one hand and read our mail as quickly as possible with the other.

Now, you would think we'd be pretty upset about the turn of events that evening. I mean, wouldn't you if your body was hungry, cold, and wet, and you knew that tomorrow and the next day and the next would probably bring the same thing? Maybe worse? We were also facing the distinct possibility that our rucksacks might not be delivered again because of the weather, meaning another night spent completely exposed to the elements. Oh, and let's not forget our sneaky little adversary always lurking just out of sight. Well, a letter I received that day put the reality of our situation into a totally different perspective for me. It made me realize I was experiencing something I would have never thought I could survive, let alone tolerate, only a few short months before.

I was reading a letter from Ed Helmuth, a high school buddy who was attending a small college in upstate New York. Like most other friends who sent letters from back in the world, he hoped everything was okay in "Vet Num." With good intentions, advice, and concern for my safety, he hoped I wasn't getting sunburned and that the barracks were okay, and he warned me to stay away from the women and not to get drunk because it could be dangerous. The opening paragraph hit a funny bone almost immediately and had me smiling. We had only seen the sun a few hours that month, and that was when we were still in base camp with our hooches set up. The temperatures were in the forties and fifties every night, and we were sleeping in the rain and mud because that's what grunts have to do sometimes when their packs aren't brought out. And the only women we'd seen so far that month were two-hundred-year-old, seventy-four-pound Vietnamese peasants with brown teeth. But then again, they did wear these sexy little black pajamas all the time. I hurriedly tried to eat dinner and read the letter at the same time but just couldn't. I started choking on the corn-laced green Jell-O while laughing.

His letter went on to explain about how hard it was at school. It sucked being away from home without knowing anyone there and staying in his cold room most of the time to study. The girls were okay, but he hadn't met any yet. *Poor guy*. I thought. He went on about going home for Christmas and a shopping trip he had taken into our small town of Pompton Lakes. It was on a cold, drizzly day, and he'd driven around our one and only main street until he could find a convenient parking spot. He described how the sidewalks were covered with slush and puddles and explained how he didn't want to get his head and feet wet by walking too far. *Yeah, I know the feeling, Sport*. I laughed to myself. He continued his story, how after five minutes of horrible stop-and-go driving, a car pulled out directly in front of Gelman's department store, where he wanted to go. He pulled past the spot in order to back into it, and in the time it took him to stop his car, put it in reverse, and turn his head to look out the back window, an elderly woman in a Volkswagen had already occupied the space. He was furious because he had to park a half block away and walk without his umbrella! *Horrible, Eddy, just horrible*, I thought. The letter went on about how the store didn't even have what he wanted, his feet got wet for nothing, and to top it off, a few days later he came down with a cold. The experience did, however, provide him the time to write me while resting in bed.

I lost it at that point, and the guys around me thought I had cracked up, when in fact, I had. They were asking me if I was okay, if everyone at home was okay, showing real concern for my well-being. All I could do was hand them the rapidly smearing letter and contin- ue choking. It was definitely infectious to each guy who read it. Here they were, standing up to their ankles in mud and water, rain beating off their heads, fingers and toes puckered like little prunes, no place to sleep or get out of the rain because our packs hadn't arrived yet, no dry clothes to change into, and they were laughing. It seemed we all got the same feeling from that letter. We also knew that, had the circumstances been reversed, we'd have probably written about the experience the same way.

Between gasps for air during the laughing jag, guys were yelling, "Tell your buddy to get that woman's li- cense plate and we'll find her; see how she'd like walking a half block in the rain!" "Hey, let's save our tissue-pa- per packs and send them to him in case he runs out of Kleenex." "Why don't you guys cut it out and leave him alone. I bet those dormitory rooms really are cold and lonely with those coeds running around in their miniskirts." "Yeah, and his cafeteria probably doesn't deliver hot food directly to him like we get!" The barbs continued into the night, even when I was woken up for guard duty. "I'll bet your friend probably has to stay in bed all night, instead of having a friend yanking on his pants legs at two forty-five in the morning. No won- der why he's so lonely!" During guard duty that night, we all took the time to think of something clever to wake the next guy up with, to make it easier for them to keep their eyes open while they shivered in the rain.

I actually carried that smeared, wrinkled letter with me until I left the field. It helped to reread it once in a while and remind the guys about how much worse our plight could be. It was also good because it reminded all of us of the comforts we would hopefully return to someday and that all things in life should be appreciated, no matter how bad they appear at the moment. To this day, when I'm walking down a street and the rain is blowing under my umbrella, or my newly polished shoes are getting white streaks from salt-laced slush, I always think of that letter, the conditions grunts have always endured, and suddenly life isn't so bad. I also keep a photo on my desk, taken on a not so good day, that keeps me humble with the memory.

Thank You, But . . .

Packages from home were especially great to receive. Sometimes they contained things we had asked for, like a sweater, Kool-Aid, tea bags, or instant oatmeal. As I mentioned earlier, Kool-Aid was a critical need for many grunts. Packages usually contained other great things that we didn't necessarily ask for but would accept nonetheless, like salamis, pepperoni, fruitcakes, cookies, stuffed animals, umbrellas, large framed photos, beautiful Bibles, white boxer shorts with red hearts on them (my favorite), bright argyle socks, boxes of pasta, and so on.

We loved getting packages from home, but they sometimes created a problem. Books were good to get by those who enjoyed reading, but more than two in a backpack could mean excessive weight. The same held true for *Playboy* magazines for the guys who didn't like to read. Any more than ten issues in their pack could become excessive. Some foods that we loved at home, sent to us for that very reason, sometimes created unique difficulties, like if they had to be mixed with milk. Pasta was great too, but no one had a pot large enough to cook it, except maybe a metal helmet, but they were used almost exclusively for shaving.

The intense heat a package was exposed to while in transit usually had its effect on the contents. Some guys probably wrote home that they would love to taste butter again, so naturally it was sent to them in their next package. At least that's what we guessed, because empty wrappers found inside their box were labeled "butter" and the rest of the contents were well lubricated. Holidays were interesting because almost everyone received a package containing foodstuffs and occasionally something made of chocolate. We had to guess at those—if a blob of chocolate was found melted in the bottom of a clear plastic wrapper, and it had arrived just weeks after the holiday, it was probably an Easter bunny. At least we assumed they were rabbits, because we'd find candy eyes floating in the brown gooey mess. They still tasted okay but were just a little more difficult to eat without using a spoon.

Sometimes the same thing would happen to cheeses, but that was okay because melted cheese always worked better when mixing it in a can of C rations. You might not realize it, but if carried long enough in high heat, salami and pepperoni also melt. On one occasion in late May, I received a pint of Southern Comfort that I had asked for in February, just to help take the chill off at night while we were "back at our barracks." I received it in a box filled with other goodies while on a stand-down. The sweet nectar had been removed from its glass container and poured into a plastic bottle so it wouldn't break in transit. It was a great idea, but unfortunately, the combination of alcohol, heat, and plastic just didn't work well together. I took a swig of what I expected to be "comfort" and spit it out immediately, gagging for air. If you think Jolly-Ollie Orange Kool-Aid, iodine, and warm river water sounds bad, try cutting the lawn on a hot August afternoon and having a satisfying warm Southern Comfort–and–polyethylene cocktail. I was going to dump it out, but a guy offered me two packs of crushed Fig Newtons in trade. Such a deal as this I could not refuse.

Packages often prompted trades and mega feasts the day before we were to leave an LZ to begin a new operation. Some guy who didn't like to read would trade a book he got for a box of smashed Oreo cookies. A can of Spam would be traded for a box of beef bouillon cubes, a knife for a pair of sunglasses, a hot salami for a can of cold chili. The dealing would continue right up to dinnertime, and then whatever was left over, couldn't fit in a rucksack, couldn't be traded, or didn't look appetizing enough for the owner to eat it himself was free for the taking. We'd eat into the night until the dew destroyed most of the perishables or our stomachs gave out.

I can clearly remember a package delivered just before Easter. While on an operation traipsing through the mountains, Big Joe got a package labeled "Fragile." None of us could believe that such a small cardboard cube had made it that far without being crushed. Amazed, we all stood around waiting to see what was inside. Joe was really reluctant to open the box because he knew if it was indeed fragile, he would have to rewrap it and send it home. It would never be able to survive being repeatedly dropped to the ground from a helicopter while stored in a flimsy rucksack. We could see the concern on his knitted forehead while debating with himself before finally saying aloud that he had better open it to at least see what it was before returning it. We watched Joe with growing interest and speculated as to what could possibly be inside such a small box. Taking his heavily muscled physique into consideration, guys were guessing that it was probably a big chunk of leather he could chew on, maybe finger weights or pieces of lead to put in his pants cuffs so he could stay in shape on our little hikes. As usual, he would just smile with his little-boy charm and chuckle.

Joe first checked to see if anyone had something he could use to reseal the box before he could open it. Once assured by one of the radio operators who had some electrical tape, Joe began to gingerly open the package. A bunch of us were leaning over his shoulders, but his hands were so big, we were having trouble seeing what was in the tiny box, especially when he started removing the thin tissue paper and cotton used to protect its contents. Our guesses immediately started changing to things like mascara and a compact mirror, a crystal paper weight for his desk, perfume in a fancy crystal bottle, a gold-plated M-16 round on a necklace for the grunt who has everything, nylon stockings for R and R in Taiwan. We were all having a good time at Joe's expense, as often happened when anyone got a care package, but we weren't prepared for what came next. His eyes got very big, then glassy, and he whispered, "God, I don't believe it."

He very carefully put his thumb and index finger into the box and pulled out a beautifully hand-painted Easter egg. We all stood in awe looking at it, wondering how long it must have taken to paint, the patience and love involved to do it, and how the hell it had ever survived the ten-thousand-mile trip from Philadelphia. It was as if we had all just experienced a miracle. The egg was actually empty, making it that much more fragile and brittle, and it looked like a fancy Fabergé egg, without as much as a single stroke of paint or decoration harmed in transit. Joe held it and slowly turned it as all the guys standing around him praised how beautiful it was and asked who bought it for him. With tears welling up in his eyes, he said that his father had painted it for him, and that in turn brought a tear to most of our eyes, thinking of home and family. Everyone soon turned and walked away and left him to his own thoughts with what little privacy we could afford him. Almost two months later, after reading a letter, a very happy Joe told us the egg had made it home without any damage, much to the relief of all of us.

Most everyone would have a need for some type of understanding or compassion during their combat tour of duty. For many of us, it was the first time we had displayed or shared real emotions with another male, which was very awkward and uncomfortable back then. Though we didn't know how to handle it or what to say most of the time, we tried to give comfort as best we could. At times we wanted to unload feelings brought about by a letter or event but felt we couldn't because everyone there had their own problems. So, as great as letters and packages were to receive, they could sometimes also create the loneliest of times. They could prompt feelings of sadness, elation, or frustration, sometimes in the same letter, painfully reminding us that we had very little if any control over the events shaping our lives. As I've mentioned, weeks could pass before the response to a question was received, and by then the answer could be too late. It was often very difficult to write letters home as well. We tried to keep them positive and upbeat, when very often we wanted to scream out in agony for some peaceful comfort and tenderness. No mention of hardships, danger, living conditions, and depravations were ever mentioned, unless to a close buddy also in the service.

Sometimes a letter, either sent or received, could provide a good deal of healing or harm just by the way the reader interpreted it, like emails today. Even something as seemingly harmless as sending a photo home could evoke different feelings. We rarely got any pictures of ourselves in the field, so when one did come along, it usually meant a hard decision as to who it should be sent to without hurting someone's feelings. Was the last one sent to my parents, wife, best friend, sister, grandparents? It didn't matter, because whomever you sent it to, the others might write back saying they were hurt for not getting the photo. I guess that should have been understood, because everyone at home thought we were working in supply and had lots of pictures in our footlocker. Mail could be tough, and after a time many guys didn't write home as often. Some became reluctant to read letters from their loved ones, just because of the stress and depression it caused them. When someone is looking for compassion, they don't want to feel attacked.

Congratulations, My Condolences

My time of need came when I received a letter from a very close high school friend. The time was late June, and fortunately we were on a stand-down, pulling "guard duty" along Route 1 just northeast of Camp Evans. It was an area where boots and pants were optional, where one could sleep for a whole day if he so chose, maybe catch up on letter writing or drink all of the stored-up cans of warm beer he'd been carrying. Our hooches were put up without the worry of taking them down for four days, and overall, we usually felt relatively secure. Of course, we still had a perimeter, had dug holes for defense, and knew where every weapon was at all times, and everyone pulled guard duty every night.

The weather was extremely hot, so most of us washed our clothes and just lounged around in our bathing suits or fatigue pants rolled up to the knees. In fact, that was about the only thing we did there because it was so boring. The intense sun had baked the ground dry, leaving it in a state where the slightest breeze would pick up loose grit and plaster it to any sweat-covered exposed skin. It felt more like the lazy, hazy days of summer back home instead of a free-fire combat zone. Overall, that stand-down was used primarily to "recharge our batteries" and allowed us to feel almost safe around friendly civilians.

Joe Kochman, Jack Teakle, author

A betting pool had been started in our company as to which guy would become a father first, me or a guy named Bob in our company who hailed from West Virginia. Our wives were expecting our first children around the same time—mine in mid-May, Bob's the beginning of June. Everyone had gotten a kick out of my wife's last letter in May when she wrote she had just finished polishing her car on her due date because she felt fine. Naturally, we all looked forward to each letter with special anticipation, and according to the calendar, both wives were overdue. Neither of us had heard anything from the Red Cross or home for over a week, so all we could do was hope and pray everything was okay. Those times were especially hard, because although we were sometimes overly concerned during combat, the painful thoughts of our own mortality were overshadowed by what it would mean to our wife and unborn child.

We had mail call as soon as we had settled in on the first day of the stand-down. I was excited when my name was called because it could be "the" letter. I rushed up to get it and found it was from my mother-in-law, immediately thinking it had to be *the* one because she had never written me before. In fact, she never liked me before, either. As I started walking back to my hooch, tearing at the envelope, my name was called out again. Whoa, two letters at the same time could only mean big news! The guys in my squad started to hoot and holler as I turned to get the second one, saying the good news had to be in one of the letters or my wife was probably going to be entered into the *Guinness Book of World Records* for the longest pregnancy. The second letter was from a high school sweetheart who had married a friend of mine, himself already a Vietnam veteran. We had all remained good friends, and they had written me a few times already. I again started back and tore at my mother-in law's letter, quickly scanning it for any news. And there it was: "Judy had a baby girl and all is well." All I could do was stare at the words and yell at the top of my lungs, "I'm a father! I'm a father! I have a daughter, a little baby girl! I'm a father!"

Guys came over to give their congratulations while I was grinning from ear to ear, saying it over and over, "Can you believe it? I'm a father! My wife had a baby girl!" Everyone seemed genuinely happy for me and asked questions as to how much the baby weighed and when she was born. I realized then that I hadn't even finished reading the letter yet, but I figured I had the news I wanted. First things first—we were all going to celebrate and get drunk. I ran over to a street vendor who was standing with his small pushcart next to the road. I ordered a case of American beer and a box of cigars without giving any thought to the cost. The frail little Vietnamese man said he had no cigars but did produce a warm case of Hamm's beer. When he told me the price, I almost had a baby myself because it was more than I made in a month! I told Papa-san I had just become a papa-san myself and not to sell the beer to anyone else, that I'd be right back with the money. I ran back to our company and looked for all of the new guys who didn't know about lending money to a grunt, hit them all up, and ran back with a fist full of MPC monopoly money to collect our "champagne" for the party.

I gladly passed a couple of beers to each guy in my squad and anyone else who came over to congratulate me, including Bob, the other expectant father, who had lost the "first born" pool. Other guys came over to celebrate and brought their own beer, so we had the makings of a real party. We kidded around and laughed for the remainder of the day, but unfortunately, after not drinking alcohol for so long and not having any body fat to absorb it, three cans of warm beer had me and more than a few others pretty wrecked.

During a lull in the conversations, I reread the letter, attempting to memorize the details of my new daughter Michelle's birth—time and day she was born, weight, location, and such. I was surprised to learn that my wife in fact had given birth three weeks earlier and neither the Red Cross nor the US Army had notified me. The rest of the letter was like most others—hoping I was okay and that type of stuff. Something about the letter, though, was slightly odd. My mother-in-law mentioned that she was "sorry to hear about your friend," but I didn't understand what or who she was referring to. Heck, we'd lost so many guys already, none of whom I thought I had ever mentioned in my letters home, certainly not to my wife. I shrugged it off and opened Diane's letter, continuing again to laugh and drink with the guys as I did so. Diane too congratulated Judy and me on the birth of our daughter and went on to say how sorry she was about Donny because she knew how close we were.

I was definitely feeling the effects of the warm beer and the good news by that time, so I didn't fully understand what she was referring to. I assumed she was alluding to the fact that my best friend Donny Miller, and I had beaten the system all along until we were separated when we got to the 1st Cavalry. Then the words of my mother-in-law's letter came to me: "Sorry to hear about your friend." I must have gone into shock because I kept reading both letters over and over, thinking I was confused because of my beer-induced state of mind. When I could no longer ignore what both letters were trying to say without using the word "killed," I was crushed.

My best friend had indeed been killed in action almost a month before, but no one had written to tell me.

I just lost it. I didn't know how to react, because my mind and emotions were on overload. My best friend had died. My first child had been born. Do I laugh, cry, what? I don't know which I was doing when Big Joe and Jackie asked me if I was all right. Regaining my composure a little, I tried to act tough by holding back my emotions, saying only that the second letter had some bad news. My closest friend, the LRRP, hadn't made it, and the war sucked. Everyone there was pretty drunk by then and started to curse the war, the army, the politicians, everything—just trying to think of something that would make sense of it all.

After a short while, I just couldn't stay with the guys, trying to be the host of the party with false bravado but really hurting inside. I said my good nights, excused myself, and tried to find someplace where I could be alone, try to sort the whole insane thing out in my head. It was by then dark, and I found a secluded spot behind an old building just out of sight of everyone. Dropping to the packed clay, I leaned against the concrete wall still hot from the afternoon sun and sat for hours, staring into a black sky filled with billions of twinkling stars. I found myself suddenly very much alone in a strange place, having no control of my fate. I had been cast from the secure fantasy world of invincibility all teenagers create in their minds. Instead of beautiful visions and wonderment of what my future held, I was forced to see the harsh reality that nothing in life is fair. For the next several hours, every emotion imaginable swept through me while I prayed, questioned, pleaded, and swore until finally falling asleep with eyes swollen shut. That was a very difficult night and four-day stand-down for me. Certainly the happiest and saddest day of my life.

Chapter VII
Leisure Time

Many nations have underestimated the resolve and tenacity of the American fighting man and woman. They thought we were soft back then and probably still do now. They provoke us. Then they get their asses kicked. Militarily, anyway. Prior to each of the world wars, aggressors didn't think the United States would get involved. They assumed we'd rather play tennis than fight. Funny thing is they were half right. Sure, we'd rather play than fight, but Americans have this wonderful ability to work hard, play hard, kick ass if our country asks, and then go right back to playing.

That trait still confounds the hell out of people from other nations today. They've been killing their neighbors for five thousand years. When they ask for our military help, we do it at the cost of American lives. When it's over, we're accused of being warlike, imperialistic, and a bully because we don't always allow the political negotiations sufficient time to solve the problem. Duh, if you haven't been able to solve your problem in five thousand years, why should we wait? As a nation we do what needs to be done and then move on to bigger and better things. There's a very good reason why it's an American flag on the moon!

So, it shouldn't come as any surprise that when a group of young Americans are put together in one place, even if that place is a war zone, they can still have a laugh. Sure, sometimes we wet our pants when the bullets flew, but we had fun too. When an operation ended and we were pulled out of the bush, we would normally stand down. On a couple of occasions, we were fortunate to be bivouacked along QL-1, Vietnamese for Highway 1, as we called it, the main road that stretches the entire length of Vietnam along the coast. While there we were able to mingle with Vietnamese civilians who were trying to sell us stuff. Same highway and people but quite a different atmosphere from those days during February's Tet Offensive.

But in most instances our stand-downs were on small firebases or LZs—not exactly a site one would select as a nice place to relax and enjoy a few days off. A typical 1st Cavalry firebase could be a few barren acres of red dirt surrounded by barbed wire and miles of wide-open flat plains, or it could be located on a mountaintop in the middle of nowhere surrounded by the same jungle we had just left. Regardless of where, remote outposts were usually populated with an assortment of artillery pieces, the troops who manned them, and an infantry unit defending its existence. Because of the Spartan surroundings, there was very little to do on an LZ. Depending on the weather, one could either sit on their air mattress inside their hooch to get out of the hot sun, getting covered with baked-on dirt while trying to read, write, sleep, or play cards, or they could sit inside their hooch to get out of the monsoon rains, getting cov-

ered with mud while trying to read, write, sleep, or play
cards. There were no stores, no bars, no libraries, no
ladies, nada, so we would just hang out for the three or
four days. Occasionally a guy was given permission for
emergency reasons to climb onto a helicopter returning
to Camp Evans to make a MARS[56] call home. In any
case, the stand-downs afforded the opportunity to at
least try to get some rest and relaxation—listen to tape
recordings from home or some favorite music, maybe
give each other a haircut, stuff like that. For excitement
we'd sit in front of someone else's hooch, kind of like
sitting on a neighbor's porch back home in the world.

Actually, let me clarify something about the "rest"
part. I think we got more sleep during rainy afternoons
than we did during the stifling nights. Everyone still
had normal guard duty after the sun went down—one
hour long, an hour and a half, two hours, depending
on how many guys were left in a squad to cover the
eight or nine hours of darkness. Just because we were
supposed to be out of harm's way didn't mean Char-

---

56   MARS call—Military Auxiliary Radio System, a US Department of
Defense–sponsored program used when access to traditional communications
is not available; basically, an emergency communications system. Messages
are relayed linking over three thousand dedicated licensed amateur radio
operators. Each time an individual communication is completed, the commu-
nicator must say "over." At that point, each radio operator monitoring the call
changes his radio from *receive* to *send* and forwards the transmission, then
changes their device setting back to *receive* a response. Take, for example,
Bob, who calls his wife and says, "I miss you, Babe. Can't wait until we're
together again." He ends his romantic transmission by saying "over." The last
operator in the long line of operators changes his radio from *receive*, then to
send to her, then changes back to receive to hear her response: "Who is this?!
Is that you, Rick?" If she doesn't say "over," the call is stalled. If she doesn't
hang up, she will eventually hear the operator say, "You must say 'over,'
ma'am, or the call cannot be completed." Not very intimate or private, plus
the call must be completed in no more than five minutes, but it was faster than
the mail.

lie would necessarily comply. Also, if one was not on guard duty, he and everyone else on the LZ was constantly being traumatized by the artillery guys executing fire missions directly over our heads.

Now imagine, if you will, the relief you would feel after being in the bush for two weeks, flying over miles of dense jungle that hid bad guys, and landing in a secure area. For the next three or four days, you won't need to carry your shoulder-straining heavy backpack or the twenty pounds of munitions hanging around your hips. You twist your tired body out of the straps and belts and let everything drop to the ground. Rain or shine, you push your weary body to set up a hooch with a friend, you blow up your air mattress with what little air you still have left in your lungs, and finally, after a tension-filled afternoon, you're able to lie down. Your hands are supporting your head like a pillow. You slowly exhale the tension from your body and eventually begin to scan the velvety black sky dotted with billions of twinkling points of light. Soon you can see nothing else around you in the near-total darkness. Occasionally you can hear a slight breeze rustling a few parched shrubs nearby. You know you won't have to get up until two thirty for guard duty, and your eyes are getting heavy as your mind starts to relax. You are soon in a sound, exhaustion-induced sleep from the physical and mental strain of being wired tight for two weeks, traipsing through jungles, rivers, and mountains looking for trouble. Visions of home and loved ones cautiously creep into your thoughts until the threatening world around you finally starts to fade away. You are literally floating on air. Soon you are dreaming of home, seeing your loved ones, holding your wife in your arms. The dream is so vivid it must be real. You never want it to end, and *ka-boooom!* A blinding flash of light illuminates everything around you, and the sound of ten lightning strikes shatters your eardrums when a 105- or 155-millimeter howitzer is fired directly over your head. Before you can even fully leave your dream, the ground shakes beneath you, and shock waves of hot air nearly blow your hooch over. Rest? Relax? Brutal. Freaking brutal. Just as you flinch when the next round is fired, you remember you have a few more nights of this crap.

Yeah, thanks for the rest, sirs, and by the way, my ears are still ringing after fifty-plus years. As was probably the case since the invention of gunpowder, everyone was sure their army was doing things like that on purpose to piss them off. It is always the "brass's fault." We found on more than one occasion we would have much rather been back in the bush so we *could* get some sleep. But always after that initial blast or two, it was just a matter of time before we would all eventually calm down and wait…wait for the news, hoping that the fire mission was just outgoing harassment fire, and wasn't because Charlie was picking a fight with the cavalry unit that had just replaced us. If he was, we might have to saddle up in a hurry.

On one special occasion, we went to Camp Evans for a few days' rest. The routine at the 1st Cavalry's base camp was pretty much the same as on the small LZs—no PX or shops. Even at Camp Evans, we set up our hooches within the base's perimeter and lived just as we normally would in the field. It would be seven months before I'd sleep on a bed mattress with sheets again. I can't say being at Camp Evans was all bad, because we did enjoy ourselves the one time we were there. It was the first week of March after our Tet operations when just to remind us they still had some guys left, Charlie fired a couple of 122-millimeter rockets into the new base camp. Unfortunately, one of them hit a new ammunition dump and a fuel storage area being prepared for the division's squadrons of helicopters. Instead of placing the munitions within individual protected areas surrounded by dirt revetments, they had to stack and relocate everything later. In any case, the rocket exploded very near the only tin roof on the base, coincidentally a barber shop run by a Vietnamese national. It just happened to be located adjacent to dozens and dozens of fifty-gallon barrels filled with highly flammable aviation fuel. That one rocket instantly set off the greatest fireworks display any of us had ever seen—different-colored star clusters bursting in air or flying sideways, red tracers everywhere, fuel drums launching off the ground like rockets with long flaming tails, huge plumes of orange flames. It lasted for a full day and a half without ever stopping. Great colors and sound, but it got on our nerves after a while because it kept us awake. So much for the safety and solitude of a big base camp.

Interestingly, a few weeks after that attack, I received a letter from my terrified mother, including a small newspaper article detailing how "Camp Evans, a large military base used by the 1st Cavalry Division (Airmobile) in Vietnam's I Corps region, has been bombed by suspected North Vietnamese MiGs, heavily damaging the base and its large detachment of helicopters. Total amount of damage and casualties has not been released at this time." I'm pretty sure that was the day I stopped believing things printed in newspapers. Only baseball box scores are real. Everything else is made up to terrorize, sensationalize, placate, or mislead the public, thereby selling more newspapers and feeding the public's need for more information.

Yeah, life in the field and on stand-downs was pretty basic, the amount of fun being dictated by where we were.

The Good Life

Usually at LZ Jack, where we spent most of our stand-downs, life was pretty predictable. We would wake up in the morning whenever we wanted. A teenager's dream. But it was usually when the sun beating down on our hooches reached a sufficient temperature to start baking our brains. We'd get up, brush our teeth, and maybe start some water boiling for coffee. Someone might forsake coffee, slip into his untied boots, put a helmet on his head, and grab an M-16, some toilet paper, and an entrenching tool. He would then walk toward the barbed-wire perimeter, well past our foxholes, dig a suitably deep hole, face away from the maddening crowd to make sure Charlie wasn't lurking about, and then go about his business, so to speak. That was often a trial for whoever went first, but it signaled the beginning of fun for some of the others.

If that wasn't humiliating enough, a couple of guys would always throw some rocks or cans or something just to make sure the guy felt even more vulnerable. So, while squatting and thinking about the "boredom, cold, exhaustion, squalor, lack of privacy, monotony,

ugliness and the constant teasing anxiety about the future,"[57] or maybe just trying to read a two-week-old *Wall
Street Journal*, rocks and stuff kicked up dirt all around
him or bounced off his steel helmet. This scene was repeated daily and was always accompanied by yelling
and laughing from the guys in the perimeter. Great
way to start the day, don't you think? Once back to the
hooch as if nothing had happened, he would look to
see what was left of the C rations for breakfast, cook it,
take a bite, throw it away, and then sit back down on
his air mattress, write letters, or do other stuff until the
next meal. Pretty exciting, huh? At least it was better
than having people shooting at you.

If it was payday or a day or two after, poker games
were rampant. Guys borrowing money, guys lending
money, old-timers warning new guys that if they lend
money, don't expect to get it back. Any borrower could
be here today and gone tomorrow. By the end of the
four-day stand-down, one guy in the company would
have everyone's money. The poker games would be replaced with rummy or hearts and the stakes were lower,
the losses payable on the next payday. All card games
were pretty interesting because like in the Old West, everyone was armed and dangerous, meaning there was
definitely no cheating. There were some very verbal
"misunderstandings" though. It wasn't the loss of money but the principle of trying to screw a brother grunt.
Actually, money didn't mean much, so most guys received very little pay in the field. You determined how
much you wanted when processed into the division. I
was getting ten dollars a month and sent the rest home.
If we needed fifty cents, we ripped a dollar bill in half.
As far as most of us were concerned, compared to food,

57   Scannell, Vernon, *Not Without Glory*.

clothing, and shelter, money was useless. We couldn't buy anything because there was no place to buy anything from. Besides, once we flew out for our next mission, the money usually deteriorated from the water, humidity, and everything else we put it through.

Speaking of clothing, changing wardrobes could be humorous or downright funny as hell. We would receive clean clothes every two weeks or so, usually when on a stand-down but not necessarily. The way we selected our new wardrobes was rather interesting. We might be lying around waiting for a log bird to deliver our hot chow and would be notified that clean clothes would also be arriving. The CO determined which platoon would be first, second, and third. Platoon leaders would give their squads' order. After crawling around in rivers, mud, dirt, and sleeping in them for two weeks, clothing had a tendency to become a little soiled, especially when you consider we couldn't bathe very often. Most guys didn't wear underwear because of the effect tropical weather had on it. If cotton underwear was worn, the only thing that would be left after a few days would be the elastic waistband; the rest of the material just seemed to mysteriously disappear.

When clean clothes arrived, they were distributed one squad at a time, the same way chow and pay were doled out. Though that may sound democratic in principle, in reality it created an embarrassment for the last squads, who had to select from a scant, tangled pile of trampled leftovers scattered around on the ground. You see, once the original mountainous supply of clean clothing had been rummaged through by eighty, ninety or so guys, it was hard to find anything that a) had a size label, b) had all its buttons, c) had no holes, or d) all of the above. When our squad's turn came to pick, the selection process really didn't matter much to me. At 112 pounds after only three months in-country, the only size that would fit me was an extra-small, and those were normally reserved for the Vietnamese army. In fact, my web belt once belonged to someone in the North Vietnamese army.

Clothing day was always good for a laugh though. For instance, I had a twenty-seven-inch waist and a thirty-inch inseam. Needless to say, I looked ridiculous wearing a thirty-six/ thirty-eight. If that was the only size left in the pile, that's what I got. But, hey, at least it meant wearing clean clothes for a couple of days. If you could visualize ten naked guys stomping through piles of clothes and tossing them around on the ground while "shopping" for the right article, you can appreciate the humor in something as simple as getting a clean shirt and pants. Sometimes, though, I got lucky, and the entire pile was size small. In that case, Big Joe and the other hulks looked pretty funny, especially the Rooster. Shirt sleeves reached their elbows, while shirts and pants could not be buttoned. As you might imagine, we were not exactly the best-dressed army, even after we received a clean change of clothes. If for whatever reason you needed something, everyone was issued a "line number" and could order what they needed—cloths, canteen, helmet strap, whatever. The request was sent back to supply, and it might take a few days before it would arrive, but hey, fashion was not a big thing in the bush.

Hygiene sometimes had its lighter moments too. Showers were a rarity because they took so long to prepare. If on a stand-down, we would set up a tall tripod made from hooch poles and hang a large feedbag-looking device from the center. Then all you had to do was

fetch five-gallon cans of water from a water truck, carry or drag them hundreds of feet to the tripod, climb
up a makeshift ladder to pour the water into the bag,
wait while the sun heated the water, and then take your
shower. Of course, there was never enough water in
the feedbag, so a shower was rarely finished. With the
exception of being in a "secure" area, near a sufficient
water source, baths could not even be considered. It
didn't matter, though, because body odor is a relative
thing—we all stank, ergo no one smelled bad.

We were often at LZ Jack, a small firebase located
five or six miles from Camp Evans, positioned on a low
rise in an otherwise flat, open plain area that stretched
for miles. Far to the west, the flatlands suddenly ended,
and the high, rugged mountains dominated the landscape. We experienced an interesting weather event

that usually took place every day around five in the afternoon during the hot seasons: It would rain. Each day we would watch clouds forming around the mountain peaks miles in the distance, when the cooler air of evening sank into the river valleys and the warm, humid air was forced upward. The clouds would grow, darken and start to drop the condensed water right back down into the valleys and onto the grunts that were out there. For anyone at the LZ, though, it was beautiful to see. We'd stand in the bright, hot sunshine and watch the storm approach from the mountains, a solid silvery sheet of fresh water falling straight down like a wall of mercury, slowly working its way across the wide, open plains toward us. The dry, sunlit plains between us and the mountains would be slowly blackened by clouds passing over them, as if in the throes of an eclipse. Afterward, in the rains' wake, massive rainbows grew upward and filled the sky as the sunlight reappeared.

Judging the speed of the approaching storm as best we could, we would strip and start soaping up with a little water spilled from our canteens and then look to the heavens while the downpour rinsed us off as the bloated clouds reached us. It usually worked rather well, and I say "usually" because there were times when the rain stopped before it reached us or veered off in another direction. On occasion our timing was off, and the rain would be on us and gone before we could finish. In all of those cases, we'd be ten or twenty naked guys standing in the bright sunlight, covered in rapidly drying soapsuds. A picture would look as if taken for a *National Geographic* magazine. Maybe a primitive tribe decorated in white ashes and doing a ritual dance to the gods. In any event, we sometimes did smell better on a stand-down.

For Music Lovers Only

We usually listened to music on stand-downs, supplied by guys who carried little transistor radios or small reel-to-reel tape recorders, powered by old batteries from the PRC-25 radiotelephone. You have to remember; this was during the pre-Walkman era. In fact, the pre-eight-track era! Regardless of the source, the only problem we had with the music was that we were limited to Armed Forces Radio and the small, two-inch-diameter tapes we had. Therefore, whoever supplied the sounds chose the music. That created problems at times, because for those of us into rock and roll, someone's selection of C and W music would drive us nuts, and of course vice versa. Saturday nights were especially brutal for many guys because the only thing on the radio was the Grand Ole Opry, coming to you live from the Ryman Auditorium in Nashville, Tennessee!

I carried tapes of the Doors, Beatles, Beach Boys, and Four Tops, while other guys had their favorites, including a lot of Motown, which was very much the in thing before most of us had left the world. The only problem with the tapes was that after seven months of playing the exact same artists and songs, they started having the opposite effect they were meant to provide. Instead of sitting back and enjoying the music, someone might complain that it was getting on his nerves, causing an ugly scene between the guy who liked the tape and another who was at his wit's end because of it. Besides music, some guys received tapes from home recording their loved one's voices instead of reading a written letter. They would play them over and over and over and over and over until you started to either dislike the people who recorded them or love them as your own family. It all depended on your perspective or how much brainwashing you were willing to take.

One day, after discussing how tired we were of the same music, Little Joe and I decided to write our own song. We were having a lot of fun with it after we got the lyrics down, but we needed some melody. There were about six guys sitting around, listening to us "singing" the lyrics using a Beach Boys song, then to a Dylan tune. Actually, we were speaking the words like Arlo Guthrie doing "Alice's Restaurant" but sounding more like Dylan. I can still remember the song today and the great laughs shared with a bunch of great guys.

Around last summer I was raising some hell,
Making some money and doing real well.
But a letter came for me one fateful day
Saying they wanted to take me away.
I got drafted.

Now, the Sarge and me, we both agree
That the army needs me like a dog needs fleas.
But I made it through basic without a sin

And even got my ninety-day wonder pin.
I'm a grunt.

So, it's off to the war across the sea,
To keep for us sweet liberty.
Fightin' through the paddies and into the bush,
I could hear from behind me the brass yellin'
"Push!"
This ain't fun.

Well, I got for me some nice Purple Hearts,
Seemed I stopped a bullet, got hit with some darts.
So, they sent me to the rear and a nice soft cot,
Where I tripped away my tour with baggies full
of   pot.
War is hell.

Now it's back to the states where this all starts
And I'm lauded a hero for catchin' those darts.
So I'm thankin' the army and all the big brass
For making me go and scaring my ass!
I'm a hero.

We were all laughing and carrying on when at some
point, one of the guys said, "It's too bad we don't have
any instruments. We could work the song out better by
jammin' with them." No problem. There were plenty
of "instruments" around, so we improvised and entertained ourselves as only grunts or drunk teenagers can.
One guy assembled a set of drums from C-ration boxes, cans, helmets, and metal ammo cans, varying the
amounts of rounds in them to change their tones. Another had a long-handled ax that he was holding like
a bass guitar, plucking imaginary strings with his right

hand, while someone else had a D-handle shovel and was also holding it like a guitar, but he wanted to be the lead player. He was shredding the "neck" of his "Stratocaster" with the fingers of his left hand, looking like Jimi Hendrix, complete with headband, playing and singing "Foxy Lady." There was a horn section composed of barrels from M-16s, 60s, 79s, and a shotgun.

Of course, the more everyone improvised, the more we fed off each other and the more hysterical we got. Two of our black brothers were trying to choreograph foot and arm movements like the Four Tops, but the white guys kept tripping over the drum set. At some point, someone yelled for everyone to calm down so we could tune the instruments and get underway. With a semblance of seriousness, the guys with the "guitars" started making the sounds of a musical scale, something like der, derr, derrr, while turning their imaginary tuning nuts to adjust tones. Not to be out of tune with the strings, the horn section was doing the same thing with their "mouthpieces." The drummer just looked around with amusement and adjusted the "heads" on the tom-tom and snare. The more we looked and listened, the more hysterical we got. Foghorn came over and wanted to play with us, holding an entrenching tool like a ukulele, but one of the guys in the band called him an idiot and told him to get lost. Everyone was a little surprised at the rejection because we all liked Shelby, but when the guy gave his reason, we couldn't argue with him. After all, who ever heard of a banjo in rock-and-roll band?

Photo 1st Cavalry Division Assoc.
Probably sounded better than us.

While everyone was tuning their instruments, going bing, bong, boing, boom, bang, ding, dong, ding, der, derr, doo, doo, dee, daa, the company's first sergeant, "Top" Carroll, walked up and was standing in the background chewing a cigar and watching the band get ready. He had caught us while we were actually being "serious" and must have thought the combat was finally catching up. His face was etched with confusion and concern as he looked at everybody tuning...nothing! Guys were leaning over and helping other guys next them who couldn't quite get a note right, or who had slippery fingers and couldn't tighten the imaginary tuning nut on their guitar. Even other guys who were just sitting around to listen to us were giving their advice as to whether a note was sharp or flat. When I looked up from my guitar, I noticed Top standing there and invited him into the circle to listen or jam with us if he wanted to. It was beautiful because the guys picked up on it right away and offered him a "sax, trumpet, or clarinet." Looking somewhat concerned and telling us to hold the "music" down, he asked if we were all okay. Everyone was very serious, and I said, "Sure, Top, what's the matter? Don't you like rock and roll?" He stared very intently at us to see if there was a hint of humor in our eyes. Then Little Joe broke the uneasy silence by saying, "No, Top, everything is not all right. I need new guitar strings because they rust up so damn fast out here!"

We all lost it at that point, complaining about drumheads stretching, mold growing in the sax and trumpet, a chip out of the bass guitar's neck. Still somewhat concerned with our well-being, Top said, "If you guys are serious, give me a list of the instruments you want, and I'll order new ones for you—keep them back at supply until you want them brought out. What do you think?" We thought he was nuts because we didn't sound good enough to warrant brand-new instruments yet.

Ye Ole Swimmin' Hole

I think I might have mentioned a place we called "the bridges." Actually, it was just one large metal bridge on Highway 1, built by the French many years earlier to span the My Chanh River. In fact, the place looked very much like a scene in the Oliver Stone movie *Platoon*. When our stand-downs were at that location, and I think we were there two or three times, we really enjoyed ourselves. All of our routines were the same as if we were at an LZ, except we were allowed to go down to the river for about an hour a day to swim, wash, do laundry, or whatever. That was always a blast because for that one hour, it was probably the only time we didn't feel like we were in a war. Sure, our weapons were always nearby, and some guys holding M-16s with a bag of loaded magazines at their sides were sitting on the riverbank looking for potential trouble. And of course there was the ever-present sound of helicopters, something no one who served in Vietnam, and especially with the 1st Cavalry Division, will ever forget. The artillery fire in the distance kept us ever mindful that we were in a war zone, but life there was very tolerable and somewhat safe.

Because of the "safe" location and the convenience of the highway, civilians would stop by on their Vespas or bicycles just to say hello. As in "GI want haircut? I do numbah-one job." "Hey, Joe, have numbah-one girl. Want boom, boom?" "Who need bayding suit or chorts?" For the most part they were all friendly, but it *was* a war zone. What was a lot of fun was when we got hot chow, either breakfast or dinner.

All the little kids, we're talking five and under, would come down the road in swarms hoping for some GI food. There was a folding table or two set up just off the roadway where insulated marmite cans containing hot food were placed, along with paper plates, plastic utensils, and napkins. After we went through the line, it was tough glancing at your plate and looking at all of these smiling kids staring at you, so you hurried away and ate. Seems most guys cut way back on their calorie intake when we were there. When it was announced "Who wants food?" the swarm grew larger and attacked the table. "Whoa! Whoa! Get in line!" we'd say, and line them up just as we had done, and as soon as a server dipped a ladle into a can, the swarm exploded and crowded at the table. "No! No! Back in line!"

A couple of guys would escort them back, some holding their hands, and steer them back into line by their shoulders. We'd walk alongside of them, making sure they stayed in a straight line, one in front of the other, while they danced and giggled. For whatever reason, mostly because of a shortage of food at home, they didn't understand the concept of patience or not invading the space of someone standing next to you. It was the same way every day, but we made sure everyone had something to eat.

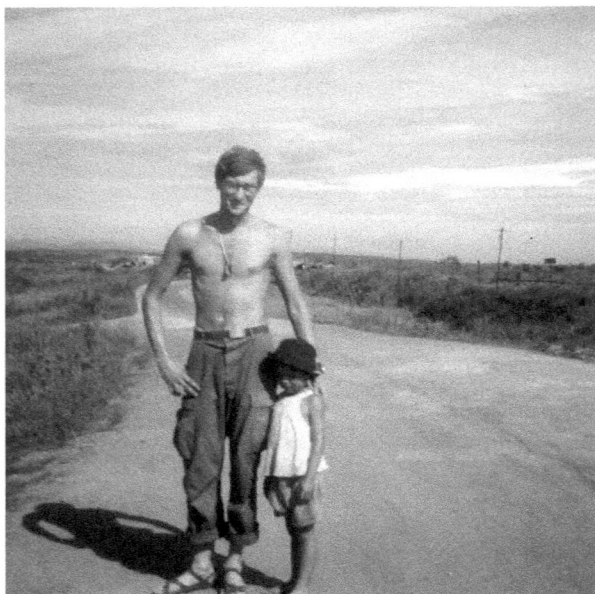

Bill Ebel with a friend

When it was our platoon's turn to go swimming, we'd walk down the highway from our campsite, wearing bathing suits purchased for one dollar from the Vietnamese kids hawking their wares. It was probably a ridiculous sight—deeply tanned, hardened troopers of the much-respected 1st Cavalry Division walking down Route 1, wearing helmets, clothed in only bathing suits and unlaced jungle boots. Each guy carried a weapon in one hand and an inflated air mattress tucked under the other arm. Topping off our trendy beachwear ensemble and slung across our bare chests were satchels of munitions that sometimes looked more like beach bags because of the towels and poncho liner hanging out of them. For some reason, I always seemed to be the hit of our parade, among both the grunts and the Vietnamese. My air mattress was decorated like a Hobie surfboard, my helmet was adorned with flowers drawn with ink on the camouflage cover, and my bathing suit was actually a pair of white boxer shorts with big red hearts that I had received from my wife for Valentine's Day. Hey, laughing is good, even when it comes at your own expense sometimes.

As soon as we reached the water and shed our articles of war, we became a bunch of eighteen-to-twenty-two-year-old guys at the ole swimmin' hole, some even skinny-dipping but all having a great time. The Vietnamese kids in the area loved to play and swim with the GIs, creating a family-like atmosphere. We would float around on our air mattresses sunning ourselves or straddle them like horses, trying to push each other off. Once we exhausted ourselves, we would get our strength back by pushing the little kids around on them, making noises like motorboats while they giggled and laughed. When we weren't doing that stuff, there were always "chicken matches" in deep water, where teams made up of one guy on another's shoulders would fight to be "King of the River." I always tried to team up with Big Joe, because with his strength, he didn't even know anyone was on his shoulders, especially when that anyone was not much over one-hundred pounds.

While we played in the water or lounged along the banks, we'd see the Vietnamese women doing laundry across the river, laughing and pointing at the antics of the crazy GIs. The very old women with their brown teeth would just stare at us with distrust, while the younger ones would laugh and cover their mouths with their hands or point at their sons and daughters playing on the air mattresses. Giggling adolescent girls gathered together, clutching at each other and pointing at the GIs who were showing off for them, or the few who were naked. It was hard to believe we were in a war zone sometimes, until we heard the all-too-familiar "Saddle up!"

When we weren't at the bridge swimming, we'd be back at our small encampment catching up on rest. The days were then usually monotonous, the nights either spent doing a typical guard duty shift or taking a single squad outside the perimeter into the bush to create a forward listening post to protect the perimeter's safety. If we weren't resting at the bridges or the LZs in the field, we would stay near a small hamlet along Route 1 just up the road from Camp Evans, where I received the letters about my daughter's birth. In any case, our stand-downs were always pretty much the same: no stores, bars, distractions, planned entertainment, sports programs or equipment, beds with sheets, or solid buildings with roofs to sleep under. But most importantly, no one shooting at us.

Arts and Crafts

I can remember the first operation where every grunt in our company was told where we were going, what kind of support to expect, and what to do if the helicopter you were on was shot down. *Wait, did he just say shot down?!* We were told that on April 1, the 1st, 2nd, and 5th Battalions of the 7th Cavalry, which comprised the entire 3rd Brigade of the 1st Cavalry Division, would have the honor of spearheading Operation Pegasus.[58] We would air assault into a mountainous area east of the US Marine Corps Khe Sahn Combat Base (KSCB). There would be 240 slicks available for the operation, supported by lots of Chinooks.[59] The main objective was to stop the North Vietnamese Army's artillery and rocket attacks on the combat base. Oh, and while we were there, get rid of the NVA soldiers too, stop the threat of them over running the five thousand US Marines and five hundred rangers on the base. *Hmm, Pega-*

---

58   Operation Pegasus—A joint US and Vietnamese effort to break the NVA siege of the marines' Khe Sahn Combat Base .

59   CH-47 Chinook—A large twin-engine medium cargo/transport helicopter.

*sus, huh? The winged horse? Seems like an appropriate name
for an air-cavalry mission.*

This was all explained to us on March 31, so naturally we thought it might be a sick April Fool's joke, just
to break the monotony and add a little levity after our
traipsing through the mountains for a week. *Not funny,
Boss!* But there was no doubt it wasn't a joke, because
we and three other companies of our 5th Battalion had
been airlifted from different AOs[60] in the mountains
and dropped off near a huge grassy field that looked like
it was close to a mile by a half mile in size, code-named
LZ Pedro. Each company marched off to an assigned
area and set up their own perimeters. There were a lot
of guys already there that we would find out to be the
four companies of the 1st Battalion.

The more we learned in the briefings from our
CO,[61] Capt. John Taylor, and platoon leader Lt. Tim
Pasquarelli, and by the concerned looks etched on
the faces of our platoon sergeant, SFC Marion Green,
and squad leader, Sgt. Sam Byrd, the more nervous we
became. "There won't be an artillery prep of the area
around the LZs. They were bombed before, but our
gunships will be there to help. We will have more air
support throughout the operation than they had on
D-Day," the CO offered, trying to bolster our confidence. "Four US Air Force jets will be above us at all
times in case they're needed." *If I recall correctly, there
wasn't much Allied air support over any of the beachheads on
D-Day, so of course we'd have more air support!* Anyway,
the briefings continued for an hour, and yet for those
of us who had survived the actions in February around
Hue during Tet, we just couldn't imagine anything be-

---

60   AO—Area of Operations.

61   CO—Commanding Officer; in this case, company commander.

ing worse. But we had all seen the *Life* magazine photos of the mountains and valleys that almost surrounded the combat base. The NVA artillery and rocket attacks were causing a tremendous number of casualties for the marines, something like twenty-five hundred over the past couple of months, and it was feared the base could be overrun.

Also, for the first and only time prior to an operation, everyone was given a small topographical map of the areas where we'd be working, instructions for "escape and evasion," and the chain of command to be followed if your chopper went down. *There he goes again with the "shot down" stuff.* We were told we would be issued extra equipment in the event we couldn't be resupplied for a week. *Gee, now this is getting scary…*Everyone would carry, in addition to the stuff already in their rucksack, plus their weapon, ammo, grenades, flak vest, and steel helmet, extra pounds of munitions, grenades, LAWs, trip flares, explosives, spare radio batteries, Claymores, a twenty-five-pound case of C rations and double the amount of water. That would probably be around seventy pounds, plus or minus. *Holy crap! And they want us to jump off a hovering chopper with all that weight?! Good Lord! How many blown-out knees and broken ankles are we going to have?!* We crawled into our hooches that night with a lot to think about. Things that probably kept some guys awake. Especially the new guys.

At first light on the morning of April 1, we awoke, had a hasty meal, and did the same things we did every morning. Though unlike other mornings, there were boxes of equipment and rations lying everywhere for us to resupply. Kind of like Christmas, but no wrapping paper or bows. Lieutenant Pasquarelli and Sergeant Greene roamed through our positions, making sure everyone was okay and had what was needed for the operation. So, three battalions of 7th Cavalry troopers waited in assigned areas around the grass field. We had already been told what helicopter to board when they landed, plus positioned to take the least amount of time to climb aboard. But there was a hell of a lot of grunts there, and it would require a hell of a lot of helicopters to lift them out for a combat assault. We all guessed it would probably be a very long day of "hurry up and wait." Things rarely go as planned.

I don't think anyone was ready for the arriving spectacle when an increasingly loud rumble filled the air. Each guy on the ground eventually turned to look up when the rumble got louder, and they could see more and more of the dots in the sky coming into view. When the massive formations of Hueys grew larger and the rumble changed to a roar, jaws started to drop. It wasn't long before the sky got darker and everyone on the ground watched in awe as a swarm of eighty slicks, followed by an untold number of big Chinooks spread out in various formations, came within full sight and hearing range. Flanking them was a host of gunships, and above it all was the battalion commanders riding in their C&C choppers, watching the complex logistical plan with so many moving parts being executed. Things only got louder and windier when groups of approaching slicks dropped lower toward different-colored smoke grenades indicating which flight went where. Guys on the ground wearing black baseball hats and a PRC-25 on their backs were roaming around to different areas, pointing and directing the ships, always in radio contact with the pilots to keep things orderly.

Photo: 1st Cavalry Division Association

In no time, everywhere we looked, it was like it was raining Hueys. The muted olive-green choppers would break from the big formation, come down in smaller groups, and flare their ship's nose up to reduce speed. Looking up, we could see the pilot's and navigator's legs behind the clear Plexiglas nose cone, the slick's doors wide open, and door gunners on their seats, scanning the area for trouble. In other locations slicks were leveling off or hovering over their "parking space," some almost on the ground, rocking a little in the air like a boat on water until their skids softly touched down, flattening the grass around them with the downdraft. Not only was the sound level deafening, but the tones kept changing as rotor blades slapped the air with different sounds during each maneuver. Just an awesome sight as one group after another dropped from the sky until almost the entire area of LZ Pedro was covered.

Not to be outdone, the big twin-engine Chinooks followed and started landing in another area of the grassy field closer to our location. Their addition made the decibel level rise even higher. The entire area was soon completely covered with helicopters, and four companies were ready to board the slicks. Deafening might be an understatement, until…"Hold on, everyone. We're going to hold up for a short weather delay because the mountains are hidden by clouds." The mountains were always shrouded in clouds in the mornings until the sun rose a little higher and burned them off. We went from hearts pumping gallons of adrenaline and adjusting our pants, to looking around for a place to lie down for a nap if this was going to take long.

And so, we waited. And waited. And as expected, we had to hurry up and wait. But our eardrums were being taxed to the max by nearly one hundred idling helicopters! Until suddenly it started to get quieter as all of the chopper engines were shut down. So, there we were. Seven-man groupings standing around the slicks and other guys in larger groups stooped over wearing giant rucksacks while kneeling around the perimeter. That was our cue to drop the damn rucksacks.

As expected, the sun eventually rose higher, the clouds dissipated, and everything was on again. At 1330 hours, all of the one-hundred-plus helicopters of different sizes started up their engines and started idling. At 1331 hours, we all lost our ability to hear again. Everyone there, regardless of age or rank or military discipline, had to be a proud member of the "First Team" and its awesome capabilities. We could not help but be impressed looking at the immense amount of firepower preparing to take off.

And with that, Phase I of the battle plan finally began when two companies from the 5/7 carrying only their weapons and munitions, already in groups of seven, quickly boarded forty slicks, and two other companies from the 1/7 boarded the other forty slicks. The C&C birds went airborne to watch everything again, while the gunships and observation helicopters followed. The rest of us waiting on the grassy field were lucky enough to watch. The amazing sight and sounds were chilling when forty Hueys, carrying well over 250 grunts from the 1/7, gunned their engines and lifted off almost in unison. The higher they rose, the darker the sky grew overhead. Everyone watched the airshow, whether already airborne or still on the ground, as the first flight circled aloft, waiting for the other forty slicks carrying the same number of 5/7 troopers to lift off and form up with them. That there were no accidents with that many helicopters flying in all directions at the same time said a lot about the discipline and abilities of the pilots and the foresight of the planners of the operation.

When all eighty choppers carrying half of each battalion's troopers were aloft, the two flights of forty lined up single file and adjacent to each other. Well-spaced Huey and Cobra gunships added more darkness as they joined the formation on both sides, providing support from the lead Hueys all the way to the last ten. Within a matter of minutes, the long formations soon spaced themselves into short groups of ten helicopters, still in-line. In a matter of time, the long line of choppers disappeared from view, continuing on a forty-five-minute flight heading west toward the Khe Sahn Combat Base. If you like watching large flights of Canada geese migrating in formation, you would have loved this. Pretty

impressive. Now we knew how Charlie would feel looking up at an armada that size, knowing each helicopter
was full of heavily armed troopers ready to look for
him.

Phase I of the operation was to have the eighty loaded slicks stay on a parallel flight route until nearing
their assigned AOs. At that point they would split off
and simultaneously execute forty slick air assaults onto
two mountaintop objectives, secure the perimeters, and
begin clearing the LZ. The 5/7's would be called LZ
Cates, after Gary Cates, a gallant trooper who had giv-
en his life back in February during the Hue campaign.
The newly created LZ would be high atop Hill 691,
1,950 feet above and north of Highway 9 overlooking
the KSCB. The 1/7 would land south of Highway 9 on
Hill 248, designated LZ Mike. Once Phase I was complete, the eighty slicks would head off for a twenty-minute ride to LZ Stud, another staging area near Dong Ha,
located ten miles east of Khe Sahn and about fifteen
miles south of the DMZ.[62] That would put us all closer
to Hanoi than Saigon by about 150 miles.

Soon after the dark cloud of slicks had departed LZ
Pedro, it was our time to leave in the hooks[63] and begin
Phase II. We were ordered to saddle up, and a lot of
grumbling soon ensued. The guys who left on the slicks
were traveling "light." Meaning they only carried weapons and munitions. They had left their rucks with all
of the extra gear behind to be slung out to them later.
Whaaat?! What about us?! We'd be carrying a full load. So,
with a little help from our friends, we were able to lift
our rucks, crouch down into a sitting position, and rest

---

62   DMZ—Demilitarized Zone separating North and South Vietnam.

63   Hooks—CH-47 Chinook, a large twin-engine medium cargo/trans-
port helicopter.

the ruck onto a knee. A quick twist of the body allowed us to get an arm through a shoulder strap. Then, by quickly standing up and whipping an elbow back to the bulging side of the ruck, we pushed it around to a point where we were able to jam the other arm into the other strap. At that point all we had to do was bounce up and down a few times to quickly hike the heavy packs up onto our shoulders. Even though staggering under the weight, everyone was bouncing up and down, pulling and pushing straps and the rucksack's aluminum framing until balancing the load evenly. That was the easy part. The helicopter loadmasters helped us shuffle up the angled rear ramp single file, making sure we were boarding our assigned idling Chinook.

After we cussed out the military brass, we could only but pray that army knew what it was doing. The packs were so heavy and bulky that it was difficult to start or stop moving, let alone walk and fight. Filling the long canvas seats on both sides of the big twin-engine transport helicopter, starting from the front and filling seats to the rear, we literally fell or were pushed backward onto a seat when the guy in front stopped walking and turned. The fact that it was a large aircraft didn't matter because, as with all helicopter seating, they weren't designed to hold a human being wearing a Volkswagen Beetle–sized rucksack on his back. Every guy was left in a sitting position dangling in space while their backpacks were tucked comfortably in a seat.

Our platoon rode the noisy beast twenty minutes to LZ Stud. No one could see anything outside the windows of the Chinooks, so we relied on our other senses and past experiences of how the huge choppers reacted in certain situations. We tried to doze or reflect on things that would keep us loose during the cold flight.

So, in effect, while we were flying to our destination, the entire 1st and 5th Battalions of the 7th Cavalry were in the air at the same time—eighty slicks with gunship escorts on a forty-five-minute flight to execute two air assaults into two LZs simultaneously, and twenty-some Chinooks with gunship escorts on a twenty-minute flight to another LZ staging area. Over a hundred helicopters heading for three different LZs.

When we felt the vibrations in the Chinook change and the noise intensify, we knew we were nearing the landing zone. Soon, the rear ramp started to lower as the big bird prepared to land. Turning to look out of the rear opening, we saw what looked like a sandstorm outside. Following standard operating procedure, no matter what type of chopper we were riding in, was to get out as fast as possible because they make really big, tempting targets for Charlie. Unfortunately, we found that we had a big problem because no one could stand up!

The tremendous weight of the rucks was so far behind us, we couldn't get our feet and legs far enough under ourselves to lift it. A couple of guys were able to force an arm into the tight space between them and their neighbor to push themselves up with some help from their friends. Before a Chinook's ramp even touched the ground, we would typically be running off the chopper. Instead, we were all grunting and straining, flailing our arms and legs, rolling our shoulders left and right, looking more like turtles trying to right themselves than a combat team about to go into a big operation.

For most of the guys, we found the only way to get up was to stretch an arm across the aisle, grab a guy's arm or rifle, and stagger out of the way to pull each other up without knocking each other down, like sumo wrestlers smashing bellies together. That worked but created another problem, because standing became dangerous in the confined aisle. If someone pushed back while standing, he could cause a serious "domino effect," and everyone would have to try to get back up again. We supported each other as best we could and waddled off the chopper. No one knew where we were going nor where the rest of our company was until directed by the helicopter crew chief or loadmaster standing next to the ramp. Once all of Chinooks were emptied, they took off to make room for the original eighty slicks returning from the air assaults to complete Phase I.

We had landed in a huge open area where the 2/7 was also being staged. By the looks of it, there was definitely going to be a massive helicopter assault around the Khe Sahn base. The LZ was a beehive of activity everywhere we looked. There were stacked pallet loads of supplies and howitzer rounds, rolls of barbed wire, trucks and forklifts racing to or from another load. Helicopters of every variety were either already lined up on the ground, were about to land, or were lifting off. Troopers were either boarding assigned slicks or just getting off Chinooks. Huey and Cobra gunships were checking armaments and refueling, while heavy equipment and artillery pieces were being moved to a different staging area, where they would be airlifted out by Chinooks as soon as the infantry cleared and defended the LZs for their arrival. Controlled chaos. Each step taken gave us a greater appreciation for the logistical nightmares for the D-Day invasion at Normandy and

the Pacific island-hopping during World War II.[64] This
operation was the first division-sized heliborne assault
ever attempted, and it was flawless.

Like every other Chinook idling with troops departing, the guys in our platoon slowly shuffled in the
general direction toward our company's area as instructed. The huge LZ looked like a wasteland. Hundreds of boots, jeeps, trucks, tracks, and helicopters
were breaking down the bone-dry soil into smaller and
finer particles of sand that was covering everything like
a new-fallen snow. With every step toward our destination, we were attacked by an environmental plague
that was being blended and dispersed by every type of
helicopter landing, idling, or lifting off. We kept getting
buffeted by the changing air turbulence, making it more
difficult just to maintain our balance on straining, wob-
bly legs. It looked like every guy had a raised arm bent
at the elbow as an only defense through the storm. We
squinted and turned our heads, but it was nearly impossible to protect our eyes from the blinding sunlight
breaking through the swirling clouds of soil and debris.

All of our senses were being attacked—deafening
noise, eyes blinking and burning from blown sand laced
with a volatile chemical cocktail of aviation, creosote,
and diesel fumes. It didn't take very long before everyone's sweat-covered skin, mouth, and ears were being

---

64   Around 2005 I met Joe Kinser, a retired US Marine Corps general
who in April 1968 was the logistics officer in charge of LZ Stud. In preparation for the 1st Cavalry's helicopters, he said he had to "come down hard on
the marines doing the work to prepare the landing site. They didn't believe
more than eighty helicopters would be coming, let alone landing at the
designated time. Later in the day, they heard the roar of all those helicopters
approaching that looked like a big black rain cloud, and right on time. They
couldn't believe it. Hell, I couldn't believe it! The sight and sound of that
was unforgettable, and I was Army Airborne before I switched to the Marine
Corps!"

coated with grit. With the weight we were all carrying, and the unstable environment, every guy was probably mumbling to himself, "One step at a time. Just stay focused and follow the bootheels in front of you. Turn your body a little more. Maybe that'll help. You think this is bad? Wait until the eighty Hueys come in! Keep moving!"

The short but taxing five-minute walk from our Chinooks brought four companies of troopers to our designated company areas. We shuffled around bumping into each other until told we could drop our packs in slings laid out nearby. *Happy days!* The sudden fifty-plus-pound weight loss made us feel like we could leap tall buildings in a single bound. Everyone quickly prepared to move out "light" for the actual air assault and started staging by individual squads, ready to load up when our rides landed. And it was a good thing we did, because after a surprisingly short wait, the slicks started arriving. Each squad was notified about who would be on what bird and the order of insertion for the assault. We were finally able to move but not overly thrilled about where and why we were about to be moved to. Each guy made last-minute preparations, making sure they had everything they would need, everything was where it needed to be, everything was secured for the jump, and the map was readily available. The small talk ended, and thoughts and prayers were started. It was time to go to work.

We were all ready when "saddle up" was shouted over the din of eighty idling Hueys. Our platoons quickly headed toward a grouping of assigned slicks, squads dispersed into fire teams, and seven troopers mounted their idling Huey. There was a certain amount of tension and anxiety about any combat assault, but this one was serious based on the size and preparations. And as always, we'd be going into unknown territory, but this place was already known to be dangerous. After a few minutes lost in thought, we felt our excitement and adrenaline take over when the Hueys started to shudder and sway the moment their skids lost contact with the ground. Surrounded by other slicks lifting off, we were pelted with needles of sand coming through the open doors. The steady drone of idling Hueys quickly morphed into a roar, making both vision and communications momentarily impossible. Once well above the LZ, we saw the vastness of the departing slicks loaded with grunts; different types of gunships loaded with full complements of rockets, miniguns, grenades, and machine-gun ammunition; command-and-control birds carrying commanding and operations officers to monitor the operation; Loaches;[65] observation and spotter fixed-wing aircraft; diesel engine trucks belching plumes of black soot trying to get out of the way. It was a spectacle the marines had not seen before. Nor had we.

Photo 1st Cavalry Division Assoc.

---

65   Loaches—LOH, or light observation helicopter; Hughes OH-6 "Cayuse."

We watched the impressive display around, above, and below us through the open cabin doors. Choppers flew in all directions while gaining altitude until the eighty slicks regrouped into the same formation used earlier: two rows of forty slicks running parallel to each other headed for the same two LZs they had just left, only this time they'd be going in using a different approach in case Charlie was preparing to greet newly arriving helicopters. We were in position to once again fly off into the unknown and hopefully to bring a safe and successful close to Phase II of the operation. As nervous as we were for our own safety, it was the only operation where I felt like we had a real purpose. We were there to help other grunts—no politics, no questions, with no more casualties. If only the marine's artillery sitting idle in Hue would have helped us out in February, things might have been different[66] for us and them. But that's another subject.

Once Phase II was completed, two 7th Cavalry Battalions would be at full strength at two LZs. After dropping us off, Phase III would begin immediately when the same eighty slicks returned to LZ Stud and picked up the 2nd Battalion of the 7th Cavalry in its entirety. Again, using a different approach to the mountains, they would air assault near LZ Mike and temporarily share the LZ for the night with the 1st Battalion of the 7th Cavalry. The following morning 2/7 would head out toward Highway 9 and the KSCB. By the end of the day, the 1st Cavalry's 3rd Brigade had landed three full infantry battalions, well over fifteen hundred men onto two different mountaintops overlooking the KSCB, in five hours; the two lead battalions in a little over an hour. Over the next few days, lots of Chinooks would

---

66   Baker, *Gray Horse Troop.*

follow loaded with supplies, sandbags, ammo, water, and so on, plus artillery, bulldozers, and shells brought in attached to slings. The completed artillery firebases would be ready to support infantry operations less than two days after the initial air assault. Over the course of the operation, individual companies were picked up for combat assaults into different areas or moved where needed. Our company was spread around the battalion headquarters for security atop Hill 691. War correspondent Michael Herr noted, "Everywhere you went, you could see the most comforting military insignia in all of Vietnam, the yellow-and-black shoulder patch of the Cav. You were with the pros now, the elite. LZ's and firebases were being established at a rate of three and four a day, and every hour brought them closer to Khe Sahn."[67]

Fortunately, the operation involving many other US Army units, including the 101st Airborne and South Vietnamese marine units, was very successful, with few casualties. NVA supplies and equipment were found abandoned in many locations and included a good number of AK-47s, 12.75-millimeter machine guns, and thousands of rounds of ammo for each, plus mortars and other items. Besides large quantities of rice, B Co. actually found a mess hall. Charlie had everything he needed but apparently had left in a hurry. In some areas of the gorges and valleys, the terrain was so torn up and cratered, it was obvious the B-52s had done the work already. On April 7, the 2nd Battalion of the 7th Cavalry ended three days of contact with an NVA force blocking Route 9 east of KSCB by defeating them soundly. Later that day two of the 2/7 companies walked in at the east end of the base. They were given

---

67   Herr, *Dispatches*

the credit for lifting the siege of the KSCB. Operations continued with 1st Cavalry and US Marines hopping from one mountaintop to another, clearing the areas of any enemy concentrations.

The 1st Cavalry Division was assigned operational control of the KSCB. A few of our companies were air-lifted from their LZs and relieved some marine units on the base perimeter. It freed up those units to go outside the wire to search the mountains, valleys, and gorges around the base. A Co. of 5/7 was flown onto the base late on April 11 to be on the perimeter that night, a defensive perimeter that was so impressive to us that it seemed impossible for the enemy to be able to success-fully overrun the base like the media had exaggeratedly described. Could they have been overrun? Not likely. Not with the wide-open flat terrain surrounding the base. Not with the advantage of our US Navy, Marine, and Air Force capabilities.

There was more barbed wire on the perimeter than any other base I had seen. Hanging and lined up on the ground, protected by the rolls of the slinky-type con-certina wire and rows of double-apron[68] barbed-wire fences, were hundreds of trip flares and antipersonnel mines of different varieties. Behind the wire and mines and Claymores was a zigzagged trench line almost five feet deep, with shelves dug into its sides that held crates of ammo and "baseball"-style hand grenades, a type we had never seen. There were reinforced machine-gun bunkers spaced along the trench line, albeit infested with rats and garbage lying around, and just to the rear of them were 105-millimeter howitzers, some pointing

---

68   Double apron—A six foot tall fence with barbed wire running di-agonally down to points on the ground on both sides, with rows of horizontal barbed wire attached to the diagonal wires.

up and loaded with high explosives, others with their barrels level to the ground and loaded with flechette rounds, very nasty stuff. Add to those defenses artillery, jets, and helicopters with miniguns for ground support and we just could not understand how that base could ever be taken, even with human wave attacks. Of course, we had no idea how long the perimeter actually looked that way.

Apparently, the sense of danger and impending disaster was more a factor of the newspeople wanting to sell more newspapers, and the nightly news stations wanting higher ratings to get more advertisers. Most news correspondents and camera crews were only on the base for a day or two, if that. It was a snapshot, not the whole picture. The marines were in a bad situation because of the horrific artillery and rocket attacks they had endured for months, which had taken a heavy toll. They had suffered over twenty-five hundred casualties during the previous months. Our decision about the KSCB wasn't from what we read but from the proof around us. We could not help but feel that the sensationalism of how vulnerable the marines were was a government-planned media misinformation campaign to draw the NVA en masse to the surrounding areas. That made it easier for US B-52 bombers to destroy him. That feeling was enforced by a few facts. On more than a few nights while on LZ Cates, we watched distant "Arc Light"[69] strikes on the surrounding mountains and valleys from our location overlooking the base. A single B-52 dropping a payload of over eighty 750-pound-or-larger bombs is terrifying. You can't hear them coming, so you can't run from it, dig down far

---

69   Arc Light—Name used for nighttime B-52 bomber strikes, referring to the brilliant light emitted when welding metals.

enough, or hide. The first strike is followed immediately by more bombers trailing along. The night sky flashes from each explosion as if someone is using a huge strobe light or has the ability to switch a full moon on and off. From a distance you eventually hear and feel the deep rumble from every bomb, exactly as you would experience thunder in a severe lightning storm. The shock waves of each detonation have a ripple effect. And just like in lightning storms, the explosions produce a rolling thunder. Terrifying to watch and hear, more so if you're in the target zone. Validating the success of the bombing campaign around Khe Sahn, there were numerous companies working the surrounding mountains and valleys who couldn't, wouldn't or didn't have to enter some areas because of the obvious devastation and unmistakable odor.

Results of a B-52 strike.

To us who pulled guard duty on their perimeter, the whole thing seemed like a sick ploy, using marine grunts as bait to destroy Charlie in a statistical game of attrition. A terrible strategy that worked and pissed a lot of guys off. We were not too happy either about going into someone else's base camp to pull guard duty for them, but they were brother grunts who probably needed the rest. Our wrath was instead directed at the marine brass for letting Charlie get so many people so close to begin with, and at the politicians and military brass in Washington for allowing it to happen. Even in the time of Julius Caesar, there was an old maxim that read, "The soldier has a right to competent command."

On the morning of April 13, our company walked between rows of tents and was amazed at what we saw. Despite the obvious garbage and disrepair everywhere that made it look like a slum, marines were playing basketball with a real pole, hoop, net, and ball. We couldn't quite grasp why they weren't outside the wire looking for Charlie, or cleaning the place up, because it looked like a dump. The further we walked, the further our mouths dropped. There were stacked crates of Sunkist oranges, some opened with their contents just rotting on the ground and some still unopened and left to rot. There were cases of Campbell's soups, Coca-Cola, and other delicacies none of us had enjoyed since we left the world. The farther we walked, the more jealous we became because of all the goodies we saw. We had never seen supplies even close to the stuff the marines were getting, and we weren't bashful about saying it aloud. We half complained and half bragged that because of all the actions we had been in, we were never in one place long enough to get supplies by the crate and pallet load. If the marine grunts deserved it, we reasoned we did too. We were just grunts passing through, not offi-cers, but it was obvious their command was wanting.

We watched with interest as we neared a clearing when some marines climbed into a few 1st Cavalry Hueys instead of the larger, slower varieties. They were grinning from ear to ear, looking around at the door gunners and all, just like any other FNG on his first combat assault. We were sure they'd enjoy the ride. The difference between a Huey and marine light-to-medium transport helicopters was like riding in a high-perfor-mance sports car compared to a school bus. We con-tinued our walk through the base with occasional good-natured barbs thrown at us. "Why'd ya bother comin'? It's all over now." "Ain't it just like the army, huh? They show up when it's safe and try to take the glory." Of course, our return volleys alluded to the fact that they could now come out of their bunkers because we had just cleared the roads and the areas around the base, doing their job for them. "If you had spent as much time outside the wire as you do playing games, we wouldn't have to be here!"

We eventually reached the KSCB runway and sat in rocket or artillery craters trying to pass the time while waiting for our extraction. I was whittling on a three-inch-thick piece of soft wood, or maybe it was some type of packing material, while Big Joe heated a can of beans over rolled-up marble-sized pieces of blazing plas-tique. While concentrating on my knife blade, I heard Joe say, "I don't believe it. Here comes a general, Bano."

"Yeah, right, Joe. If it's Patton, get his autograph for me, will ya?" I said without looking up from my work of art.

Then Joe scared the hell out of me when he sudden-ly jumped up, shouting, "Attention!"

I was about to yell at him because I had almost cut my finger off when I heard a stranger's voice say, "At ease, troopers." I looked up over my right shoulder, and the first thing I noticed was two stars on each collar. Damned if it wasn't the Commander of the 1st Cavalry Division, Maj. Gen. John Tolson, and a captain carrying a radiotelephone.

Joe stood at attention while I sat in the dirt agog as they both hurriedly slid into our crater and sat down on the edge as if we were old friends who hadn't seen each other in a while. General Tolson's easygoing manner and our surroundings put me at ease, but Joe remained a little uptight and formal. I wanted to tell Joe to relax because, after all, what could the general do to us, send us to Vietnam? (It was a line certainly every grunt and probably most REMFs had used at some time during their tour of duty in the RVN.) We talked and laughed a bit, Joe eventually relaxing enough to ask them if they wanted some lunch, but they graciously declined.

Through the course of conversation, General Tolson commended us for the great job we were all doing, as well as said how proud he was of us. He asked Joe and I how long we'd been in-country. When we answered four months, he nodded knowingly. "Yeah, Hue sure was bad." He continued the conversation, asking how things were going, what we needed, and stuff like that. I kept expecting them to get up, continue on to another hole, and talk to other grunts, but they remained sitting in the dirt talking while Joe cooked and I nonchalantly whittled. I occasionally glanced up at LT and our CO sitting in a couple of other craters and had the feeling they were getting a little antsy. I don't think generals normally sat with grunts one on one for extended periods unless they were getting an earful. And if that were the case, I'm sure it wouldn't help someone's military career.

When I finished with my project, I had a perfect full-scale replica of a 1st Cavalry patch that looked like a big rubber stamp. I offered it to General Tolson as both a memento of the war and a reminder of the Cav's actions at Khe Sahn. I was surprised when he graciously accepted it. Then, with a mischievous grin, he said, "Too bad we don't have any yellow paint. We could have some fun with this. After all," he added with a big smile, "we just took temporary command of this base." While he explained the transfer, Joe left the hole to pass the word around. Within a few minutes we had a five-gallon pail of yellow caution paint delivered to us, with word that there was plenty more where that came from. General Tolson, with his grin getting bigger handed the stamp back to me and said, "Why don't you try it out for me?"

Well, try it I did. Hesitantly at first, not sure if I should start walking around in the open at a base that was a prime target. I approached a marine jeep and "stamped" the side, leaving a perfect 1st Cavalry Division patch where it used to read "US Marines." The guys in the other craters loved it and started to cheer. I ran around with the pail, dipping the stamp and sticking it onto everything that said marines. Other guys slowly joined me and wanted to try it themselves. I figured I could mass-produce the stamps if I didn't make them so perfect and we could all have fun, so I gave the original back to the general while I started whittling in earnest. As soon as I finished one, I would hand it to the first guy nearest to me, who would then go on a stamping rampage. Guys actually started queuing up near us as I frantically whittled. As soon as I finished one, another trooper would run off, dip the stamp in paint, and head in a direction where no one had been.

I just had to get back to the fun, so I finished one for myself, said goodbye to General Tolson, and ran toward the runway, figuring arriving journalists should know who had been there. While leaving bright yellow patches on the runway's steel plating, I could hear hysterical laughter and cheering behind me. At some point when I turned and looked up, I just couldn't believe my eyes. There were Cav patches on everything—marine jeeps, trucks, water blivets, a destroyed C-123 cargo plane on the side of the runway, heavy equipment, sandbags, tires, tents. Everyone was running around going nuts, laughing as if possessed. I looked over at the general to make sure we weren't getting too carried away, but it appeared he was having a good time too.

I turned my attention back to the edge of the runway, where a couple of other guys joined me, but I felt the little patches of paint just weren't doing enough justice to the "First Team's" efforts. I asked some guys to help me find a mop or broom and more paint. In no time, they found a storage shed alongside the runway, and I had everything I needed. I was ready for some real arts and crafts fun at the expense of the US Marines. While trying to contain my own laughter, I explained what I wanted to do, emphasizing that we should do it as fast as possible so as not to spend too much time exposed in the middle of the metal runway. The plan was agreed to unanimously, and we immediately jumped into action. I ran onto the runway with a broom while another trooper followed carrying a five-gallon pail of yellow paint. Once satisfied with the perfect location, I started to outline an enormous 1st Cavalry patch right smack dab in the middle of the runway where the occupants of every plane coming or going from the base at Khe Sahn could see it. The two of us worked fast until the outline was completed. Another guy ran out, a much better artist, and started outlining the horsehead portion of the patch.

Painting a 1st Cavalry patch on the runway at Khe Sahn Combat Base

With a wave to the others, ten more guys ran out to us and started carefully pouring yellow paint from their own five-gallon pails into the outlined areas that required filling, while others began spreading it with

mops, brooms, and shovels until the twenty-five-foot-
long patch started to take shape. It was hysterical watching and listening to everyone yelling to hurry, the paint
being splashed all over and frantically pushed around
while carefully "staying inside the lines" of the picture.

From the corner of my right eye, I caught a movement that caused me to swing around. There, coming
at a high rate of speed with horn blaring, was what appeared to be a yellow-polka-dotted olive-green jeep. Inside were four marines, yelling and flailing their arms
and fists over the vehicle's dropped windshield, driving up the runway right at us. Instead of stopping and
scattering for safety, everyone naturally painted faster,
throwing the paint right from the pails to fill the voids.
Just when the jeep was almost on us, the driver locked
its brakes, causing it to go into a four-wheel skid across
the wet paint in an attempt to smear it. Two marines
in the back seat of the sliding jeep dumped five-gallon
pails of sand onto our masterpiece, yelling something
about how much they enjoyed our presence there. As
soon as the driver regained control of the jeep, they
sped off and our guys went back to work, easily covering the sand piles with more paint.

We thought nothing could stop us except for our incoming choppers, but over our laughter and shouts to
hurry, we heard the roars of huge diesel engines. When
we looked around to see where the noise was coming
from, I was suddenly concerned all of our work was for
naught and we might lose the battle. This time steering
directly toward us wasn't a jeep but a convoy of huge
road graders, dump trucks, forklifts, and bulldozers,
all blowing out massive columns of black diesel smoke
as each was shifted through its gears. Painting became

even more frantic and the game a little more serious when some guys started yelling over the laughter to call in an air strike or get some LAW rockets to stop the approaching enemy armor. Not really wanting to risk a full escalation of the "battle," we figured our fun was over. Besides, most everyone was out of breath from laughing so much.

As the heavy equipment rumbled close enough for our reserves to attack them with hand stamps, the driver of the front bulldozer yelled, "Yo, hurry up. Dare's more marines comin' in more jeeps!" Standing in the middle of the runway to protect our work, we watched, stunned, as the convoy veered off left and right at the last instant. Just like the cavalry of old arriving in the nick of time, they circled their "wagons" around us to protect the patch! Drivers and passengers hanging out of doors and windows were yelling and cheering for us to finish, barely audible over the deafening noise of the monstrous diesel engines, huge whining tires, and blaring air horns. We couldn't figure out why they were doing it until a guy screamed, "We're Seabees, and we don't like them jarheads either."

Everyone was having a ball as more marines arrived, jumped out of their jeeps, and tried to get through our paint, toting defenses. Naturally, skirmishes broke out all along our lines as paint, sand, and bodies slipped and slid trying to get at the Cav patch, which was almost complete. Occasionally a "yellow" marine made it through and dumped what little sand he had left. Not that it mattered, because there was so much paint on the patch by then, the sand instantly turned yellow. Everyone was laughing hysterically, relieving a lot of pent-up tension, I'm sure. I vividly remember[70] looking over at General Tolson and seeing him standing with his hands on his hips, head thrown back and his face bright red from laughing so hard.

Despite the heavy, overcast sky, aching muscles, and almost empty bellies, it was a great day, and appropriately, at the apex of our fun, we heard, "Saddle up! Inbound!" All of the troopers immediately scrambled back to their gear to get ready for the extraction. I think subconsciously all of us wanted to show off for the marines and Seabees, give them a real show of what the 1st Cavalry sounded and looked like when a huge flock of Hueys, noses adorned with bright, yellow-painted crossed sabers, burned in for a landing, loaded up with grunts, and lifted off in a minute. Unfortunately, it was a flight of USAF C-123's. The extraction was flawless, and once airborne, we continued to grin from ear to ear while looking down at the marines, Seabees, and General Tolson, who was saluting us. We watched the big 1st Cavalry patch[71] on the runway, all of the yel-

---

70   I remembered the event so vividly that I brought it up to some guys at a mini reunion of our 5th Battalion, 7th Cavalry Association. I was stunned that no one remembered it. Maybe they weren't there. So I brought it up at other reunions over the next ten years, and not only did no one have a photo taken from the air, but they didn't even remember it happening. I knew it did but started to wonder, "Did I make this up?!" Eventually enough guys must have brought the subject up with others and asked around, because Vince Laurich, back then a lieutenant, A Company's 1st Platoon leader, found a guy who had a photo.

71   Baker, *Gray Horse Troop*. A validation of my memory by the then S-3 Operations Officer of the 5/7 Cavalry, Maj. Charles Baker: "Adding to our problems with the 26th Marine Regiment was the issue of the patch. . .. One such 1st Cav patch appeared on the airstrip. It was huge, extending halfway across the PSP surface of the runway. The first observer of this piece of art was a B-52 pilot who called into the Marine CP at first light, remarking how clear the 1st Cav patch looked from thirty-five thousand feet. I had to go up to the Regiment HQ and apologize for that one, which was well worth it."

low-polka-dotted equipment, and the Khe Sahn Combat Base until the rear ramp on the plane closed.

We flew all the way to Phu Bai where I had first landed. This time, our whole company would have the pleasure of riding in a truck convoy to Camp Evans. We would eventually pass right through the middle of Hue and the locations of some really bad days spent months before. The first time I had taken the route, I was excited and drank in the exotic scenery and friendly people. The second time, just outside the city, the scenery was dark and threatening, the people terrified and displaced. This third time, I felt disoriented. Same scenery, same people, same smiling kids, but obvious pain and destruction.

Chapter VIII
To the Rear, Har!

Most grunts, artillerymen on a remote firebase, or basically anyone who wasn't stationed on a large military base or in a city never got to see and experience the difference between those two worlds. I had some strange experiences in the relative safety of a few base camps and was struck by how very different the war and life were for some rear-echelon troops. Don't get me wrong, anyone who serves in a war zone can be traumatized by one event. For them the war was very real and terrifying, even though their job might have been behind a desk.

I extended my tour in Vietnam as a courier assigned to the 93rd Military Police Battalion Headquarters, located on a small remote base miles outside of Qui Nhon. As a result, I saw a lot of the country flying from Qui Nhon to Nha Trang and back every day over a seven-month period. I had a friend, actually a neighbor who lived across the street from me back in the world, who was stationed in Nha Trang, a medium-sized city located along the South China Sea. A beautiful place back then, but now mostly high-rise condos and casinos that run along the entire beach. My neighbor lived in a French-built hotel made of brick and mortar, not wood or canvas. Good restaurants within easy walking distance, and a Vespa for shopping and commuting. Nice place, decent-sized room, comfortable chair for reading, a real bed with linens and a mattress, large walk-in, white-tiled shower, hot and cold running water, women knocking on the door every night. And that was the tough part of his tour.

He worked in a French-built office building with a wonderful rooftop bar and restaurant. The folding glass rear wall of the Sky High Lounge opened onto a charming balcony, adorned with beautiful flowering tropical plants that overlooked the beach. Always a soft sea breeze, and the sound of gentle waves washing up on the sand could be heard through the swaying palm fronds. A quiet place that had probably hosted white-dinner-jacket affairs in bygone years. Anyway, he was out for a ride in his jeep one weekend and heard mortar rounds exploding nearby. He was very traumatized by that single event, an event that changed his life forever.

View from Sky High Lounge in Nha Trang

I'm not trying to put down the type of tour or job discipline someone had in country. Nor am I referring to the amount or degree of danger each discipline was exposed to on a daily basis. Trauma experienced in a combat zone is still trauma regardless of one's military status. I'm referring to the difference in lifestyle, comfort, entertainment, and convenience. I left the company a few times for different reasons, three times while on a stand-down so as not to desert the guys in the bush—once for sick call, once to make an emergency MARS call back home, and once to have glasses made. Oh, and one week for R and R.

Toon Town

On March 1, 1968, we were picked up while still in the field after the Hue Tet Offensive and flown to Camp Evans. Keeping with the weather pattern we were exposed to throughout February, we walked down the rear ramp of a big two-engine Chinook into a torrential downpour to be greeted by a sizable US Army brass band, complete with formal marching uniforms. I was shocked by the sight of them totally drenched, standing in ankle-deep mud while being blasted by torrents of water blown by the two huge rotor blades. Jim Robbins heard me mutter something about "those poor bastards" and explained that when a full battalion of the 7th Cavalry leaves the field, the lead unit is greeted by a division band playing "Sergeant Flynn" to welcome them home. I bet those guys wished we hadn't come home on that particular day! As we walked down the ramp, I asked Jim, "Who's the older guy with the big smile? Said he's proud of us for a job well done. He simply answered, "Oh, that's the division commander, Gen. Creighton

Abrams." [72] I wondered how he became a general when he didn't have enough sense to get out of the rain.

Unlike the first time I arrived at Camp Evans, slightly more than month before, I now felt like an old-timer stepping off the chopper. We slogged through the mud and rain with what was left of our platoon and headed toward an area where we'd set up our perimeter. The conditions were already atrocious due to February's prolonged rains. We were fighting a losing battle digging in the pouring rain. It was a double whammy. Besides the rain pouring down, our foxholes were filling with groundwater seeping up. *Ride on, Trooper.* Although soaked to the bone, after completing the defenses, we gladly erected our hooches and crawled inside to escape the chilling rain. We were then finally able to inflate our air mattresses with what little breath we had left after digging the pool off our veranda. To add to our comfort, we knew we would be staying at Camp Evans for a few days to get some desperately needed rest. And almost as important, it would also mean enough time would pass to dry our lightweight nylon poncho liners so we could finally sleep under a dry, warm "blanket" for a change. The twenty-eight days in the field for the Tet Offensive had taken their toll on everyone, as well as our equipment.

Knowing we probably wouldn't be ordered to do anything immediately after we set up camp, it gave us an opportunity to relax and check to see if we had any

---

72   Creighton Williams Abrams Jr. (September 15, 1914– September 4, 1974) United States Army general who commanded military operations in the Vietnam War from 1968 to 1972. He was then Chief of Staff of the United States Army from 1972 until his death in 1974. In 1980, the United States Army named its then new main battle tank, the M1 Abrams, after him. General George Patton said of him: "I'm supposed to be the best tank commander in the Army, but I have one peer—Abe Abrams. He's the world champion."

body damage that required some TLC. Like most of the other guys, I was covered with scratches, punctures, and abrasions, plus blisters on my feet because I still didn't know what size boots I needed. The pair I wore fit me a month earlier when the temperatures were in the upper nineties, but not in the wet lower fifties.

Looking into the open hooches near us, it appeared no one had any finger- or toe prints left. The continuous rain had kept our skin almost permanently puckered for a month, making our digits look more like white raisins than skin. I went to sleep that first night thinking everything would heal and return to normal as long as I stayed dry and didn't have to play soldier in the mud too often. Unfortunately, after only one night on the stand-down, I awoke just after dawn with an odd problem—my right hand had blown up like a balloon while I was sleeping.

You know the feeling you get when one of your arms has gone numb because you laid on it while sleeping? Without knowing, you roll over and the dead arm is simply dragged into a different position. You half wake up from a dream because someone is trying to choke you to death until you realize it's you who are cutting off your air supply. You typically get mad at yourself for screwing around in the middle of the night and waking up. That's exactly what happened to me on the first morning of the stand-down.

I awoke in a semiconscious state from the odd feeling of a boxing glove slapping me around. My half-opened eyes tried to focus in the darkness of the hooch, and my half-awake brain tried to figure out what the hell was going on. I stared down and concluded that one of the guys had slipped an old-fashioned leather baseball glove on my hand as a joke. Groggy from the stored-up month of exhaustion, I stared at the fat shiny thing that should have been my palm and tried to move my fingers to check it out. The more I tried, and nothing happened, the more concerned and awake I became. I sat up, confused, realizing it was indeed my own hand and not a joke. I decided to wake Randy lying next to me because he had been in-country for eleven months and might have witnessed something like my predicament before.

I hated to wake him, but I was starting to get nervous. Had Charlie sneaked into our perimeter and shot us with poison darts from blowguns, thus rendering us incapable of self-defense? Had I broken my hand while wrestling with my arm in my sleep? Randy would know, so I nudged him awake. He immediately rolled over on his mattress, semi alert to potential danger, braced himself up on one elbow to face me, and asked what was wrong. I felt guilty, thinking I had probably scared the bejesus out of him, so I first calmed him down. Once he realized we weren't under attack, he whispered something about already pulling guard duty and to let him sleep. Before he lay back down, I started to babble about dreams, fighting with numb limbs, and Charlie sneaking up on us, then showed him my hand, asking if he knew what was wrong with it. He shook his head from side to side and looked at me with a frown of disbelief. I guess he heard the panic in my voice, because he eventually took my hand in his and turned it over this way and that, looking at it very closely in the dark. After a couple of tense minutes, he finally said, "New kid, I've only seen something like this in the movies, on TV, and in a place in California." I really started getting nervous, because all in all, I was a pretty healthy kid who rarely got sick, had no allergies, and had just survived Hue!

Wanting an answer, I pleaded with Randy for an explanation—if he knew what it was, what had caused it, if it was serious. Still examining my hand, which was by then numb and looked like a new softball with Italian sausages sticking out of it, he said, "You know, I've seen this before, but I never thought it was real, just some kind of Hollywood special effects stuff. Yep, I know what it is—looks like Mickey Mouse's hand."

My mind immediately started to go through its data banks to brief me on the medical terminology he had just stated, but nothing registered. I then realized in my half-awake, panicked state that it was his idea of fun, and I was being had for waking him. "Cut the crap, Randy," I demanded as he flopped back down and rolled over, "this is serious! Suppose I just woke up in a firefight and couldn't get my finger in a trigger guard? I can't move my fingers, dammit, they won't bend!" I was getting really concerned because the hand continued to swell.

"Doesn't matter, Bano," he said coolly into his poncho liner covering his head, "you'd learn to shoot with your feet, pull grenade pins with your teeth, and throw with your left hand."

"Oh, that's great, Randy, thanks." I complained as I slid my feet into my boots and yanked my balloon hand up to my chest, cradling it in my left forearm as I prepared to find a sympathetic ear, or someone more knowledgeable. "I'm about to become a goddamn cartoon character and he's breaking my chops." I mumbled to myself. I could hear his muffled high-pitched cackle as I shuffled off my air mattress, stepped outside into a huge newly formed lake, and splashed off to find some help in the early morning rain.

I walked over to our new medic's hooch and called to him, not really expecting much help. He was new in-country, having arrived only days before, and had not experienced much yet. Eventually he came out, asking what the problem was. I could hear his "room-mate" complaining inside the hooch about waking him up. The unseen body then ordered someone to close the hooch opening because rain was getting him wet. I explained my dilemma in a shortened version while offering Doc my right hand. He seemed surprised when he took it from me and saw the size of it. After a brief examination, he said he suspected a bite of some kind—spider, scorpion, maybe a centipede. He then added that there was nothing to worry about because there were no signs of any blood poisoning. I again explained my concern about waking up in that condition without be-ing able to protect myself, and although he agreed with my reasoning, he added that he never thought much about that stuff because he was a conscientious objec-tor and didn't carry a weapon. Doc then suggested I see Sergeant Green to request sick call to see the doctor. I naturally agreed without hesitation, thanked him, and apologized for waking them up so early.

I left in the constant rain, being careful not to step into any of the well-camouflaged foxholes, since they had filled with muddy water during the night and looked like any other puddle. I found Sergeant Green's position and, hoping he was awake, called through the poncho hanging over the front of his hooch. I heard the squeaks of the air mattress as he stirred and mum-bled something about "bein' too ole fo' dis booshit, babysittin' a bunch o' kids, runnin' roun' in da rain

an' mud, ain't no food, no sleep, no booze, peoples Ah
doan eben know tryin' ta shoots me."

I had a feeling it wasn't a good beginning as he
shoved the poncho away and slid into view, sitting
on his air mattress inside the dry hooch with the camouflaged poncho liner draped over his head, looking
something like Mother Teresa on safari. I apologized if
I woke him and went through the same explanations, I
had given Randy and Doc, waving my growing hand in
front of his face. I must have said the right thing when
he asked me what I expected them to do if I went on
sick call, because he let me go. "Bano," he asked, "what
dey gonna do fer ya back dare? You ain't tryin' ta git
outta my platoon, are ya?" His slow southern drawl was
fatherly and sincere.

"No, Sergeant," I reasoned, "I've got a responsibility
to myself and the other guys, and I won't be able to do
anything with this ridiculous-looking thing!" I shook it
around like Mickey saying, "Hi, kids!" "I just want to
go in and see if they've got some kind of medicine for
it."

"Makes sense," he said, nodding, "but don' let dem
try ta talk ya outta the infantry, son. We needs ya out
here."

Yeah, right, Sarge, I thought. *No one will ever be able to
get me out of the bush!*

I finally got to the medical tent about an hour and a
half after waking up with the problem. There was another hour wait to see the doctor because of the line of
"Remington raiders," or REMFs, who had gotten there
before me. I thought we had it bad in the bush, but
those poor guys had all types of terrible maladies—like
sniffles, acne, hangovers, stiff backs from sagging bunk
mattresses, and indigestion from eating too much hot

chow the previous night. I almost felt guilty taking up a seat.

By the time it was my turn to see the doctor, the swelling had already started to subside. I jumped up on an examination table and showed him my hand, explaining what our medic had suggested, but he seemed reluctant to get too close to me. I calmed myself down by reasoning that it was not because I had some kind of contagious disease but rather because I had not showered in over three weeks. I guess he took a deep breath or something because he eventually came over and started to examine my hand, turning it over this way and that just as Randy, Doc, and Sergeant Green had done. Finally, he said, "Looks like Mickey Mouse's hand, doesn't it?"

My gaze went from my hand to his face, and I couldn't help but ask, "You don't happen to have a younger brother who's a grunt, do you, Doc?"

Everyone seemed to be having a lot of fun at my expense, but I was genuinely scared about the condition. I never had anything swell up like that. Well, maybe something, but I couldn't help but wonder what would happen if whatever it was that had bitten me got me in the forehead the next time. I pictured myself with eyes swollen shut, staggering around in the middle of a firefight with everyone laughing at me, making jokes about Jake LaMotta or some other boxer from the past. The doctor asked me what I expected him to do, because by then my hand didn't look so bad, and I was able to bend a finger a little. I had to go through the whole story again, showing how big the hand had been hours earlier. I described how small a trigger guard is on an M16, that I was a grunt, and suppose it was my eyes swollen shut? He was probably feeling me out to see if I

was shamming and finally understood my honest concern. He agreed that the swelling could present a problem or even a danger at a bad time. I could not help but
think at that precise moment that this was going to be
my ticket out of Vietnam.

The doctor moved across the tent to a large medicine
cabinet, rummaged around, found what he was looking
for, and returned to where I was sitting. While he doled
out the proper dosage to me, he explained that I had
probably had a severe allergic reaction to a spider or
mosquito bite and that it was nothing serious enough
to worry about. I couldn't disagree with him more and
felt my ticket home slipping from my semi swollen fingers. "If it should happen again," he instructed as he
handed me the small bottle of cough-medicine-looking
stuff, "take a tablespoon of this immediately and the
swelling will subside." I felt relieved that the condition
wasn't serious but disappointed that there was no mention about getting out of the bush because of potential
danger to myself and others. Shrugging and sliding off
the exam table to leave, I slipped on my shirt and asked
how long it would take for the medicine to kick in once
I drank it. His reply about floored me: "About three or
four hours."

I stopped in my tracks and blinked a couple of times;
not sure I heard him correctly. "How long will it take
for the swelling to go down if I don't take anything,
Doc?" I asked incredulously. I already knew the answer
because my hand was getting smaller by the minute,
and I could by then move my fingers a little.

He looked at me and responded with all of his professional medical training supporting his answer. "About
five or six hours," he said. I was about to start all over
again, asking him what I was supposed to do if I woke

up in a firefight, but decided not to. I just shook my head and left without even taking the medicine. After all, it would have just been some extra useless weight to carry in my rucksack.

When I returned to my hooch, Randy was sitting on his air mattress inside, grinning, and asked what the doctor had said. Instead of answering, I asked him if he had an older brother who'd gone to medical school. He laughed, knowing full well that I had wasted my time. "Bano, there's only a few ways to get out of the bush. One way will keep you in the army longer because you'll have to enlist for more years to get a cushy job. There are a couple other ways to get out, and you already know they hurt a lot. The best and usually only way is like me—I'm *short, new kid!*" he yelled and cracked up laughing. Randy was expecting his orders soon to DER-OS—Date Eligible for Return from Overseas.

An Eye for an Aye

The second time I went on "sick call" was in late April, when I could no longer postpone my need for prescription eyeglasses. We had just returned after two weeks from Operation Pegasus and were about to stand down for a rest on LZ Jack. I had shattered my glasses during the CA into a mountainous area near the Khe Sahn Combat Base and, being nearsighted, was having trouble seeing anything at a distance. When I first entered the army, I learned to not wear them during any activities where donning a steel helmet was necessary, and that was often for a grunt. Especially when jumping out of a hovering helicopter. Better that my glasses break in my pocket rather than breaking my nose when the helmet slammed down on the top of the frames.

As before, I went to Sergeant Green and asked if I could go into Camp Evans to get a replacement pair or two. He didn't see any problem because we were on a stand-down, and he told me to get on the next log bird heading back. Fortunately, I was able to do just that the following morning after a hot breakfast when supplies were flown out to our company. I boarded the chopper for its return flight and watched my squad disappear as we flew southeast toward Evans.

After a short flight, I arrived at a rapidly growing Camp Evans. The Army Corps of Engineers was building a new runway for fixed-wing aircraft. There were now quite a few "permanent" tents erected since we were there in early March. I again went to the medical tent with some apprehension about being helped. My naive hope was that they could just call back to our base in An Khe where all of our records were kept and order the glasses. As I feared, I was told I would have to go elsewhere to get glasses, perhaps Phu Bai, a city about nine miles south of Hue with a larger US military base. If not, I'd have to fly to An Khe. I figured the whole process would probably take two days, three at most, which meant I'd be able to return before our company stand-down was over.

Nodding my understanding, I left and took advantage of the beautiful weather by taking a nice leisurely stroll back to our supply tent, soaking in the sights and sounds, fantasizing about how great it must be to be stationed in the rear. After entering the supply tent, I asked if anyone knew how I could get a ride down to Phu Bai. After suggesting a number of methods, they finally reached a consensus that the MPs[73] would probably know best. Sounded like good advice, so I told the supply sergeant he'd know where to find me and followed the directions to the Military Police Operations area.

Another nice leisurely walk through the creosote-saturated dirt, eye-burning diesel, and helicopter exhaust got me there. I spoke to an MP desk sergeant and arranged to hitch a ride with a few couriers heading

73   MP—Military Police.

south. I meandered toward their carpool area to find my transportation without a care in the world, naively thinking I would be able to go to Phu Bai, get examined, and have my glasses made in a few hours, just like back in the world. That wasn't quite the army's way of doing it though. My search for glasses would take about two weeks, cover over four hundred miles, and let me experience the tremendous difference between what grunts were experiencing in the bush and what rear-echelon troops took for granted. At the same time, without my knowing, it would also keep me out of some terrible action in a place called the A Shau Valley. A very dangerous place where no "friendly" troops had entered in over two years. The last group was a Special Forces camp with indigenous Vietnamese militia support that was overrun by combined Vietcong and NVA regular forces. The entire area was strictly NVA territory.

No one would be traveling off the base until the following morning, so I bunked the night with some MPs. Turned out to be my first experience with marijuana. But I didn't inhale. The following morning, I rode in the back of a bouncing jeep behind two MPs and watched the familiar landscape go by with a totally different perspective than I had earlier. Vietnam was a whole new experience for me. I was awed by the exotic beauty everywhere—small huts covered in brown grass, huge expanses of rice paddies, and the wide, slanting roofs of beautifully adorned shrines. There were sleek little sampans on the Perfume River, decorated rickshaws pulled by men wearing black silk "pajamas" and traditional conical straw hats. There were bicycles and mopeds everywhere, Coca-Cola and Esso billboards, water buffaloes, ancient French Renaults. There was so much to see, it was hard to soak it all in.

Only few weeks later, on February 22, the second time I went down the highway, I traveled on foot, and everything looked ominous because of the Communist offensive during Tet—each hamlet, building, wall, and shrine meant potential danger from an ambush. The flooded rice paddies represented our vulnerability in the sucking mud and the constant rains. The people were all suspect now instead of being the friendly, smiling Vietnamese I had witnessed earlier. Even the aged mandarins with their wispy white beards might be vicious Communist spies instead of gentle sages.

My third trip was only a few days before when we returned from Khe Sahn. The sights were not as exotic, nor too threatening. But on this, my fourth trip traveling down Highway 1, I saw things somewhere between beautiful and ugly, threatening and friendly, magically exotic and boringly familiar. When we passed the cemetery less than one kilometer from the city, where three of our companies were bogged down for a couple of days, where innocence and many lives were lost, chills ran up and down my spine.

Soon passing through the Imperial City of Hue again, I could not believe the difference from just a couple of months earlier. The destruction of the beautiful buildings in and around the city was terrible; seemingly 75 to 80 percent were destroyed or damaged. We had fought outside the city, but I couldn't help but feel slightly guilty for having taken part in it, even though we were doing our jobs—repelling Communists who had left a trail of graves from mass murders. But as we continued south, my guilty feelings changed as I thought of the guys we lost, reminded by the gutted Hueys resting in the paddies. Shot-up trucks, jeeps, and APCs left abandoned along the roadway. The roadside ditches were littered with twisted mopeds, bicycles, and splintered wooden carts. They represented the material losses and terrible sights of a battlefield's aftermath but not the human tragedy. Everyone took a beating there, and by our company's kill ratio alone, we all knew the battle was very, very costly for the enemy. February 1968 had been an ugly month in more ways than just the weather.

I arrived in Phu Bai around midmorning under an intense sun and immediately started asking for directions to the hospital. As each guy offered his best guess with a surprised look, I walked toward the general direction offered. My senses were the first to register a difference in the war—the sounds and smells were very different as I meandered through a maze of tents, cabin-like barracks, and office buildings. Rather than the sweet and pungent smells of vegetation and fresh rain experienced in the mountains and jungles, the air was instead filled with the sickening odors of diesel fumes and oil burning human waste, mixed with aviation fuel fumes wafting from the airport runways, and laced with the evaporating creosote vapors from the freshly coated dirt roads. Instead of the crystal-clear skies we grunts took for granted in the bush, the air there had a translucent yellow haze of sand and soot particles that assailed the nostrils and lungs, burned the skin and scratched the eyes. With each step toward my destination, my body and mind seemed to notice and compare every environmental difference between experiencing the hard, dangerous fight for survival in the boonies, and the soft unhealthy life away from the fighting on a large but safe base camp. I grew up in the country and worked in Newark, NJ, so it seemed ironic that the safe, healthy environment back home was in the boonies, and not in the dangerous, unhealthy life on a big "base camp."

I glanced over at the two-and-one-half-ton trucks being staged and loaded with troops and supplies. The half olive-green-painted metal, half dirty brown canvas lumbering beasts, were, as before, preparing for their next dangerous trip along the unprotected roadway. The deep growl of their big diesel engines occasionally drowned out by the din of huge four prop-engine C-130 cargo planes taxing past on the runway, or the shrieking roar of a jet-assisted takeoff of the smaller twin prop-engine C-123 workhorse. Each plane most likely full of supplies and troops, either coming or going, all using the same runway I had landed on in January.

In stark contrast to the dull browns, dusty greens, and red earth-tone surroundings, were people wearing brightly colored tropical shirts and pants, others with starched jungle fatigues, even some young female American nurses that stood out like neon signs. I felt as if I were visiting New York for the first time, totally awed by the sights and sounds of a big city. As large as Camp Evans was to us and represented the rear, this place by comparison made Evans look like a small LZ, which I guess it was to these people. After only three months in the field, I had turned into a country bumpkin just because I was a grunt, deprived of the simplest of human comforts.

Continuing my search, I eventually found people walking around wearing scrubs and assumed I was in the hospital area. The big red crosses painted on the sloping tent roofs reminded me of how lucky I had been so far. As before, when someone approached, I stopped and asked directions to where I could get glasses made, but either no one knew, or my odor and slovenly appearance scared them away. I continued walking around, going into different tents and buildings that were suggested, but with no success. While passing through one area, I came upon two young doctors walking toward me and again asked for help, repeating my predicament for the hundredth time that day.

Unlike the countless others I'd asked, they seemed to take a genuine interest in my situation and, I was certain, they could see by my appearance that I definitely wasn't from around those parts. It was obvious because I was wearing ill-fitting, torn, and filthy sweat-stained jungle fatigues, and scraped-up muddy boots. I desperately needed a shave and haircut, and had no orders, overnight bag, or any sense of where I was. Other than that, I would have fit right in. For all practical purposes, I was completely winging it, and they knew it immediately.

I was relieved that someone was going to help and that I'd finally found the right place. Unfortunately, I didn't know it when I stopped them, but they were probably Vietnam's answer to Hawkeye Pierce and Trapper John. In fact, I was so relieved that I never thought their blood-stained scrubs suggested they weren't optometrists. The tall guy with dark hair asked his friend, "What do you think, Og, can we help him?" Og had been staring at my eyes intently, then reached out to turn my head by the jaw and seemed to be doing some kind of cursory exam. "You know, Skip," Og started to explain, "I think we can help our lost friend here."

I was smiling from ear to ear because I thought I had finally found the right people. Stepping back and saying something to Skip, Og turned to me and asked where I was stationed and with what unit. I told them I was with the 1st Cavalry up north and had just come out of the field from an operation in Khe Sahn. They both nodded with that serious, understanding gaze that doctors always seem to demonstrate when telling them what's been ailing you. Skip studied my facial features again and asked me if I had been wounded yet, if I had a girlfriend back home, and made some small talk to divert my attention from his prodding around my cheekbones and eye sockets. I began to think it was a little strange for two doctors to conduct an exam outside but figured they were checking to see if my eyes were dilated.

They backed away from me for obvious reasons, primarily the body odor, and began a brief consultation with each other, nodding and discussing something very seriously. After a few minutes, it appeared they had arrived at some type of conclusion. While Skip stood back, one arm across his waist supporting the elbow of his other and slowly tapping his cheek with a finger, he finally said, "Well, soldier, after consulting with Doctor Ogdon, I am sorry to inform you that we cannot make glasses here. However, we can remove one of your eyes."

I stood confused, not expecting the diagnosis, when Doctor Ogdon added, "We've been studying your facial features and bone structure and think you'd look great with an eye patch. You'd love it, and the girls back home think they're sexy. And take into consideration the fact that you would get monthly disability payments for the rest of your life, a Purple Heart, and could go home as soon as the healing from the surgical procedure was complete. We can take care of all the necessary forms and paperwork. So, what do you think?"

Doctor Og added, "Do you have a preference for which side? I would suggest the left eye because your right one is usually more dominant."

Finally realizing more doctors were having fun at my expense, and still not knowing where to get glasses made, I stood mute as if seriously thinking about their offer. What the hell, it would get me out of the bush, definitely prolong my life expectancy, and get me home to my expectant wife. Who knows, I reasoned to myself, maybe I *would* look good with a patch. Besides, it had to look better than wearing glasses. But I thought better of it after a few milliseconds because if I got out of the field, it would leave my squad one guy short. Deciding to play the game a little myself, I asked with a serious look, "Would it hurt much?"

They tried to hold straight faces but lost it and started to grin. Finally, Og said, "God, it must be bad out there if you'd even consider something like that!"

"Consider it?" I answered incredulously. "I already had the money spent and was making up the story of how I lost it!"

They, like everyone else I'd met that day, admitted they couldn't help, adding they didn't think there were any military facilities there to get glasses made. Their suggestion was to go to Da Nang or An Khe, where they thought I could get the necessary help I sought. I thanked them, hoped I would never have to see them in the future, and started walking again, this time back towards the airport.

It was by then late in the day when I reached the terminal and found myself in yet another dilemma. Because I had no formal written orders to fly anywhere, I was instantly refused a ticket and told to go back to my CO. I explained to the desk jockey that my company was in the bush, and I had no way to get back to Evans. If I could find a way to get there, I would have to wait for a chopper to bring me out, then another to bring me back in, and get another ride back to Phu Bai, and I had no idea of the procedures or what the hell was going on. An air force desk sergeant finally just shrugged and cut me orders to fly to An Khe, the 1st Cavalry's primary base camp for records. I boarded a C-123 heading south at 4:30 p.m., hungry, confused, exhausted, still nearsighted, and still smelling like a grunt.

Two Different Wars

After arriving in An Khe, I hitched a ride over to the somewhat familiar supply area where I had been processed into the division in January. Again, the search continued as before, and I asked everyone I saw if they knew where I could get glasses made. But just as in Phu Bai, no one did, though a couple guys said they knew people who had gotten them there. That made me feel a little bit better, knowing I was at least on the right military base. It had been a very long, frustrating day, and I realized I had nowhere to sleep and no money for food nor any toiletry items. Because it was very late and I knew my search for the "one-hour" glasses had failed, I made my way over to supply for some desperate help. The supply sergeant listened to my strange story, then suggested I go to the transient barracks where guys stayed when they were processing in or out of country, adding they'd probably be able to put me up for the night and get me a meal. So, I continued my quest, seeking out yet another unknown area in an unknown place.

I found the processing center shortly and again was met with suspicion because I had no orders and had

obviously just come out of the field. The specialist on
duty acted as if I were taking up his precious time and
he couldn't be bothered with the lowly creature standing in front of his desk. I was about to begin my long,
woeful story but was too tired and hungry to argue with
anybody, especially some REMF. With a look of disgust, I told him to call the MPs and have me thrown in
jail because I had just traveled half the length of Vietnam and was not going to put up with any more bull
from anyone. I felt a grunt should be treated with a
little more respect because we were sacrificing the most.
Maybe he saw the look in my eyes, because his attitude
changed. Cordially, he pointed up a hill to a barracks
and handed me a note to give to the mess sergeant so I
could get something to eat.

After dining alfresco on wonderful army fare, I
dragged my body through the sticky, humid night and
found my way to the same weather-beaten transient
barracks I had been in before. Upon entering, I let my
eyes adjust to the dark, dust-filled air and barely identified a few occupied beds. With the help of the moonlight passing through the screen door, I was quickly
able to claim an empty one for my own not very far
from the door. The chipped and worn metal bed frame
had an old threadbare mattress on it with a folded wool
blanket lying at the foot end. Walking around to the
side, there was a dented metal locker standing slightly
askew. To me the place looked like the Ritz Carlton. I
removed my boots, socks, shirt, and pants, quietly placing each article in the locker as I undressed. Crawling
onto the bunk, I realized that for the first time in almost three months, I was without my M-16 and was
about to sleep inside a building. So what if it was on a
filthy, musty-smelling bed? Basking in my luxury sur-

roundings, I drifted off into a coma, knowing I would not have to get up at no o'clock in the morning for guard duty.

I awoke the following morning around seven, ready to renew the search for my Holy Grail. Sliding off the bunk, I stretched from a great night's sleep and looked around at my posh surroundings. Standing completely naked, I opened the locker and found it empty except for my worn-out jungle boots! I immediately went berserk, losing what little sanity that had survived my ordeals. I felt completely betrayed, robbed of my dignity and what few possessions I had to my name. The army had finally succeeded in making me nothing more than an animal, naked to the world, with no earthly possessions. *I remember every second of the next hour as if was tattooed on my brain.* Feeling like Wile E. Coyote— "Patience my ass, I'm gonna kill somebody!"—I stormed out of the vacant building and headed for the military police barracks, wearing only my unlaced boots and the old blanket thrown over my shoulders.

I received a lot of curious looks as I stomped downhill to the processing area, kicking rocks and mumbling to myself. Wearing a five-day growth of beard, my hair a tangled mess, and looking like Jo-Jo- the Dog-faced boy at the circus, I did nothing to prevent the moth-eaten blanket blowing open in the breeze. So, it was no wonder I'd get someone's attention. Upon reaching the MP barracks, I kicked in the screen door, making the desk sergeant jump about five feet. When he landed, his eyes looked like they were having trouble identifying what was in front of him. Without waiting for any snide remarks from another REMF, I screamed, "Somebody stole my fucking clothes and I want an M-16 with two magazines, *right now!*" A couple of other MPs came running to the front of the building to see what the commotion was and probably couldn't believe what they were looking at either. While I continued yelling about how low someone could be to steal a man's clothes, they were trying to calm me down to find out who I was, where I was from, did I take any drugs, did I have any mental illness in my family...

Unable to calm me down, they took me outside, and we started to walk toward the scene of the crime while I continued to vent my fury with incoherent phrases. Guys passing near the little parade of MPs stopped and looked at me in wide-eyed amazement as if I were a lunatic being taken for his morning walk. I was flailing my arms, as all Italians do when they talk, and flashing everyone as the blanket constantly flew open with every gesture. After reaching the barracks, a search of the area recovered my empty wallet and socks but no more.

My small eight-millimeter Yoshika camera, along with seven rolls of exposed film, was gone, as were my watch, knife, lighter, and picture of my wife. I was livid. I demanded every plane leaving the base be stopped and searched, but apparently the only plane out had already left and was probably carrying the guy or guys who had stolen everything. I was so used to having complete trust and faith in my brother grunts, that I couldn't understand how something like this could happen in a combat zone. It was to be only the beginning of my education into the stark differences between people's attitudes and the war they "fought" while in the rear, away from the actual combat.

About all the MPs could do was write a report and apologize. My blood still boils just thinking about that day. I hope the bastard who stole the camera at least had enough sense to have the film developed. There had to be more than a few great shots taken at Hue, Khe Sahn, and during other operations. It is for that reason alone I have but a few pictures of my frontline experiences. Early in my tour of duty, I had sent two rolls of exposed film to Hawaii for processing. Instead of prints, I received a letter from Kodak or whoever was developing them, stating they would not release graphic pictures of war—how is that for hypocrisy? I've heard the same story from many grunts over these past fifty-something years. So I decided from then on to carry all my exposed rolls of film and the camera rolled up in an "elephant rubber" until I went on R and R. I could then hand them to my wife for safekeeping and have them developed when I got back to the world. Seemed like a good idea at the time.

The MPs drove me over to supply to get some clothes so I could at least walk around without drawing a crowd. Once I was presentable to the public, they later brought me to where I could have my eyes checked. I thought my quest was finally over, but as fate would have it, the dated note on the building's door informed everyone that the doctor would not be back from his R and R for seven more days. I had just missed him leaving by a day or so. With the seventh day being a Friday, it meant I wouldn't be able to see him until Monday, over a week away. Thoroughly disgusted, I returned to the guy who had given me the clothes, towel, and directions to where I could take a shower. He seemed friendly enough and might be able to help me out with some of the other things I needed. As it turned out, he was a former grunt, a former dog handler who had two Purple Hearts. Or maybe he'd spent too many rainy nights hugging his German shepherd. Because of that, he had been transferred to the rear to spend the remainder of his tour. We hit it off really well and hung around together for what turned out to be over a week.

Jim Stanton was my age and size but had a tremendously deep voice. When I entered the supply tent, he was sitting on a pile of stuffed laundry bags, playing a guitar and singing the Peter, Paul and Mary song "Stewball." It immediately reminded me of being back in the world with Dave Stewart, a Vietnam veteran and high school friend who was given the nickname after we had heard the song. I joined in the chorus, and we had a few laughs together. Jim understood the plight of a misplaced grunt and helped me out tremendously. His demeanor was slowly restoring my faith in mankind, with him helping me rather than ignoring my problems or taking advantage of my situation. But then again, that was pretty much what I had come to expect of all grunts. He explained that he had not been in the rear very long himself and had trouble adjusting to the way REMFs acted and treated each other. There was no tight brotherhood like we experienced in the bush, just everyone looking out for themselves. Their existence revolved around the same petty, self-centered greed, prejudices, and problems they'd brought with them from the states.

Jim eventually instructed me as to how and where to get some money from the finance group, as well as where I could get a real haircut and some other things to make me feel human again. He also directed me to the USO and Red Cross buildings to get some writing paper and something better to eat than army chow. We agreed to meet later in the day after he got off duty, making plans to go to the EM club and have a couple of beers. It all sounded good to me.

I left Jim to his "work" and walked around the base. I passed the "golf course," a huge, cleared area about the size of a mall parking lot where the 1st Cavalry's hundreds of helicopters and planes had originally been based. The airfield was so named three years earlier when the area just north of An Khe was designated to become the base camp for the 1st Cavalry Division. The division's assistant commander at that time, Brig. Gen. John M. Wright, ordered that the thick, overgrown jungle vegetation should be cleared and left as "smooth as a golf course." I couldn't help thinking of all the work and sacrifices that must have gone into securing the area and building the base, only for the division to leave and move north to I Corps. A feeling of pride swept over me as I walked. Looking up, one could not miss the huge yellow-and-black 1st Cavalry patch painted on Hon Cong Mountain, an outcropping overlooking the base. I felt I was now truly a part of the "First Team."

I walked ten minutes to the Red Cross building, where I'd be able to write some letters home, and was amazed at not only what I saw but how much I had changed in the few months I had been in Vietnam. Where before I was awed by the sights and sounds of so many helicopters and the rhythms of a combat base, I looked at the few remaining choppers now as if they were just taxis, lined up and waiting for a fare. The guys walking around with jungle fatigues were not the hardened combat troops I thought I was looking at in January but instead mostly REMFs with cushy jobs compared to what grunts were experiencing in the field. Later in my tour, though, I realized those guys in An Khe had it a lot harder than other guys, such as those stationed in Cam Rahn Bay, Nha Trang, or a couple of hundred other places in Vietnam. What was misery for some would have been glorious to others.

I felt completely out of place in the Red Cross building because it looked like a library, tables full of clean-cut guys with starched fatigues, insignias and stripes on their sleeves, all clean shaven and with professional haircuts. By comparison, I probably looked like a homeless bum. I found a place to sit off in a corner and was writing a letter home when I looked up and saw the back of some guy who I thought might be a grunt. He was big, broad shouldered, and had long, scraggly hair touching his collar. There were no stripes, bars, or any indication of rank or unit on his wrinkled jungle fatigues. I noticed guys walking over to him, shaking his hand and talking, but didn't know why until he turned around. The instant I saw him, I probably had the same incredulous look on my face as those who'd witnessed my Jo-Jo the Dog-Faced Boy impression earlier that morning. I stared, mouth agape, not believing my eyes. Standing only twenty feet in front of me was my childhood hero, Davy Crockett!

I was speechless. It was him! Davy! I wanted to run over and show him I still knew all the words to the Davy Crockett theme song. I had to tell him how much I liked him, and that I had outgrown my coonskin cap but still had my Davy Crockett cereal bowl and cup! Before I made a complete ass of myself, I suddenly realized I was now like the real Davy Crockett, Injun fighter, more so than Fess Parker, the actor in front of me who portrayed the legendary frontiersman and statesman. Still, I had to tell him how much I enjoyed his work and how much it had meant to me growing up. *By the way, I'm looking at my Davy Crockett drinking glass on my desk as I type this.*

I eventually got over the shock and mustered enough courage to walk over and ask for an autograph, for my wife Judy, a big fan of his! We had a nice talk with a few laughs, and I thanked him for coming to Nam, helping us with some moral support from home. A short time later, we shook hands, and I headed back to my solitary corner, where I continued my letter, feeling better about the state of things in general, and listening to the Davy Crockett theme song echoing in my head. Once finished, I included the autograph with the letter and sent it home. I left the Red Cross building after writing a few more letters and made my way back across the base to meet Jim. While walking alone on a dusty dirt road, I couldn't help but reflect on the events of just a few hours earlier. I had started the day as if I had just come into the world—naked and without any possessions. Now I had clothes and Davy Crockett's autograph. Life was good again.

That night, Jim and I went over to the enlisted men's club, where I had my first cold beer in months, and it was fabulous. We sat and got to know each other better until things started to get ugly. A touring band from the states was performing on a small stage, and a bunch of drunk REMFs were really ragging them for being so bad. The female lead singer stopped playing and was obviously hurt by their insensitive remarks. She suggested they should just appreciate the fact that people from home were coming all the way over here just to entertain them. The grunts in the audience agreed, telling the REMFs to shut up the fuck up! For grunts, the only thing we ever heard "live" was the Grand Ole Opry coming out of a small transistor radio on Saturday nights. After a couple of more beers and a few aggressive verbal exchanges, a couple of "uncouth" grunts with very southern accents knocked over their chairs getting up, and everyone knew what was about to happen.

Instead of calling their bluff, the instigating REMFs wisely left, mumbling about dirty hair and wrinkled fatigues. Jim quickly stood up and asked if any of the transient grunts wanted to see a movie. We all thought he was kidding, but with a huge grin, he assured us there was a drive-in theater up the hill, right next to the baseball field. You know, just across the road from the swimming pool! There was a hesitation by most guys before they finally answered with what they thought he was full of. I could tell he was enjoying the stunned look on everyone's face. I answered him the way Carlos would have. He insisted it was true but couldn't stop laughing at our disbelief. It was worth the walk, so a number of us left the club and en route passed the baseball field and the pool. I could not believe guys were humping rucks in the boonies, losing their minds, limbs, and lives, while other guys were being entertained and having all the comforts of home. I started to understand why Jim didn't feel comfortable back at a base camp— the feeling was guilt.

We reached the drive-in theater, which turned out to be a grassy slope with a whitewashed cinderblock "movie screen" at its lowest point. Grumbling about the disparity and our misfortune in drawing the short straw and being assigned to a combat company, we sat down in the dirt and grass, unfazed by our seats. I watched in amusement as jeeps having two or three guys in each lined up in a designated area for vehicles, as if they were back in the world parking with their sweethearts. Other well-groomed and tailored guys showed up on foot, some carrying beach chairs and popcorn.

We grunts were in culture shock to be sure, watching in disbelief as a few REMFs carefully stepped through the area, concerned about getting their boots dirty, while others were getting as comfortable as possible using the blankets they had brought in case it got too chilly. Jim seemed to have a permanent grin while he watched and listened to our reactions to the sideshow. I finally turned to him, asking to be slapped because we couldn't possibly still be in Vietnam. My astonishment caused him to laugh even harder and say, "Wait till you see the pool show tomorrow." Seriously?! While we waited and took in the sights around us, I could not help but think of what my squad was doing at that very moment back at LZ Jack. Something was not right here.

Everyone waited for the show to begin while a very clean-cut, nervous guy at the top of the little knoll set up a small wooden table behind us and prepared to load a sixteen-millimeter projector with a movie called *Doctor Zhivago*. There was a chorus of moans when he announced the title because many of us thought it was some type of army training film on hygiene. In spite of a constant flow of jeers, taunts, and popcorn being thrown at him, he went about his job in a disciplined manner. He stacked seven large blue film cans on the small table, threaded a film reel into the camera, and waited for it to get sufficiently dark to turn on the projector.

Eventually the show began, and we grunts sat mesmerized, as if viewing a movie for the first time. I watched the magic screen in wonderment, probably like folks during the movie industry's early years. I was hanging on every word and staring at the beautiful scenery of a Russian winter that quickly reminded me of the snow-covered lawns and trees back home when I had left in January. I was awestruck by the magnificent music. *Right, and I bought* Playboy *magazine to read the articles.* Well, the music was nice, but good Lord! Julie Christie's flowing golden hair and big, gorgeous round eyes! By the remarks and panting of the grunts around me, I assumed they were enjoying the scenery and music too.

Our fantasies were suddenly interrupted by some REMFs who started to leave after a half an hour, tripping and stumbling over us in the dark. Compounding their disregard for anyone, they climbed into a jeep and peeled out onto the road. As if throwing dirt and gravel all over us with their spinning wheels wasn't enough, they positioned the turning vehicle's headlights to wash out the movie on the wall, shouting all the while about some of the attendees to drown out the movie's dialogue. More than a few grunts were infuriated at the REMFs' antics and yelled out the same challenge they had said to the guys in the EM club. I turned to Jim and asked why anyone would walk out on a good movie. "The dew is probably getting their uniforms damp." was his whispered response. I couldn't see his face in the dark and wasn't sure if he was serious. Nothing I had seen or heard all day seemed real. I wondered if I would ever get that "soft" again—the idea of leaving somewhere because my pants were getting a little damp.

When the dust finally settled, everyone's attention returned to the screen, and they immersed themselves back into their own little worlds. In keeping with a grunt's luck, a little over an hour into the movie, it started to rain, and the projectionist shut it down. A very nervous new kid apologized and explained that the rain might damage the projector. He would show the rest of the movie on another night when the weather was better. Grunts in the audience besides Jim and me didn't want to hear it and let the new kid and everyone else know what we thought about rear-echelon guys having it so soft. While REMFs were packing up their beach chairs, mumbling about how we were uncouth and like animals, and the jeeps were peeling out behind us, the grunts who had come straight from the EM club with us would not allow the projectionist to leave.

He pleaded that it was his first day there and he didn't want to break anything. Wearing ugly looks, they ordered him to stay put because they'd find a tent or something to protect his precious equipment. One grunt took his shirt off and threw it over the projector, then left with three others to find some type of shelter so he could continue the movie that night. While staggering away, the four guys were yelling at the night sky, to no one in particular, "We're grunts! We adapt, we survive!" Then another added, "Yeah, we're drunk grunts. We watch movies in the rain while sitting in the mud." Laughing, they disappeared into the dark, appreciating the absurdity of it all as only a grunt could.

Within five minutes, we heard an enormous boom, like the crack of far-off thunder or a muffled explosion. Jim and I tried to figure out what the noise was, fairly certain it didn't sound like "war" noise. We heard it again about ten seconds later and every ten seconds thereafter for a couple of minutes while the rain increased in intensity. The explosions got closer and louder, and while the remaining REMFs with umbrellas started to run, yelling, "Incoming! Incoming rounds!" Jim and I knew better and kept the projectionist, who was by then terrified, there in the rain. We tried to calm him down, explaining that grunts were regular draftees just like him. They just didn't have many opportunities to enjoy the pleasures that guys in the rear took for granted. The new kid was jumpy as hell. Every time there was another explosion, his head disappeared into his collar. He must have trusted our field experience that they weren't mortars, and he calmed down a little more when Jim told him if they were incoming rounds, the grunts would've been the first to dive for cover.

We finally saw what all the noise was when the four staggering grunts who had left, and few other guys they had picked up along the way, came into view. They were rolling an olive-green shipping container down the hill toward the "drive-in." They kept putting their shoulders against a side and at the count of three, pushed in unison. Slowly the big box would lift up on one edge, tip over, and slam down with a reverberating *ka-boom!* The guys, laughing hysterically in what was by then a downpour, would then walk down to where it had landed and repeat the action. We told the new kid to stay put and ran up to help the other guys, rolling the container over again and again until we had it positioned right where the projector could be carried into it. Laughing and exhausted, and probably still a little drunk, we sat back down in the mud. Once everything was set up correctly, we happily started to watch the movie when it began anew.

It was strange that everyone was having trouble following the action once the movie was restarted. Regardless of how much we concentrated or asked the other guys near us what we had missed, the movie just wasn't making any sense. The old people became young, the dead alive, the good bad. We began yelling out questions to no one in particular, making jokes about how fast we had forgotten our history lessons on the Russian Revolution. Everyone was asking what was going on, had we missed something, or did we just forget how to watch a movie? Not that the plot really mattered, because no one wanted to stop looking at the angelic Julie Christie, even in the heavy downpour that was almost washing out the projected image on the block wall.

Most everyone eventually calmed down and just watched the movie for the sake of entertaining themselves. Sometime later when the movie finally ended, and the new kid had to rewind the reels, we found out what had happened. When the film cans were carried into the new "projection shed," their sequence had been mixed up. Simply put, there was no following the story line because we had seen reels one, two, five, seven, three, six, and four—in that order. Every time I see *Doctor Zhivago* advertised on TV, I can't help but remember a bunch of drunk grunts laughing their asses off while watching it in a downpour back in 1968.

I spent the week having a great time with Jim and all the "wonders" of the An Khe base. I went swimming at the pool and lounged in the sun, had delicious hamburgers at the USO Club while listening to Otis Redding singing "Sittin' on The Dock of the Bay," and heard more bands from the states at the EM club. Each band seemingly had the same repertoire of songs: "The Letter" ("Give Me a Ticket for an Aero plane"), "Green, Green Grass of Home," "San Francisco (Be Sure to Wear Flowers in Your Hair)," "Satisfaction." Of course, it really didn't matter, because the beers were cold every night. I caught up on my mail, eventually saw the eye doctor, and even ran into a guy from my hometown of Pompton Lakes, Don Krom, who had graduated a few years before me.

On my last day there, I found out the LRRPs' barracks were located there, and on an outside chance I might be able to find my best friend, Donny Miller, or possibly one of the other guys I came into country with, I headed for their location. Incredibly, Donny was there, and we couldn't believe we were actually together again. We sat around under a billion glittering stars in the clear night sky, talking for hours about the past, our families, and what was new from the different friends who had written. He talked about starting his own auto body repair business when he got home, and we joked about different names for the business using Vietnamese words. After a time, we started to compare notes on what we'd seen thus far, and I was amazed to find he had just finished his LRRP training and hadn't gone into the field yet.

I couldn't believe that I'd experienced so much in three months, and he hadn't gotten into the field yet. All the while I was worrying about him, thinking he had a much more dangerous job than I, he was actually worrying about me because of my location. I tried to explain to him how bad it really was in the field, telling him not to rush, in fact to sign up for something else if it could keep him from going into the bush. He just shrugged and said he'd wasted enough time and was ready to earn his pay. We continued talking long into the night while sitting on an old, sandbagged bunker. And even though I knew I had to wake up just after sunrise and head back north, I could not get myself to leave. Something inside was telling me to stay and keep talking.

I talked about the guys in my squad, the fact that the stand-down was probably over, and my CO thinking I was AWOL. In fact, I really wasn't sure if I was or not, because I never had any official orders, just permission to go on sick call. Around three in the morning, we had exhausted our conversations and said our good-byes, promising to write each other more often in the future. We hugged, gave each other a pat on the back, and asked to give our best to each other's parents, to whom we both felt very close. That was the last time we saw each other.

Sadly, a couple of months later, only two weeks after I received the letter telling me of my daughter's birth and Donny's death, his LRRP squad was em-bedded with our company, intermingling with us for a jungle insertion. I was at least able to talk to the guys in his squad about what had happened, try to make some sense of it all, and get some closure for my own peace of mind. His sergeant said, "I'm sure you know, we can't get too close to anyone out here, but he was one guy you couldn't help wanting to be with. He kept everyone's spirits up and made us laugh. A great guy. We'll all miss him." In spite of us having experienced so much hardship and loss already, we both had tears in our eyes as I thanked him and walked away. I felt somehow better having talked to him.

That morning I left An Khe and flew back to Phu Bai, hitched a ride on a truck heading north, and eventually made my way to our supply tent back at Camp Evans. In a way it was almost like a relief to get "home." Walking into the shade of our supply tent, I happily joked with a couple of guys sitting on C-ration boxes, who had just returned from R and R in Thailand. We laughed about our travels a bit, but they seemed a lit-tle hesitant to really get into the discussions on their fun. With the conversations over, I asked Rabbi when the next chopper was going out. Harold and the guys got suddenly very serious and visibly upset, saying the news was pretty bad. The company had to cut their stand-down short, had air assaulted into a place called the A Shau Valley over a week ago, and were hitting it pretty bad every day. My mouth dropped and heart skipped a few beats, thinking of my friends out there and worst-case scenarios.

I looked at the others for signs of confirmation on their faces, wondering why they were still sitting there in the rear. I asked when the next log bird was going out, but no one knew for sure, adding that over twenty choppers had been shot down already. I felt almost panicked as the events were being told to me, knowing I was letting the guys down, that my place was with the guys in my squad. I still didn't have my glasses, it might take a while, but I needed to at least know if the CO wanted me to come out. A radio call assured me the CO had enough problems without a blind man walking around and was told to catch the first bird as soon as the glasses arrived. I looked at the other guys monitoring the different radio frequencies, and one of them said, "Bano, you better pray those glasses don't come too fast. And whatever you do, don't do anything stupid. Your whole squad and I think the platoon are okay, no problems for them so far." Though somewhat relieved, I was consumed by the helpless, guilty feeling inside me for not being with them. It still does to this day.

The other two guys had to fly out the following day, while I stayed and helped around the supply tent. Surprisingly, the glasses arrived a few days later, but I was informed the company was coming back in the following day. After taking a log bird out, I met them later that afternoon at LZ Jack, and everyone looked really beat and shaken. The stories they told me of what was found along the Ho Chi Minh Trail surprised the hell out me. Choppers going down in flames, ambushes, spider holes and dug-in bunker positions, trucks, antiaircraft guns. . . As bad as I felt about letting them down, no one held it against me, only saying they were happy everything had turned out okay for the squad but sadly not the platoon.

After everyone settled in, I told them of my escapades, and we all had a good laugh, though the one thing that bothered everyone was how different the war was in the rear. Here we were, black, white, yellow, and brown, Catholic, Protestant, Jewish, Baptist, Italian, Puerto Rican, Native American, Pole, farmer, college student, inner-city kid, auto mechanic. Not only did we get along, but we would also put our life on the line to help each other. We all cried, laughed, sweated, and bled the same. We learned there were people you didn't like, but it was because of who they were, not what they were. In the field, we were brothers in the truest sense of the word. We talked about home and life, politics and social problems, sports and girls. We were all one and the same, even Charlie.

Things somehow changed in the rear. Blacks fought with whites, southerners with northerners, cowboys with surfers. To us young, naive grunts, it was sad, because we knew we could all live together. Heck, grunts had been proving it through many, many wars. We didn't steal, lie, or try to take advantage of anyone. There was too much at stake. It was interesting in 1968 when guys went to the rear and returned from R and R. They would bring everyone up to date on current events, new music, and how incredibly short hemlines were getting back in the world. Once the conversation turned to how people were acting at the big base camps and at home, the talk ended, because no one wanted to hear it, or maybe because no one could understand it at twenty years of age. As much as we all wanted to get back home, I think we all knew deep down inside that the adjustment was going to be hard. All we could do was shake our heads about the insanity of civilization and try to help each other survive.

Remembering the good times, the laughs, funny incidents, and the guys helps me to focus on the positive and be able to share the lessons learned so long ago. Though we were all somewhat traumatized by it to different degrees, I believe the combat experiences made us all better people. We should focus on that and pass those lessons on to others whenever we can. Respect those who serve in the military. Our fallen brothers deserve that much.

Breaking Up Is Hard to Do

By late July and on into early August, we continued to work the mountain regions farther and farther to the west. Though the weather was getting hotter, the action fortunately was not. It had become very sporadic—sniping, small ambushes, and short firefights. The conditions were very different from earlier in the year when during the Tet we made some type of contact with large NVA concentrations almost daily and the constant rains kept us shivering and wet. But the gnawing fact always remained: Anything could happen, anywhere, at any time.

It was an August morning on yet another nondescript mountain, dawn of the fourth day of a new operation. A lot of guys were already up, while others seemed to be moving in slow motion, having trouble crawling out of their hooches. Everyone looked bleary eyed and complained to no one in particular about the conditions. Even though we were high in the mountains, the unusually humid night air had been stifling. And with little to no air movement possible under the umbrella of towering hardwoods, we all suffered from a restless sleep. And with the oncoming sunrise, conditions were only getting worse.

Okie, Ski, and I were preparing something to eat and going about our morning routine of breaking camp, packing rucksacks, and making sure nothing was left lying around. We could only hope the CO had experienced the same restless sleep. If so, maybe he and the battalion commander would consider the weather when moving us throughout day. By the time eight in the morning rolled around, it appeared we just might stay for a while—get some water and strength back into our systems. Doc had been having a holy fit because of the poor physical condition we were already in after only four days. He reminded the CO of the last time we were this exhausted and low on water—not a pretty sight.

On a previous mission, one of our guys had to be medevacked because of the heat. We removed his gear, enabling him to climb to the top of the mountain where there was an open area large enough for a chopper to land and get him out. Big Joe was irate because LT ordered him to bring the gear up. Joe was a fire team leader, half of the squad, but took the order literally. It was one of the rare times when we were packing heavy, so you can imagine how Joe felt when he thought he had been personally ordered to carry two packs. Before we knew what was happening, being the good trooper that he was, Joe simply threw the second pack over his left shoulder, then grabbed the other guy's ammo, grenades, and helmet. He just put his head down, threw it in low, and plowed his way uphill, mumbling to himself as he knocked down trees and shrubs with his shoulders.

We couldn't yell for him to stop or slow down, so it took us a bit to catch up to him and share the load.

Jackie told Joe to drop the pack and everything else so we could split it up, but Joe was furious and almost in a trance. He kept mumbling, "Joe, do this. Joe, get that. Joe, carry everything!" Jackie finally stepped in front of him and told him to stop or he'd jump on his back. We were all strung out and very much on edge because of the forced march, the heat, and the fact that we were traveling heavy. Joe just said, "LT told me to carry it, so I am. Now get out of my way." Joe never talked to anyone that way, so we knew it was going to be a touchy situation. Jackie, with his thin smile and slow Texas drawl, said, "Well, okay, Joe, but Bano's gonna git on yer back, too." I was standing on the other side of him and said, "Yeah, come on, ya big lug, bend over so I can climb up on your shoulders. I'm hot and exhausted too. Jackie, sit on his ruck facing back in case someone else needs a lift. You can help them climb up." The chiding worked, because he broke into his little-boy grin and started to drop stuff all around him, still mumbling about the army and its ways. As the rest of the guys caught up, we divided the load as best we could and started our climb again. Joe, of course, felt bad and wanted to carry the extra pack, but Jackie convinced him they could both carry it, each holding a shoulder strap. By the time we reached the summit, we were all ready for a chopper ride to the battalion aid station.

So, on this particular morning when no one said anything about our moving out right away, we all sat around trying to stay cool, an impossibility, of course. Usually, once we awoke in the bush and had something to eat, we walked from morning until night for two weeks looking for trouble. "Move to contact" they called it. Naturally we appreciated every minute we weren't. Unfortunately, around eight thirty we had gotten word that we would be moving out soon. Before anyone complained, the following order was a relief: Load your rucks and get them ready to sling out. It was little things like that that raised our spirits. But in the back of everyone's mind was the question, "Why are we suddenly traveling light? What's up ahead?"

I noticed Top and Mac, his RTO, walking in our direction and thought nothing of it while I continued with my packing. When I heard Top Carroll's gravelly voice bark out, "That ain't the guy I thought it was. Somebody must have screwed up again." I glanced up to see whom he was referring to and did a double take. He was standing almost in front of me, feet spread and hands on his hips. He was wearing his trademark flattened steel helmet with a torn camouflage cover hanging in shreds, chewing on a cigar and staring down at me. I looked over at Mac for some clarification, but he too stood there very serious. As usual, his thick glasses sat slightly askew above his bushy red mustache. He broke the silence and said in his Maine accent, "Well, maybe he'll volunteer for it. Why don' cha ask 'im?" The guys sitting around didn't know what to make of the situation either. We just looked at each other, up at Top and over to Mac, and back again waiting to hear more. Mac broke into the big grin he always seemed to have, waiting like the rest of us for Top to say something.

My first thought was there was something wrong at home—my wife and daughter, mother or father. Then I wondered if I'd screwed up somewhere, somehow, wasn't carrying my load. Lord knows, after losing one new father in the platoon, most of the guys would argue with me when I was about to do anything remotely dangerous. After an uncomfortable pause, Top finally said, "How'd you like to go to the rear—permanently?"

That confused me and I still had no idea what he was talking about. A million things started to go through my mind as I stared at him, speechless, remembering Randy saying, "There's only three ways to get out of the field, and two of them hurt." *This has got to be a mistake*, I thought, *a sick joke or they want me to run an errand*.

Frowning, Top said, "That's what I thought you'd say. Finish packing your ruck. Give out your two-quart canteens and see if anyone needs ammo or anything else. Then come over to the CP." He turned and walked away while I remained stunned, confused, my mouth still hanging open like the rest of the guys. I knew it had to be a mistake because I still had a little over four months left in-country.

As I stared at Top's back, Mac came over with his right hand extended and said, "Congratulations, Bano, you're going in. You're outta the bush."

We were all in shock. "Mac," I asked, "what the hell is going on? What did I do wrong? Don't they think I'm doing a good job? Christ, Mac, I'm a fire team leader! What did I do wrong?" We all wanted to know.

Mac, shaking my hand and still grinning, said, "The old man said he didn't know he had guys out here with expectant wives or newborn kids. I told him about you, said we could get along without one guy for a while now that things are slower. All he said was 'Get him out of here. I'm not going to lose another one.' We did it, Bano. You're getting out of the field, going to the rear."

I was in shock and slightly embarrassed as the guys came over to congratulate me, one at a time. All I could think of was catching up to Top and hearing his side of the story, because it still didn't sound right. When I reached him, I said, "What's really going on, Top? What did I do wrong?"

He looked at me and smiled, something a hard-ass first sergeant rarely does. "Son, there's some kinda thing called a MAC-V levy or something. It allows us to get guys out of the field for any reason—too many Purple Hearts, can't adapt to the army, burned out. The 5/7th was allowed to let two guys go in. You're one of 'em."

Already feeling guilty about leaving the guys, I said, "Can't we do this when we go on stand-down? My squad's going to be two guys short because of yesterday's medevac."

He looked at me and replied in a no-nonsense manner, "Bano, if you're not on that log bird when it leaves here this morning, the deal's off."

I felt the same way I did when I received my "Congratulations, my condolences" letter. As I slowly walked back toward the squad, the positive side of it finally hit me: I was going to the rear. But I'd have to leave my closest friends. I didn't know whether to jump for joy or cry. It wasn't supposed to happen like this. Joe and Jackie were supposed to leave before me so I would know they made it. Then I would leave, and Bill Ebel, Little Joe, Mac, Ski, Okie, and the rest of the guys would know I made it, and so on. I was walking in a daze but kept hearing Top's last words: "The deal's off." By the time I reached the guys, I was embarrassed as hell but had accepted my fate.

I guess we were all happy to some degree, but there was no time to really say anything to each other. I had been through heaven and hell with Joe and Jackie for over seven months, and in a matter of minutes, we would probably never see each other again. Same for the "new" guys who had arrived after me. Somewhat in a daze, I walked over to each guy to say my goodbyes personally. There were hugs and pats, punches and daps. While trying to leave on a high note, we distributed my gear and joked around about how I was going to be a REMF. The thought of it made me shiver, but I said, "I'll always be a 1st Cav grunt at heart. Hell, I'll probably have to do some rotten job like keeping the beer cold at the EM club." We laughed, but something was missing.

I felt an emptiness, a deep sorrow, and pangs of guilt for leaving my friends, leaving my squad a man short, and leaving every guy out there in harm's way. Everything was happening too fast. We all heard the familiar sound of rotor blades slapping the heavy air and knew it was time. Picking up my ruck and M-16 and saying one last goodbye, I turned and walked away, embarrassed and feeling guilty. I made my way down toward the landing zone, trying not to make any eye contact, and arrived just as the Huey was about to touch down. A few guys were already there and immediately started to offload a mail sack, fresh water supplies, and another bag with ordered items. They gave me a curious look, probably wondering why all I had was my ruck and weapon—no ammo, canteens, frags, nothing. As I climbed aboard the idling Huey, one of the guys reached up and handed the door gunner some outgoing letters before giving a thumbs-up. After only fifteen minutes since being told of my good fortune, I felt the familiar vibrations and the sound of the rapidly increasing engine but not the accustomed rush of adrenaline. I just felt numb. I sensed being jostled by the ship's rapid ascent, its nose dropping, the speed increasing, and the difference in the air temperature on my arms, but I just couldn't comprehend the finality of it all. I watched the clearing below and the men getting smaller until there was no sign of any human activity, only a mountain hidden behind green leaves. Tears welled up in my eyes, as they are now, and I said a prayer for a quick end to the lousy war. And just that quick, my combat days were over.

I was eventually transferred south to the Central Highlands, about forty miles east of An Khe to a small base outside the city of Qui Nhon. Assigned to the 93rd Military Police Battalion Headquarters, I eventually extended my tour of duty and spent another seven months in-country, flying each day as an armed courier. I was fortunate to witness both sides of the war—how bad it was in the bush and how soft it could be in the cities or on one of the large base camps. Don't get me wrong, there were some bad experiences in the rear as well. I had this one flight on an old C-119 Flying Box Car, a WWII plane donated to some obscure Vietnamese airline. We were on the tarmac, mostly Vietnamese peasants who had the cabin full of pigs and chickens, when...

About the Author:

John Montalbano, a Vietnam War veteran, served in the 1st Cavalry Division and later as a courier for the 93rd Military Police Battalion Headquarters. His experiences have been published in various outlets, including Vietnam Magazine. Raised in Pompton Lakes, N.J., he now enjoys retirement in Coastal North Carolina with his wife, Helen, and their pets. A proud father and grandfather, Montalbano is also a member of the 5th Battalion, 7th Cavalry Association. His book, Bullets in My Bottom Drawer, reflects his military experiences and aims to provide solace and understanding for fellow veterans and their families.

Milton Keynes UK
Ingram Content Group UK Ltd.
UKHW041632240924
448733UK00002B/130

9 798822 950856